THE

ACT OF

WRITING

THE
ACT OF
WRITING

JESSIE REHDER

WALLACE KAUFMAN

University of North Carolina

THE ODYSSEY PRESS

NEW YORK

Acknowledgments

Acknowledgment is gratefully made for permission to reprint the following material:

Appleton-Century-Crofts. Passage from *Understanding Fiction* by Cleanth Brooks, Jr., and Robert Penn Warren, copyright 1943 by F. F. Crofts & Co. Inc. Reprinted by permission of Appleton-Century-Crofts.

Edward Arnold (Publishers) Ltd. Passages from *Aspects of the Novel* by E. M. Forster, published by Edward Arnold (Publishers) Ltd. Reprinted by permission of the publishers.

The Atlantic Monthly Company. "Vulture Country" by John Stewart, copyright © 1959, by The Atlantic Monthly Company, Boston, Mass. Reprinted with permission.

Atheneum Publishers. Passage from *Confessions of an Advertising Man* by David Ogilvy, © 1963 by David Ogilvy Trustees. For passages from *A Long and Happy Life* by Reynolds Price, © 1960 Encounter Ltd., © 1961 Reynolds Price. For passage from *Names and Faces of Heroes* by Reynolds Price, © 1963 by Reynolds Price. These passages reprinted by permission of Atheneum Publishers.

The Bobbs-Merrill Company, Inc. Passage from *The Southpaw*, copyright © 1953 by Mark Harris, reprinted by permission of the publishers, The Bobbs-Merrill Company, Inc.

The Dial Press. Lines from "The Death of the Ball Turret Gunner" by Randall Jarrell, from *Little Friend, Little Friend*, published by The Dial Press.

John Dos Passos. "The Body of an American" from *Nineteen Nineteen*, second volume of the U.S.A. Trilogy, by John Dos Passos, copyright by John Dos Passos 1932 and 1960, published by the Houghton Mifflin Company. Reprinted by permission of John Dos Passos.

Doubleday & Company, Inc. "Flower Dump" by Theodore Roethke, copyright 1946 by Editorial Publications, Inc., from *The Collected Poems of Theodore Roethke*. Reprinted by permission of Doubleday & Company, Inc. Lines from *The Summing Up*, by W. Somerset Maugham. Copyright 1938 by W. Somerset Maugham. Reprinted by permission of Doubleday & Company, Inc.

Esquire Incorporated. "James Agee, by Himself" by James Agee, *Esquire Magazine*, December 1963. Reprinted by permission of *Esquire Magazine* © 1963 by Esquire, Inc.

iv

Farrar, Straus & Giroux, Inc. "Jealousy" by Colette. Reprinted with the permission of Farrar, Straus & Giroux, Inc. from *My Mother's House* by Colette. Copyright 1953 by Farrar, Straus & Young, Inc.

Elaine Greene Ltd. Passage from "The Wall" by William Sansom, from *The Stories of William Sansom*, published in Canada by The Hogarth Press. Reprinted by permission of Elaine Greene Ltd.

Paul Green. Lines from "The University in a Nuclear Age." Reprinted by permission of the author.

Michael Hamburger. "The Autopsy" by Georg Heym, trans. Michael Hamburger, *Great German Short Stories*, ed. Stephen Spender. Copyright © 1960 Stephen Spender. Published by Dell Books. Reprinted by permission of the translator.

Harcourt, Brace & World, Inc. Section I from "Such, Such Were the Joys" in *Such, Such Were the Joys* by George Orwell, copyright 1945, 1952, 1953 by Sonia Brownell Orwell. Passage from *Aspects of the Novel* by E. M. Forster, copyright 1927 by Harcourt, Brace & World, Inc.; renewed, 1955, by E. M. Forster. Passage from *Night Flight* by Antoine de Saint-Exupéry. Reprinted by permission of Harcourt, Brace & World, Inc.

Harper & Row, Publishers. Passage from pp. 81–85 in *Mirage of Health* (hardbound) by René Dubos. Copyright © 1959 by René Dubos. Passage from p. 47 in *Art and Reality* (hardbound) by Joyce Cary (Harper & Row, 1958.) Reprinted by permission of Harper & Row, Publishers.

A. M. Heath & Company Ltd. "Such, Such Were the Joys" from *Such, Such Were the Joys* by George Orwell. Reprinted by permission of Miss Sonia Brownell and of A. M. Heath & Company Ltd., agents for The Estate of the Late George Orwell.

Holt, Rinehart and Winston, Inc. "Now hollow fires burn out to black" from "A Shropshire Lad"—Authorised Edition—from *The Collected Poems of A. E. Housman.* Copyright 1939, 1940, © 1959 by Holt, Rinehart and Winston, Inc. Copyright © 1967, 1968 by Robert E. Symons. Reprinted by permission of Holt, Rinehart and Winston, Inc.

Houghton Mifflin Company. Passage from *The Affluent Society* by John Kenneth Galbraith, published by Houghton Mifflin Company. "Injelititis or Palsied Paralysis" from *Parkinson's Law* by C. Northcote Parkinson, published by Houghton Mifflin Company. Passage from *The Silent Spring* by Rachel Carson, published by Houghton Mifflin Company. Passage from *The Open Sea* by Sir Alistair Hardy, published by Houghton Mifflin Company. Reprinted by permission of the publisher.

Hutchinson & Co. (Publishers) Ltd. Passage from *The Lotus and the Robot* by Arthur Koestler. Reprinted by permission of Hutchinson & Co. (Publishers) Ltd.

Mrs. Mary Jarrell. Lines from "The Death of the Ball Turret Gunner" from *Little Friend, Little Friend* by Randall Jarrell. Reprinted by permission of Mrs. Mary Jarrell.

Gyorgy Kepes. "Where Is Science Taking Us?" by Gyorgy Kepes, *Saturday Review*, March 5, 1966. Reprinted by permission of Gyorgy Kepes.

Alfred A. Knopf, Inc. Passage from *Bonanza Inn* by Oscar Lewis and Carroll Hall. Copyright 1939 and renewed 1967 by Oscar Lewis and Carroll Hall. Reprinted by permission of Alfred A. Knopf, Inc.

J. B. Lippincott Company. "The Disposable Man" from *All Things Considered* by Russell Baker. Copyright © 1962, 1963, 1964, 1965 by The New

York Times Company. Published by J. B. Lippincott Company. Reprinted by permission of the publisher.

Little, Brown and Company. Passage from "The Wall" by William Sansom from *The Stories of William Sansom*, published by Atlantic–Little, Brown and Company. Reprinted by permission of Little, Brown and Company.

The M.I.T. Press. Passage from *Language, Thought and Reality* by Benjamin Lee Whorf, copyright 1956 by the Massachusetts Institute of Technology. Reprinted by permission of the M.I.T. Press.

William Morrow and Company, Inc. Passage from *Coming of Age in Samoa* by Margaret Mead. Reprinted by permission of William Morrow and Company, Inc. Copyright © 1928, 1955, 1961 by Margaret Mead.

National Council of Teachers of English. "War Words" by Edward and Onora Nell from *College English*, May 1967. Reprinted with the permission of the National Council of Teachers of English and Edward and Onora Nell.

New Directions Publishing Corporation. Passage from *The Crack-Up* by F. Scott Fitzgerald. Copyright 1945 by New Directions. Reprinted by permission of New Directions Publishing Corporation.

The New Yorker Magazine, Inc. "Onward and Upward in the Arts: No Telling, No Summing Up" by Calvin Trillin. Reprinted by permission; © 1966 The New Yorker Magazine, Inc.

W. W. Norton & Company, Inc. Passage, "Confession and Autobiography," from *The Making of a Poem* by Stephen Spender, © 1955, © 1962 by Stephen Spender. Reprinted with the permission of W. W. Norton & Company, Inc.

Harold Ober Associates, Inc. Passage from "I Want to Know Why" by Sherwood Anderson, *Smart Set*, November 1919, copyright © 1921 by B. W. Huebsch, Inc. Renewed 1948 by Eleanor Copenhaver Anderson. Passage from *Writing Biography* by Catherine Drinker Bowen, copyright © 1950 by Catherine Drinker Bowen. Reprinted by permission of Harold Ober Associates Inc.

Oxford University Press. Passage from *White Collar: The American Middle Classes* by C. Wright Mills. Copyright 1951 by Oxford University Press, Inc. Passage from Leo Tolstoy's *What Is Art*, translated by Louise and Aylmer Maude, published by Oxford University Press. Passage from *Anna Karenina* by Leo Tolstoy, translated by Louise and Aylmer Maude, published by Oxford University Press. Reprinted by permission.

Paulist-Newman Press. Passage from *Best of NBC Emphasis* by Pauline Frederick, January 1961. Reprinted by permission of the Paulist-Newman Press.

A. D. Peters & Co. "Confession and Autobiography" from *The Making of a Poem* by Stephen Spender, published in Canada by Hamish Hamilton Ltd. Reprinted by permission of A. D. Peters and Co.

Random House, Inc. "To My Daughter" from *Collected Poems* by Stephen Spender, copyright 1955 by Stephen Spender, published by Random House. Reprinted by permission of Random House, Inc.

Henry Regnery Company. Lines from "Sue's Got a Baby" from *Just Folks* by Edgar A. Guest, Henry Regnery Company. Reprinted by permission of Henry Regnery Company.

Paul R. Reynolds Inc. "Vulture Country" by John Stewart, copyright © 1959 by The Atlantic Monthly Company, Inc. Passage from *Twelve Million*

Black Voices by Richard Wright, Viking Press, copyright © 1941 by Richard Wright. Reprinted by permission of Paul R. Reynolds Inc.

Saturday Review. "The Age of Overwrite and Underthink" by Stephen Spender, *Saturday Review*, March 12, 1966. "Where Is Science Taking Us?" by Gyorgy Kepes, *Saturday Review*, March 5, 1966. Reprinted with the permission of *Saturday Review*.

Scientific American, Inc. "Joey: A 'Mechanical Boy'" by Bruno Bettelheim, from *Scientific American*, March 1959. Reprinted with permission. Copyright © 1959 by Scientific American, Inc. All rights reserved.

Charles Scribner's Sons. Passage reprinted with the permission of Charles Scribner's Sons from *Green Hills of Africa*, pp. 49–51, by Ernest Hemingway. Copyright 1935 Charles Scribner's Sons; renewal copyright © 1963 Mary Hemingway. Lines reprinted with the permission of Charles Scribner's Sons from *Look Homeward, Angel*, pp. 86–87, by Thomas Wolfe. Copyright 1929 Charles Scribner's Sons; renewal copyright © 1959 Edward C. Aswell, C.T.A. and/or Fred W. Wolfe. "Up in Michigan" is reprinted with the permission of Charles Scribner's Sons from *The Short Stories of Ernest Hemingway*, copyright 1938 Ernest Hemingway; renewal copyright © 1966 Mary Hemingway. Passage reprinted with the permission of Charles Scribner's Sons from *A Farewell to Arms*, p. 13 by Ernest Hemingway. Copyright 1929 Charles Scribner's Sons. Renewal copyright © 1966 Mary Hemingway. Excerpt reprinted with the permission of Charles Scribner's Sons from *Scott Fitzgerald*, pp. 149–150, by Andrew Turnbull. Copyright © 1962 Andrew Turnbull.

Secker & Warburg Limited. "Jealousy," from *My Mother's House* by Colette. Reprinted with the permission of Secker & Warburg Limited, Publishers.

Simon & Schuster, Inc. Passage from *Attorney for the Damned* by Clarence Darrow, published by Simon & Schuster. Copyright © 1957 Arthur Weinberg. Passage from *A Single Man* by Christopher Isherwood, copyright © 1964 by Christopher Isherwood. Passage from *The Enjoyment of Laughter* by Max Eastman, published by Simon & Schuster. Copyright © 1936 by Max Eastman. Reprinted by permission of Simon & Schuster, Inc.

The Society of Authors. "Now hollow fires burn out to black" by A. E. Housman. Reprinted by permission of The Society of Authors as the literary representative of the Estate of A. E. Housman, and Messrs. Jonathan Cape Ltd., publishers of A. E. Housman's *Collected Poems*.

Stephen Spender. "The Age of Overwrite and Underthink" by Stephen Spender, *Saturday Review*, March 12, 1966. Reprinted by permission of Stephen Spender.

Mrs. Helen Thurber. "The Night the Bed Fell" by James Thurber from *My Life and Hard Times*, published by Harper & Row. Copyright © 1933, 1961 by James Thurber. Originally printed in *The New Yorker*. Reprinted by permission of Mrs. Helen Thurber.

Time-Life Books. Passage from "The Hidden World of the Soil" by Peter Farb. Reprinted by permission of Time-Life Books from *The Forest*. © 1966 Time Inc.

The Viking Press. Passage from Lawrence Durrell interview, *Writers at Work: The Paris Review Interviews*, Second Series. Copyright © 1963 by The Paris Review, Inc. Reprinted by permission of The Viking Press, Inc. Passage from *Travels with Charley In Search of America* by John Steinbeck. Copyright © 1961, 1962 by The Curtis Publishing Co., Inc. Copyright © 1962 by John Steinbeck. Reprinted by permission of The Viking Press, Inc. Passage from Henry Miller interview, *Writers at Work: The Paris Review Interviews,* Second Edition. Copyright © 1963 by The Paris Review, Inc. Reprinted by permission of The Viking Press, Inc. Passage from Frank O'Connor interview, *Writers at Work: The Paris Review Interviews,* edited by Malcolm Cowley. Copyright © 1957, 1958 by The Paris Review, Inc. Reprinted by permission of The Viking Press, Inc.

A. P. Watt & Son. Passages from *The Summing Up* by W. Somerset Maugham. Reprinted by permission of The Literary Executor of W. Somerset Maugham and William Heinemann Ltd.

The Williams & Wilkins Co. Passage from *Biography of the Unborn* by Margaret Shea Gilbert, published by The Williams & Wilkins Co. Reprinted by permission of the publishers.

Louis Zahner, Passage from "Composition at the Barricades," *Atlantic Monthly,* November 1959. Copyright © 1959 by The Atlantic Monthly Company, Boston, Mass. Reprinted with permission.

Contents

USING THIS BOOK   XIV

PREFACE   XV

PART ONE Finding the Material
Sources

1 Writing Out of Experience   3
   James Agee, "James Agee, by Himself"   7
   David Ogilvy, from Confessions of an Advertising Man   8
   George Orwell, "Such, Such Were the Joys"   11
   Mark Twain, from Life on the Mississippi   17
   Student Theme   23
   ASSIGNMENTS   25

2 The Uses of Observation   26
   Ernest Hemingway, from Green Hills of Africa   30
   Henry David Thoreau, from Cape Cod   33
   Margaret Mead, from Coming of Age in Samoa   35
   Peter Farb, "The Hidden World of the Soil"   40
   Theodore Roethke, "Flower Dump"   42
   Student Theme   43
   ASSIGNMENTS   46

3 The Function of Reading   47
   Thomas Wolfe, from Look Homeward, Angel   51
   Lawrence Durrell, from interview in Writers at Work: The
     Paris Review Interviews   53
   Somerset Maugham, from The Summing Up   54
   Paul Green, from "The University in a Nuclear Age"   59
   Student Theme   61
   ASSIGNMENTS   63

PART TWO Putting Materials Together
Problems of Form and Order

INTRODUCTION: Form and Order   67
4 What Is a Place?   74
  Nathaniel Hawthorne, from The Scarlet Letter   80
  Oscar Lewis and Carroll Hall, from Bonanza Inn   82
  John Stewart, from "Vulture Country"   86
  Student Theme   89
  ASSIGNMENTS   90

5 Revealing Personalities   92
  Andrew Turnbull, from Scott Fitzgerald   98
  F. Scott Fitzgerald, from The Crack-Up   99
  Pauline Fredericks, "January 5, 1960" *from* The Best of NBC
    Emphasis   102
  Bruno Bettelheim, "Joey: A Mechanical Boy"   104
  Reynolds Price, "Uncle Grant"   115
  Student Theme   118
  ASSIGNMENTS   120

6 How to Make Things Happen   122
  John Kenneth Galbraith, from The Affluent Society   128
  Margaret Shea Gilbert, from Biography of the Unborn   131
  René Dubos, from The Mirage of Health   134
  Georg Heym, "The Autopsy"   138
  Student Theme   141
  ASSIGNMENTS   142

PART THREE Uniting Idea and Emotion
Problems of Control

INTRODUCTION: From Abstract to Concrete   145
7 Anger and Jealousy: Controlling the Destructive Force   147
  Colette, "Jealousy"   152
  Jonathan Swift, "A Modest Proposal"   158
  John Dos Passos, "Body of an American"   168
  Richard Wright, from Twelve Million Black Voices   173
  Clarence Darrow, from Darrow for the Defense   178
  Student Theme   183
  ASSIGNMENTS   185

8 Love and Delight: Controlling Sentimentality   187
     Ernest Hemingway, "Up in Michigan"   191
     Leo Tolstoy, from Anna Karenina   197
     Student Poem   205
     Antoine de Saint-Exupéry, from Night Flight   207
     John Steinbeck, from Travels with Charley   211
     Student Theme   217
     ASSIGNMENTS

9 Sorrow and Laughter: Controlling Pathos and Absurdity 218
     Sherwood Anderson, "I Want to Know Why"   223
     Christopher Isherwood, from A Single Man   226
     James Thurber, "The Night the Bed Fell"   229
     C. Northcote Parkinson, from Parkinson's Law   234
     Russell Baker, "The Disposable Man"   238
     Rachel Carson, from The Silent Spring   241
     Student Theme   247
     ASSIGNMENTS   249

     PART FOUR The Writer's Responsibility

10 Your Writing and You   253
     Leo Tolstoy, from "What Is Art"   258
     Somerset Maugham, from The Summing Up   260
     Stephen Spender, "Confession and Autobiography"   261
     Calvin Trillin, "No Telling, No Summing Up"   266
     Walter Lippmann, "Stereotypes"   275
     Louis Zahner, "Composition at the Barricades"   286
     ASSIGNMENTS   294

11 What Your Language Does to Others and What It Can Do   295
     Edward and Onora Nell, from "War Words"   298
     Benjamin Lee Whorf, from Language, Mind and Reality 306
     Frank O'Connor, from interview in Writers at Work: The
     Paris Review Interviews   318
     Gyorgy Kepes, "Where Is Science Taking Us?"   319
     Stephen Spender, "The Age of Overwrite and Underthink" 325
     ASSIGNMENTS   330

     Index to Authors and Titles   331

Using This Book

The Act of Writing is intended for freshman composition courses. The central idea of the book is that good writing is an individual's reaction to the world around him. Therefore, the act of writing is larger than the act of putting words on paper. Writing must be considered as a way of handling the problems in the writer's world. In this book students are asked to study specific problems and possible ways of handling these problems in writing. Their own solutions may then be worked out with greater freedom and confidence. Text, student themes, selections from well-known writers, and assignments at the end of each chapter offer the student a great variety of explicit methods for finding, organizing, and transforming his material into writing in a way that will be meaningful to his reader. Questions both in the text and after selections give the student guidelines for criticizing his own work. By examining his own act of writing in this way, and in class discussion, the student can discover a writing process that belongs to him, one that will be both permanent and enjoyable.

A course based on this book should emphasize patterns of writing rather than rules of rhetoric. The technical aspects of writing should be seen as means of solving a particular communication problem. The essentials of this course are concerned with fostering different kinds of writing. The emphasis is unfailingly on the entire act of composition. A student who habitually makes errors in grammar and in punctuation should use a supplementary handbook.

Preface

Suppose someone told you, "Writing is not writing." You would say he was stupid, or more politely, that he was contradicting himself. But in a way he is correct. Writing is more than putting words on paper. If you have thought of writing only in terms of putting words on paper, you have probably had a lot of trouble. Maybe you have avoided writing as much as possible.

Consider writing not as words on paper, but as the result of a person's desire to communicate something which is important or interesting to him. In this sense, writing starts long before words reach paper. It is grounded in a desire that is common to almost every human being. When a person does not want to communicate anything to anybody we consider him seriously ill.

There have been many times when you have very much wanted to say something. Like most people you have probably thought, "If only I could put that in words." Maybe you envied writers who seemed to have the power you lacked. This experience too often leads us to think that some people can write while some cannot. But good writing is not an art reserved for the professional writer while all others are doomed to something called "composition." Few people can write a novel, a story, a poem, a play, or an artful essay, but good writing is possible for anyone who is firmly convinced that he or she is a thinking individual.

Everyone who speaks the English language and has learned to spell can write. But we all know there are good speakers and poor speakers. Good writing, like good speaking, will come from the development of your ability to use the language you have known since you were a baby. The idea now is to examine the act of writing—not only putting words on paper, but the very reasons and sources of writing. Then, since writing is a form of communication, you can develop your writing by weighing suggestions of the

people who read it. This means that in many ways you will be examining your own mind and life. That is the foundation of good
writing. It doesn't come out of a pen. The result of your examination will not only be clearer, more effective writing, but a writing
process that belongs to you and is best for putting your ideas and
experience on paper.

Of course you must bring with you something besides your
knowledge of the language. What everyone brings is his own
background. You must also have the power to work. Ultimately,
the only proof of a writer's art are the words he puts on paper. He
finds his material, examines it, shapes it, and gets it down in raw
form. Then by continuing the act of writing, he develops methods
that are most effective for him in communication. Finally he
learns not only how to find and use the material that belongs to
him, but how to make that material appeal to his ultimate judge,
the reader for whom all successful writing is designed.

You write out of your knowledge into your reader's. You start
with what is meaningful to you and end with what is meaningful
to both you and him. You start with what you care about, and you
try to make him care.

In this book you go through a series of writing acts in a planned
pattern, examining and discussing each act with the goal of
finding where your particular methods of communication are
weak or strong. You start with yourself in chapter one, and in thirteen chapters you move out from personal experience through a
variety of forms and methods. Finally you try to create writing
which encompasses the whole fabric of your experience—people,
places, events, ideas, and feelings. You create it not only for yourself but for your reader.

Along the way you will encounter most of the problems that beset any writer except, perhaps, he who is writing a full-length
book. Each chapter of this text is bulwarked by carefully chosen
selections from well-known authors, by students' themes, and by
definite assignments for the student in class. These selections and
assignments offer explicit methods of getting what you have experienced out of your head and down on paper.

When you have learned to do this, you will have more than the ability to write good English. You will have acquired the basic tool for exploring your own identity and you will have begun to master the most important means of conveying any kind of human knowledge.

APPRECIATIONS

The authors know this book is not theirs alone. We have borrowed heavily and gratefully from our friends' ideas. James Gaskin helped found the experimental course from which this book emerged. John Knowles supplied indispensable ideas for the units on emotion and writing. Doc Adams, Bill Powers and Jim Collier tested much of our material in class and helped us refine our thinking. Our ideas about the act of writing have often been clarified and reinforced by writers Reynolds Price, Max Steele, Doris Betts, Peter Dale, and Stephen Spender. Professor James Bryan has been invaluable as "devil's disciple." The distinguished career of William Blackburn at Duke has given us confidence that imaginative writing can and should have a place in university classrooms. Our students, above all, have helped with tough and honest criticism as well as understanding. Though they have helped us more than anyone, their names are too many to list, for among our students those who have been willing to encourage a new idea are the rule rather than the exception.

PART ONE

FINDING THE MATERIAL

Sources

CHAPTER 1

WRITING OUT OF

EXPERIENCE

Nobody ever knows where writing starts, but one place can be with an individual's desire to communicate what is most important and persistent in his thought and feeling. This may be the memory of an event, an idea, an emotion, or any combination of these things. If the desire to communicate is strong enough, then the writer—who in this case is you—will have a need to get whatever is meaningful to him out of his head and down on paper.

It is not enough just to get your material down. You have to get it down in a way that carries to the reader the meaning and force of your original experience. After you are finished writing, your experience must be there for the reader, regardless of where you are. Of course the reader will never have your exact experience, for despite the wishes of some writers, life and art are never the same. Yet if you work at selecting detail and finding words, you can convey in writing the essence of your experience. That essence, as you use it to shape your writing, is what we call your vision. Through this written vision of what seemed so significant to you that you had to write it, you can bring to a reader a new way of seeing or perhaps illuminate some parallel experience of his own. You may convey to him something he in turn will wish to convey in his own way to others.

Conveying this vision, this way of seeing, to the reader is the ultimate end for any writer. Sometimes a student objects and says, "I don't want to tell the reader how he should think." This is confusing an imperative, an order to think in a certain way, with presentation. In presenting a vision the writer does not say this is the only way of seeing a certain experience, or of communicating an idea. If the idea and the experience are strong enough they will speak for themselves. But the reader cannot even get an idea of what they are if they are not presented in a clear and precise manner. In other words, communication must take place before judgment. We must concern ourselves with communication as a skill basic to all kinds of human understanding.

But why choose *words* to communicate? As you begin to write, you are forced into the medium of language because it is the strongest bridge between one individual and another, between the individual and his society. Nothing else, not even music or pictures, carries so much force, or can cause so much understanding, or can give so much satisfaction to the man who uses it. Other forms of communication can call up associations and meanings. A symphony dominated by the beat of kettle drums may remind you of cannons. For a mathematician or chemist, letters and numbers used as exact symbols have a very specific and limited meaning. But no form of communication can combine precision and suggestiveness the way language can. So you choose to use words because you want to affect others, but you always start with what has affected you.

You start with your own experience, with what you have felt directly, or what you know through being involved with other human beings. All writing, truth or fiction, begins with some aspect of the writer's self. Katherine Anne Porter says,

> . . . I have never written a story in my life that didn't have a very firm foundation in actual human experience—somebody

else's experience quite often, but an experience that became my own by hearing the story, by witnessing the thing, by hearing just a word perhaps.

It doesn't matter, it just takes a little—a tiny seed. Then it takes root, and it grows. It's an organic thing.

There is no one way to communicate this experience. There is not even one complex way, such as studying a book on writing, or following a rhetoric book and learning four forms of discourse—description, exposition, narrative, and argument. The body of personal experience which you bring with you to the act of writing has helped make you an individual with a point of view and a way of seeing and thinking and feeling that is different from anyone else's. This is true of everyone, and it is one of the basic reasons why we can call ourselves individuals. So the writing which will be most expressive for one person will probably not be quite right for another. The differences between one person's way of writing and another's may not be very great or even noticeable, but there are, nevertheless, as many different ways of writing as there are individuals who write.

The temptation is to evade the problem of individuality by "inventing" a style, one which is clearly distinguished from most familiar writing by a special vocabulary, by slang, by unusual grammar and punctuation, or even by special typography. You can probably name professional writers who are marked by one or more of these special characteristics, but judging the validity of their writing will not help you in your present task—finding your way of writing.

You must discover your way *in you*, not by glibly choosing some premade, offbeat style. To choose the premade style is, in a sense, to hide behind a façade. It is also to put yet another barrier between yourself and the people with whom you wish to communicate.

We started talking about the individual when we said there is no one way to write. True, but there are certain directions you can follow. Let's say there are signposts, and there are roads above which these signposts are set. This book is one of those roads and its contents are signposts. No more. We are not saying this is the only road, but that it is one you can take, a road that begins with you, where you are now.

But where am I? you might say—for that is really the point with many starting writers. You are, for one thing, in possession of some experience that has happened to you in the years since childhood. Now that you are in college you have probably fifteen years or more of that experience. You can start with that. You can see how other writers, students or professionals, have shaped their own experience into language. Then, through the act of writing, you can shape your experience. This puts you on the road to finding a form of your own.

With your subject in mind you can start, if you like, simply by writing from your storehouse of memory. Get something down. But writing is not quite that simple. First you have the matter of selection, of choosing your material, even before you can put it down in the most intimate form—writing from personal experience. You must choose the experience or pattern of experiences you wish to write about. Then you must decide how much of that experience should go on paper. No experience, no matter how small, can be described in all its detail. For instance just picking up a phone to answer its ring involves all the detail of muscles, learning, hearing, and speaking; not to mention colors and smells, temperatures and textures, directly and indirectly connected with the act and its setting. Fortunately, we do not have to decide consciously on each omission when we begin selecting the material for writing. You need not decide right away exactly what will and will not go on paper. Simply get down what seems to matter; then you can decide.

The selections in this chapter and those throughout the book are included so that you can use them to analyze the working methods writers use, applying whatever you learn to your own writing. Before you begin your first assignment read the following selections, all written out of personal experience. Try to discover for yourself specific methods by which each man makes his writing unmistakably his own.

Selections

We usually think of writers as novelists, story writers, poets, essayists, and so on. James Agee was all of these, as well as being a journalist and a film writer. His autobiographical sketch for *Esquire* reveals something of his personality in its formative years.[1]

Mr. Agee, James "Rufus" Agee, was born in Knoxville, Tennessee, in November, 1909, scarcely one hundred years after the birth of Abraham Lincoln, of parents verging on the bourgeois, but honest. At three he inquired of his mother, "Mama"—he called her Mama in those days—"who made God?" (P.S.: He got the job.) At four he was run over by a bicycle, but later learned to love the irresponsible fellows. After a brief sojourn in kindergarten, for which he showed no more than average aptitude, he entered the public schools, and at these, and others, he spent no few years in ardent study of the back of the nearest head and of the nearest exit. At ten he proposed to write a monograph on torture, but lacking the training in research necessary for such a task, soon put it by. At fifteen he visited the London of Ramsay MacDonald [first Labor Prime Minister, 1924; 1929–1935] and the Paris of the *Hunchback of Notre Dame*, where he explored the "slums," watched out for American moving pictures, and climbed the cathedrals. He scarcely minded the bedbugs at all . . . an oversight which was to amaze him in maturer years.

At Phillips Exeter, whose motto is that there are no rules until they are broken, he fought Caesar's Gallic War for the third time, swam the backstroke, and was awarded ten volumes of Rudyard Kipling for excellence in English Composition. At Harvard he made many valuable contacts and spent what must always seem to him the four happiest years of his life.

[1] James Agee, "James Agee, by Himself," *Esquire Magazine* (December 1963).

A part of James Agee's method is to fit many facts into the brief account of himself as a boy. He arranges these facts around the theme of the learning process. The child's habit of questioning becomes a habit of exploring for knowledge in London, in Paris, and at Harvard, which marks the end of boyhood. Only at the end does Agee come out and tell us that the college years seemed to him to be the happiest of his life. Only here does he suggest his own deepest reaction. He is never glossy, never redundant. The quest for knowledge and experience was the center of his life. His sketch seems random, but in fact Agee has been very careful in cutting and sharpening his work. Not only do almost all the details work for his theme, but they tie this theme to a particular individual. The way in which Agee chooses his detail for both theme and personality makes this a unified sketch.

QUESTIONS

1. Why does Agee say "the London of Ramsay MacDonald and the Paris of the *Hunchback of Notre Dame*"?
2. Why does he tell the reader about the monograph on torture?
3. Why is his education at Harvard condensed into one sentence?
4. What kinds of details do you think he intentionally left out that he might have thought of including?

The autobiographical sketch below is the introduction to David Ogilvy's book, *Confessions of an Advertising Man*, about his career in advertising.[2] As a copywriter he believed in ads that contained information. As head of a large agency he set out to secure a limited number of selected, important clients.

As a child I lived in Lewis Carroll's house in Guildford. My father, whom I adored, was a Gaelic-speaking highlander, a

[2] David Ogilvy, *Confessions of an Advertising Man* (New York: Atheneum Publishers, 1963) pp. 3–5.

classical scholar, and a bigoted agnostic. One day he discovered that I had started going to church secretly.

"My dear old son, how can you swallow that mumbo-jumbo? It is all very well for servants, but not for educated people. *You don't have to be a Christian to behave like a gentleman!*"

My mother was a beautiful and eccentric Irishwoman. She disinherited me, on the ground that I was likely to acquire more money than was good for me, without any help from her. I could not disagree.

At the age of nine I was sent to board at an aristocratic Dotheboys Hall in Eastbourne. The headmaster wrote of me, "He has a distinctly original mind, inclined to argue with his teachers and to try and convince them that he is right and the books are wrong; but this perhaps is further proof of his originality." When I suggested that Napoleon might have been a Dutchman because his brother was King of Holland, the headmaster's wife sent me to bed without supper. When she was robing me for the part of the Abbess in *The Comedy of Errors*, I rehearsed my opening speech with an emphasis that she disliked; whereupon she seized me by the cheek and threw me to the floor.

At the age of thirteen I went to Fettes, a Scottish school whose Spartan disciplines had been established by my great-uncle Lord Justice General Inglis, the greatest Scottish advocate of all time. My friends at this splendid school included Ian Macleod, Niall Macpherson, Knox Cunningham, and several other future Members of Parliament. Chief among the masters I remember Henry Havergal, who inspired me to play the double bass, and Walter Sellar, who wrote *1066 and All That* while teaching me history.

I made a botch of Oxford. Keith Feiling, the historian, had given me a scholarship at Christ Church, and I was the recipient of much kindness from Patrick Gordon-Walker, Roy Harrod, A. S. Russell, and other dons. But I was too preoccupied to do any work, and was duly expelled.

That was in 1931, the bottom of the depression. For the next seventeen years, while my friends were establishing themselves as doctors, lawyers, civil servants, and politicians, I adventured about the world, uncertain of purpose. I was a chef in Paris, a door-to-door salesman, a social worker in the Edinburgh slums, an associate of Dr. Gallup in research for the motion picture industry, an assistant to Sir William Stephenson in British Security Coordination, and a farmer in Pennsylvania.

My boyhood hero had been Lloyd George, and I had expected to become Prime Minister when I grew up. Instead, I finally became an advertising agent on Madison Avenue; the revenues of my nineteen clients are now greater than the revenue of Her Majesty's Government.

Max Beerbohm once told S. N. Behrman, "If I was endowed with wealth I should start a great advertising campaign in all the principal newspapers. The advertisements would consist of one short sentence, printed in huge block letters—a sentence that I once heard spoken by a husband to a wife: 'My dear, nothing in this world is worth buying'."

My position is the opposite. I want to buy almost everything I see advertised. My father used to say of a product that it was "very well spoken of in the advertisements." I spend my life speaking well of products in advertisements; I hope that you get as much pleasure out of buying them as I get out of advertising them.

By writing this book in the old-fashioned first person singular, I have committed an offense against a convention of contemporary American manners. But I think it artificial to write *we* when I am confessing *my* sins and describing *my* adventures.

As Agee did in his sketch, Ogilvy follows his life chronologically, but here the sketch is leading to a specific image of an adult. As an adult Ogilvy is a strong believer in the value of his career in advertising. Looking back on his earlier years he chooses details that explain why he became head of an advertising agency and why he enjoys his work. He does not try to direct the reader by beginning with his present position. He lets the detail develop the important theme of his early years. While his final entry into advertising was unexpected even to himself, the reader can see it is not in conflict with his character. The reader is also prepared to find that Ogilvy's career in advertising was the career of an innovator.

QUESTIONS

1. Why is Ogilvy not angry that his mother disinherited him? How does this contribute to the sketch?
2. What common theme, if any, can you find in his experience at the three schools he attended?
3. Do you think that Ogilvy really expected to become Prime Minister? How does he relate this aspiration with his career in advertising?
4. Can you see any connection between the beginning of the sketch and the end?

George Orwell's two novels, *1984* and *Animal Farm*, are both concerned with tyranny in some form. This theme appears also in his essays and other nonfiction. The following account of his childhood schooldays, an essay entitled "Such, Such Were the Joys" reveals something of his first experiences with absolute power.[3]

Soon after I arrived at Crossgates (not immediately, but after a week or two, just when I seemed to be settling into the routine of school life) I began wetting my bed. I was now aged eight, so that this was a reversion to a habit which I must have grown out of at least four years earlier.

Nowadays, I believe, bed-wetting in such circumstances is taken for granted. It is a normal reaction in children who have been removed from their homes to a strange place. In those days, however, it was looked on as a disgusting crime which the child committed on purpose and for which the proper cure was a beating. For my part I did not need to be told it was a crime.

[3] George Orwell, "Such, Such Were the Joys" from *Such, Such Were the Joys* (New York: Harcourt, Brace & World, 1953), pp. 12–17.

Night after night I prayed, with a fervour never previously attained in my prayers, "Please God, do not let me wet my bed! Oh, please God, do not let me wet my bed!" but it made remarkably little difference. Some nights the thing happened, others not. There was no volition about it, no consciousness. You did not properly speaking do the deed: you merely woke up in the morning and found that the sheets were wringing wet.

After the second or third offence I was warned that I should be beaten next time, but I received the warning in a curiously roundabout way. One afternoon, as we were filing out from tea, Mrs. Simpson, the headmaster's wife, was sitting at the head of one of the tables, chatting with a lady of whom I know nothing, except that she was on an afternoon's visit to the school. She was an intimidating, masculine-looking person wearing a riding habit, or something that I took to be a riding habit. I was just leaving the room when Mrs. Simpson called me back, as though to introduce me to the visitor.

Mrs. Simpson was nicknamed Bingo, and I shall call her by that name for I seldom think of her by any other. (Officially, however, she was addressed as Mum, probably a corruption of the "Ma'am" used by public school boys to their housemasters' wives.) She was a stocky square-built woman with hard red cheeks, a flat top to her head, prominent brows and deepset, suspicious eyes. Although a great deal of the time she was full of false heartiness, jollying one along with mannish slang ("Buck up, old chap!" and so forth), and even using one's Christian name, her eyes never lost their anxious, accusing look. It was very difficult to look her in the face without feeling guilty, even at moments when one was not guilty of anything in particular.

"Here is a little boy," said Bingo, indicating me to the strange lady, "who wets his bed every night. Do you know what I am going to do if you wet your bed again?" she added, turning to me. "I am going to get the Sixth Form to beat you."

The strange lady put on an air of being inexpressibly shocked, and exclaimed "I-should-think-so!" And here occurred one of those wild, almost lunatic misunderstandings which are part of the daily experience of childhood. The Sixth

Form was a group of older boys who were selected as having "character" and were empowered to beat smaller boys. I had not yet learned of their existence, and I mis-heard the phrase "the Sixth Form" as "Mrs. Form." I took it as referring to the strange lady—I thought, that is, that her name was Mrs. Form. It was an improbable name, but a child has no judgement in such matters. I imagined, therefore, that it was she who was to be deputed to beat me. It did not strike me as strange that this job should be turned over to a casual visitor in no way connected with the school. I merely assumed that "Mrs. Form" was a stern disciplinarian who enjoyed beating people (somehow her appearance seemed to bear this out) and I had an immediate terrifying vision of her arriving for the occasion in full riding kit and armed with a hunting whip. To this day I can feel myself almost swooning with shame as I stood, a very small, round-faced boy in short corduroy knickers, before the two women. I could not speak. I felt that I should die if "Mrs. Form" were to beat me. But my dominant feeling was not fear or even resentment: it was simply shame because one more person, and that a woman, had been told of my disgusting offence.

A little later, I forget how, I learned that it was not after all "Mrs. Form" who would do the beating. I cannot remember whether it was that very night that I wetted my bed again, but at any rate I did wet it again quite soon. Oh, the despair, the feeling of cruel injustice, after all my prayers and resolutions, at once again waking between the clammy sheets! There was no chance of hiding what I had done. The grim statuesque matron, Daphne by name, arrived in the dormitory specially to inspect my bed. She pulled back the clothes, then drew herself up, and the dreaded words seemed to come rolling out of her like a peal of thunder:

"REPORT YOURSELF to the headmaster after breakfast!"

I do not know how many times I heard that phrase during my early years at Crossgates. It was only very rarely that it did not mean a beating. The words always had a portentous sound in my ears, like muffled drums or the words of the death sentence.

When I arrived to report myself, Bingo was doing something or other at the long shiny table in the anteroom to the study.

Her uneasy eyes searched me as I went past. In the study Mr. Simpson, nicknamed Sim, was waiting. Sim was a round-shouldered curiously oafish-looking man, not large but shambling in gait, with a chubby face which was like that of an overgrown baby, and which was capable of good humour. He knew, of course, why I had been sent to him, and had already taken a bone-handled riding crop out of the cupboard, but it was part of the punishment of reporting yourself that you had to proclaim your offence with your own lips. When I had said my say, he read me a short but pompous lecture, then seized me by the scruff of the neck, twisted me over and began beating me with the riding crop. He had a habit of continuing his lecture while he flogged you, and I remember the words "you dir-ty little boy" keeping time with the blows. The beating did not hurt (perhaps as it was the first time, he was not hitting me very hard), and I walked out feeling very much better. The fact that the beating had not hurt was a sort of victory and partially wiped out the shame of the bed-wetting. I was even incautious enough to wear a grin on my face. Some small boys were hanging about in the passage outside the door of the anteroom.

"D'you get the cane?"

"It didn't hurt," I said proudly.

Bingo had heard everything. Instantly her voice came screaming after me:

"Come here! Come here this instant! What was that you said?

"How dare you say a thing like that? Do you think that is a proper thing to say? Go in and REPORT YOURSELF AGAIN!"

This time Sim laid on in real earnest. He continued for a length of time that frightened and astonished me—about five minutes, it seemed—ending up by breaking the riding crop. The bone handle went flying across the room.

"Look what you've made me do!" he said furiously, holding up the broken crop.

I had fallen into a chair, weakly snivelling. I remember that this was the only time throughout my boyhood when a beating actually reduced me to tears, and curiously enough I was not even now crying because of the pain. The second beating had not hurt very much either. Fright and shame seemed to have anesthetised me. I was crying partly because I felt that this was expected of me, partly from genuine repentance, but partly also because of a deeper grief which is peculiar to childhood and not easy to convey: a sense of desolate loneliness and helplessness, of being locked up not only in a hostile world but in a world of good and evil where the rules were such that it was actually not possible for me to keep them.

I knew that bed-wetting was (a) wicked and (b) outside my control. The second fact I was personally aware of, and the first I did not question. It was possible therefore, to commit a sin without knowing that you committed it, without wanting to commit it, and without being able to avoid it. Sin was not necessarily something that you did: it might be something that happened to you. I do not want to claim that this idea flashed into my mind as a complete novelty at this very moment, under the blows of Sim's cane: I must have had glimpses of it even before I left home, for my early childhood had not been altogether happy. But at any rate this was the great, abiding lesson of my boyhood: that I was in a world where it was not possible for me to be good. And the double beating was a turning-point, for it brought home to me for the first time the harshness of the environment into which I had been flung. Life was more terrible, and I was more wicked, than I had imagined. At any rate, as I sat on the edge of a chair in Sim's study, with not even the self-possession to stand up while he stormed at me, I had a conviction of sin and folly and weakness, such as I do not remember to have felt before.

In general, one's memories of any period must necessarily weaken as one moves away from it. One is constantly learning new facts, and old ones have to drop out to make way for them. At twenty I could have written the history of my schooldays with an accuracy which would be quite impossible now. But it can also happen that one's memories grow sharper after a long lapse of time, because one is looking at the past with fresh eyes and can isolate and, as it were, notice facts which previously existed undifferentiated among a mass of others. Here are two things which in a sense I remembered, but which did not strike me as strange or interesting until quite recently. One is that the second beating seemed to me a just and reasonable punishment. To get one beating, and then to get another and far fiercer one on top of it, for being so unwise as to show that the first had not hurt—that was quite natural. The gods are jealous, and when you have good fortune you should conceal it. The other is that I accepted the broken riding crop as my own crime. I can still recall my feeling as I saw the handle lying on the carpet—the feeling of having done an ill-bred clumsy thing, and ruined an expensive object. I had broken it: so Sim told me, and so I believed. This acceptance of guilt lay unnoticed in my memory for twenty or thirty years.

So much for the episode of the bed-wetting. But there is one more thing to be remarked. This is that I did not wet my bed again—at least, I did wet it once again, and received another beating, after which the trouble stopped. So perhaps this barbarous remedy does work, though at a heavy price, I have no doubt.

In describing a very brief period of his childhood, George Orwell transforms ordinary details of a private school discipline into a complex picture of moral development. The transformation becomes clear to the reader because Orwell uses the boy's point of view in describing what happens.

The gods of Crossgates are Sim and Bingo, the woman being far the more formidable. The little boy sees them strangely, as if through a cracked glass, and this strangeness, this frightening sense of disconnection, gives the piece much of its strength. The twisted name, Mrs. Form, the uneasy eyes of Bingo, and the bone-handled riding crop waiting with Sim for the boy to arrive all proclaim a beating. Sure enough, he gets two.

While we are seeing with the boy's eyes, Orwell the writer is pointing every scene towards the ending of his piece where he sums up as a man what he learned as a boy. Reflecting on his acceptance of guilt, he sees clearly that he did this because he lives in a world of such moral complexity that it is impossible to be good. He did not break the riding crop, but his sense of guilt was so strong he accepted the blame. This then led to the correction of his bed-wetting. Such is the complex nature of virtue.

Orwell uses a subject that could be the brunt of many jokes, but in this case is not, because of what the boy and the reader find out at Crossgates.

QUESTIONS

1. Why didn't Orwell write this as he might have written or talked or thought at the age of eight or nine?
2. How would the effect of the piece be different if Orwell had begun with his conclusion on the nature of virtue?
3. Pick out as many small details as possible which convey to the reader the boy's emotion.
4. Study the paragraph at the end of the essay in which Orwell talks about memory. Recreate the process by which the plan of this essay might have come to him.

A common complaint among the children of a given town is that the place they live in is dull and uninteresting. Sometimes we blame this situation on "modern times." Study this sketch from *Life on the Mississippi* by Mark Twain and see what his town was like and how he makes it interesting through the act of writing.[4]

When I was a boy, there was but one permanent ambition among my comrades in our village on the west bank of the Mississippi River. That was to be a steamboatman. We had transient ambitions of other sorts, but they were only transient. When a circus came and went, it left us all burning to become clowns; the first negro minstrel show that ever came to our sec-

[4] Mark Twain, *Life on the Mississippi* (New York: Harper and Brothers, 1901).

tion left us all suffering to try that kind of life; now and then we had a hope that, if we lived and were good, God would permit us to be pirates. These ambitions faded out, each in its turn; but the ambition to be a steamboatman always remained.

Once a day a cheap, gaudy packet arrived upward from St. Louis, and another downward from Keokuk. Before these events, the day was glorious with expectancy; after them, the day was a dead and empty thing. Not only the boys, but the whole village, felt this. After all these years I can picture that old time to myself now, just as it was then: the white town drowsing in the sunshine of a summer's morning; the streets empty, or pretty nearly so; one or two clerks sitting in front of the Water Street stores, with their splint-bottomed chairs tilted back against the walls, chins on breasts, hats slouched over their faces, asleep—with shingle-shavings enough around to show what broke them down; a sow and a litter of pigs loafing along the sidewalk, doing a good business in watermelon rinds and seeds; two or three lonely little freight piles scattered about the "levee"; a pile of "skids" on the slope of the stone-paved wharf, and the fragrant town drunkard asleep in the shadow of them; two or three wood flats at the head of the wharf, but nobody to listen to the peaceful lapping of the wavelets against them; the great Mississippi, the majestic, the magnificent Mississippi rolling its mile-wide tide along, shining in the sun; the dense forest away on the other side; the "point" below, bounding the river-glimpse and turning it into a sort of sea, and withal a very still and brilliant and lonely one. Presently a film of dark smoke appears above one of those remote "points"; instantly a negro drayman, famous for his quick eye and prodigious voice, lifts up the cry, "S-t-e-a-m-boat a-comin'!" and the scene changes! The town drunkard stirs, the clerks wake up, a furious clatter of drays follows, every house and store pours out a human contribution, and all in a twinkling the dead town is alive and moving. Drays, carts, men, boys, all go hurrying from many quarters to a common center, the wharf. Assembled there, the people fasten their eyes upon the coming boat as upon a wonder they are seeing for the first time. And the boat is rather a handsome sight, too. She is long and sharp and trim and pretty; she has two tall, fancy-topped chimneys, with a gilded device of some kind swung between them; a fanciful pilot-house, all glass and "gingerbread," perched on top of the "texas" deck behind them; the paddle-boxes are gorgeous with a picture or with gilded rays above the boat's name; the boiler-deck, the hurricane-deck, and the texas deck are fenced and ornamented with clean white railings; there is a flag gallantly flying from the jack-staff; the furnace doors are open and the fires glaring bravely; the upper decks are black with passengers; the captain stands by the big bell, calm, imposing, the envy of all; great volumes of the blackest smoke are rolling and tumbling out of the chimneys—a hus-banded grandeur created with a bit of pitch-pine just before arriving at a town; the crew are grouped on the forecastle; the broad stage is run far out over the port bow, and an envied deck-hand stands picturesquely on the end of it with a coil of rope in his hand; the pent steam is screaming through the gauge-cocks; the captain lifts his hand, a bell rings, the wheels stop; then they turn back, churning the water to foam, and the steamer is at rest. Then such a scramble as there is to get aboard, and to get ashore, and to take in freight and to discharge freight, all at one and the same time; and such a yelling and cursing as the mates facilitate it all with! Ten minutes later the steamer is un-der way again, with no flag on the jack-staff and no black smoke issuing from the chimneys. After ten more minutes the town is dead again, and the town drunkard asleep by the skids once more.

My father was a justice of the peace, and I supposed he pos-sessed the power of life and death over all men, and could hang anybody that offended him. This was distinction enough for me as a general thing; but the desire to be a steamboatman kept intruding, nevertheless. I first wanted to be a cabin-boy, so that I could come out with a white apron on and shake a tablecloth over the side, where all my old comrades could see me; later I thought I would rather be the deck-hand who stood on the end of the stage-plank with the coil of rope in his hand, because he was particularly conspicuous. But these were only day-dreams —they were too heavenly to be contemplated as real possibili-

ties. By and by one of our boys went away. He was not heard of
for a long time. At last he turned up as apprentice engineer or
"striker" on a steamboat. This thing shook the bottom out of all
my Sunday-school teachings. That boy had been notoriously
worldly, and I just the reverse; yet he was exalted to this eminence, and I left in obscurity and misery. There was nothing
generous about this fellow in his greatness. He would always
manage to have a rusty bolt to scrub while his boat tarried at
our town, and he would sit on the inside guard and scrub it,
where we all could see him and envy him and loathe him. And
whenever his boat was laid up he would come home and swell
around the town in his blackest and greasiest clothes, so that
nobody could help remembering that he was a steamboatman;
and he used all sorts of steamboat technicalities in his talk, as if
he were so used to them that he forgot common people could
not understand them. He would speak of the "labboard" side of
a horse in an easy, natural way that would make one wish he
was dead. And he was always talking about "St. Looy" like an
old citizen; he would refer casually to occasions when he was
"coming down Fourth Street," or when he was "passing by the
Planter's House," or when there was a fire and he took a turn on
the brakes of "the old Big Missouri"; and then he would go on
and lie about how many towns the size of ours were burned
down there that day. Two or three of the boys had long been
persons of consideration among us because they had been to St.
Louis once and had a vague general knowledge of its wonders,
but the day of their glory was over now. They lapsed into a
humble silence, and learned to disappear when the ruthless
"cub"-engineer approached. This fellow had money, too, and
hair-oil. Also an ignorant silver watch and a showy brass watch-
chain. He wore a leather belt and used no suspenders. If ever a
youth was cordially admired and hated by his comrades, this
one was. No girl could withstand his charms. He "cut out"
every boy in the village. When his boat blew up at last, it dif-
fused a tranquil contentment among us such as we had not
known for months. But when he came home the next week
alive, renowned, and appeared in church all battered up and
bandaged, a shining hero, stared at and wondered over by

everybody, it seemed to us that the partiality of Providence for an undeserving reptile had reached a point where it was open to criticism.

This creature's career could produce but one result, and it speedily followed. Boy after boy managed to get on the river. The minister's son became an engineer. The doctor's and the postmaster's sons became "mud clerks"; the wholesale liquor dealer's son became a barkeeper on a boat; four sons of the chief merchant, and two sons of the county judge, became pilots. Pilot was the grandest position of all. The pilot, even in those days of trivial wages, had a princely salary—from a hundred and fifty to two hundred and fifty dollars a month, and no board to pay. Two months of his wages would pay a preacher's salary for a year. Now some of us were left disconsolate. We could not get on the river—at least our parents would not let us.

So, by and by, I ran away. I said I would never come home again till I was a pilot and could come in glory. But somehow I could not manage it. I went meekly aboard a few of the boats that lay packed together like sardines at the long St. Louis wharf, and humbly inquired for the pilots, but got only a cold shoulder and short words from mates and clerks. I had to make the best of this sort of treatment for the time being, but I had comforting daydreams of a future when I should be a great and honored pilot, with plenty of money, and could kill some of these mates and clerks and pay for them.

Mark Twain builds his essay around a central ambition. His town is an ordinary town of its time, but Twain makes it the container of a great dream. His use of exact detail brings the town, the loafers, the crew, and the boy himself alive for us. Through his vivid memory Twain takes the reader back to a time when the contrast between town and dream is most clearly seen—the arrival of a packet. The boat, with its two tall, fancy-topped chimneys and its wheels churning the foam, wakes the lazy town, the fragrant drunkard, the awkward sightseers on the wharf. On its arrival, the boat and its magnificence dominate the town.

One way Twain makes this essay work for us is by using every detail and every contrast to mirror the central ambition of the boy—the force that makes his life significant. Notice Twain gives us not one boy, but two: he shows us himself as he is and as the person he wishes to be.

QUESTIONS

1. Make an outline of this essay using one division for each paragraph. How does the organization reinforce the theme?
2. How is the narrator different from other boys with the ambition to be a pilot? Why does Twain make him different?
3. What function does humor serve in this essay? (Distinguish humor from comedy.)

Now that you have read the four selections, ask yourself again what the act of writing must have been like for each author. What might he have included that he did not? Why did he choose the particular segment or segments of experience he wrote about? If you were in possession of his experience would you have written differently? Do you have any personal experiences that are similar or parallel? If you do, how would you go about shaping your experience into words? Would you use the pattern that is used in the two student themes that follow?

Both students present an aspect of their experience through selected facts. This is in contrast to developing a single incident such as the bed-wetting in Orwell's work. In reading the themes try to analyze their weaknesses. Did the writers choose segments of their experience that interest you? Have they failed to distinguish their lives from the lives of other students?

I do not recall the moment but my parents and the Draft Board seem to agree that I was born in Englewood, California, approximately two weeks late on January 20, 1948. Misunderstanding Greeley's advice, I went East to Kansas City, Missouri, at the age of fifteen months. The fact that Kansas City has a surplus of stockyards and meat packing plants, to say nothing of public parks, greatly influenced my father's decision to move there. In every sense of the word, physical-mental, metaphysical-gentle, my father is a meat-cutter. Though meat-cutting is not so poetic as I might have led you to believe, it is static and reasonably comfortable.

I suffered the usual growing pains, children's diseases, and formal education in the City Public School through the eighth grade. Through a scholarship program with the city's newspaper and Phillips Academy, I boarded an early train in the fall of 1960 to sit under a Bodie Tree at Andover receiving Divine Guidance and Enlightenment. By far, these past four years at Andover have been the most memorable. I feel that I need a composition course badly before I go to Stuttgart, Germany to work on my writing while waiting to hear from my application at Chase Manhattan.

QUESTIONS

1. Does the first sentence launch us into his theme?
2. Did the author really misunderstand Greeley's advice? Why do you think he put that in? And what about the Bodie Tree?
3. Does the last sentence provide a strong ending for the paper?

Athlete, egoist, braggart, Carl Freeman was born in Gatesville, North Carolina on June 18, 1945. His father, a farmer and part time loafer, taught him the value of learning. But being the stubborn, ridiculous jackass that he was, Carl entered school reluctantly. For two years, he whizzed through grade school with no setbacks, except for an occasional amputated finger or sliced toe, a slight case of double pneumonia, whooping cough, measles, and chicken pox. Just the ordinary exciting adventures of an all-conquering second grader.

Carl's first setback came at the age of eight while he was still a brilliant third grader. He found himself unable to master the art of multiplication. When he had mastered this art, school was no longer challenging to him. Multiplication was the answer to everything.

For Carl, life took a big step backward in the fourth grade. He was faced with a teacher who wouldn't pet him, who enjoyed slapping him, and making him feel ignorant. His fourth year of school was a horrifying experience. Never had he been so dominated by a teacher.

The next four years of grade school were simply "heaven on earth" for him. Except for a small problem with long division, and a big problem with learning the facts of life, everything went smoothly for him. Life reached its peak when he discovered what a girl was. New fields of exploration were opened to him. With all his knowledge and ability, he was able to become one of the most popular boys in his class.

After completing his grammar school education, he anxiously awaited the beginning of his high school career and the chance to exploit his athletic ability. He averaged twenty points a game for the freshman basketball team and was one of the leading hitters on the varsity baseball team. His shy, good-natured personality made him well liked by his high school friends. It didn't take him long to earn the respect of everyone who knew him. He was soon firmly entrenched in the Student Government.

He spent his summers working on his father's farm and playing American Legion baseball. He developed a tremendous competitive spirit, a sense of always wanting to win, a desire to be the best at everything he did.

He began to imagine that he was good looking and desired by all members of the opposite sex. The turning point in his life came when he became interested in a certain girl. Right away, he realized that she had to be one in a million. He began to think of his future and of what he could do to make his life more complete. He knew that he and his new love could conquer everything together. His schoolwork vaulted to new heights. His athletic career was highlighted with All-Conference awards in basketball and baseball. His classmates demonstrated their confidence in him by electing him president of the senior class.

Graduation came and Carl, with tears in his eyes, left school amid the best wishes of his friends. After a hard summer's work at home he headed for the University of North Carolina where he began the four longest, hardest, happiest, dullest, most exciting years of his life.

QUESTIONS

1. Is the author really a braggart, or has he said that he is in order to belittle himself?
2. Are the clichés about his girl friend used effectively, or are they weak spots in his writing?
3. Imagine meeting Freeman. Can you say accurately what kind of person he would be?

ASSIGNMENTS

Present an incident from your childhood in a paper of not less than four hundred words. Choose your assignment from the following:
1. Agee seems to see some kind of a thread in his life. Perhaps this unifying thread is a need to use his own experience as a guide to learning. Can the different activities of your own life be strung together meaningfully in your first paper?
2. Twain had a definite ambition, which came to him because he lived by the river and was exposed to its glamor. Did you, as a child, have a definite ambition? If so, use it as a source of material for your first paper.
3. Employing an incident from your early life, a crucial one such as Orwell experienced, show in your paper how this incident changed you and what it revealed to you about your world.

CHAPTER 2

THE USES OF
OBSERVATION

To observe and describe is to use your senses and record their perceptions in words. Your senses perceive vast quantities of data every minute of your life, and even if you wanted, you could not turn them off. The senses are your basic tools in writing from observation. You can use them like harvest machinery and "go out" to gather the crop all at once, or you can simply allow them to work at their own speed, storing their information bit by bit in memory until you can sort through it with the imagination. How you work will depend on what you are observing and how explicitly you present your material.

William Sansom, a fire fighter who wrote about the fall of a burning wall, worked out of urgency, collecting his data in an almost incredibly short time. He had only the moment when the burning mass came his way. Part of his task as a writer was to choose one aspect of what he observed as the wall fell and to make his observation real for the reader. Out of what he saw, felt, and took for his own, he chose to preserve for the reader a vision of the flatness of the wall.

A wall will fall in many ways. It may sway over to the one side or the other. It may crumble at the very beginning of its fall. It may remain intact and fall flat. This wall fell as flat as a pancake. It clung to its shape through ninety degrees to the horizontal. Then it detached itself from the pivot and slammed down on top of us.[1]

A child, looking at a wave, may see only its light-blue surface and be unable to write at all about what he has observed. A poet, watching the ocean, turns what he sees into a reflection on magnitude and writes of what the wide reach of the sea makes him think. Like the fire fighter, he chooses one dominant aspect of his subject. What Baudelaire writes here is not so much an observation as the philosophy of an observer.

> . . . the sea presents at once the idea of immensity and of movement. Six or seven leagues represent for man the radius of the infinite. An infinite in little. What matter if it suffices to suggest the idea of all infinity? Twelve or fourteen leagues of liquid in movement are enough to convey to man the highest expression of beauty which he can encounter in his transient moods.

For Baudelaire, the sea becomes a symbol of size and time. It is the concrete image of abstract measures. But Sir Alistair Hardy, a scientist, sees the sea like this:

> Suppose for a moment that we live in a country which is bounded on one side by a permanent bank of fog. It is a grey-green vapour, denser even than that often known as a London particular, and it has a boundary as definite as the surface of a cloud so that it is like a curtain hanging from the sky to meet the ground; we cannot enter it without special aids except for a momentary plunge and as quickly out again for breath. We can see into it for only a very little way, but what we do see is all the more tantalizing because we know it must be just a glimpse—a tiny fraction—of all that lies beyond. We find it has life in it as

[1] William Sansom, *Stories of William Sansom* (Boston: Atlantic-Little, Brown, 1963), p. 16.

abundant as that of our own country-side, but so different that it might be life from another world. No insects dwell beyond the barrier, but other joint-legged creatures take their place. Unfamiliar floating forms, like living parachutes with trailing tentacles, show their beauty and all too quickly fade from view. Then sometimes at night the darkness may be spangled with moving points of light—living sparks that dart and dance before our eyes. Occasionally gigantic monsters, equal in size to several elephants rolled into one, blunder through the curtain and lie dying on our land.[2]

In writing out of observation, most of us start by being able to give our reader no more than a glimpse of the whole object or scene we have chosen. Even the best writer could not completely describe what he saw on a certain day or how he viewed a certain object. Take a pencil. How much can your senses tell about it if you begin to list every property? More than you would want to write. And suppose you could describe its chemical nature and molecular structure?

But that's a scientist's job, you might say. Perhaps you are right. What you are saying is that the pencil interests different people in different ways. And since no one can describe the pencil in its entirety, each person will see the pencil and write about it in a way that interests him. Think of a snake. What do you see in it—a marvelous example of nature's specialization or a dangerous and repulsive animal? Or a walnut tree—is it a storehouse of valuable lumber, a source of food, or a graceful pattern of branches and leaves in a landscape? Is a prize fight a contest of cunning and physical coordination or a brutal spectacle?

In writing from observation there are more than two sides to everything; there are innumerable sides. The writer can often combine two or more ways of seeing something, but he can never see all there is to see. And, of course, if he is not interested at all in the pencil, snake, tree, or prize fight, he will see little or nothing.

Your particular interest in your subject, what it means to you and how it fits into your life and experience, will determine how

[2] Alistair Hardy, *The Open Sea* (Boston: Houghton Mifflin, 1956), p. 1.

you write about it. Every writer has a bias, whether he be a novelist, a newspaper reporter, or a scientist. This bias shows through in every observation, whether of an object, a person, or a landscape. If your observation and writing were completely unbiased, you would get nothing on paper but a randomly selected pile of detail.

As in writing out of experience, the person who is trying to find the way to express himself must *try to describe how a thing looks to him so that it will look that way to other people. To make the reader accept the fact that it* CAN *look that way is not enough. The reader has to believe the new way of seeing.*

Writing from observation involves three main acts—selecting and limiting your subject, clarifying your way of seeing, and conveying the final vision to the reader.

Your own interests will govern the selections of subject and the limits of your description. For instance, in describing a house you like, you will have to decide whether you are going to include interior and exterior, construction and history, its uses and purpose.

Does a particular house, or car, or landscape have a special meaning for you, one that you would want a reader to share? Do you need to clarify this meaning? What makes your house different from every other one? Do you have deep, permanent, and specific associations that enhance the landscape in which your house is set? How do you really feel about this place where you have spent your nights and days? Can you isolate your own view of your house and pass it on to a reader?

You must probe beneath the quick, easy answer. It is not enough to say, "I like the way the house looks," or "I'm just interested in that kind of thing." This probing for the real answer may be a process of discovery, for often we are not aware of what something means to us until we have the time, the ambition, or perhaps even the courage to investigate honestly. This is the most difficult part of the process. Ernest Hemingway considered it his biggest hurdle when he worked as a journalist. Journalism always presented the temptation to be timely and novel rather than direct and honest about what made an event meaningful to him.

To clarify means to make pure or intelligible. In order to

achieve clarity, the writer must have some idea, or at least some bias, about the observations he himself has made. As Hemingway suggests, he must see what is, for him, *the real thing.* It is not enough to have a special interest in your subject. You must learn to focus your interest in what you see much as one would focus a camera for the clearest view of a single aspect, or related aspects, in a scene.

Selecting, limiting, and clarifying your approach to your subject brings you to the point of finding a way of conveying your vision to the reader. The selected data of the senses are only raw material. You have to arrange them in a particular form and communicate them in a uniform language. You must choose a point of view and a style. Your choices are closely related to the limiting and clarifying you have done already; at the same time, they are separate steps in the process of composition.

In the following examples of writing out of observation, each author is a recorder of how he has looked at a place or people or an object. Because of a particular bias or interest, each sees his subject in his own way. In the simplest sense he is trying to make others see what he saw and respond as strongly as he himself responded.

SELECTIONS

During Ernest Hemingway's later years many readers came to think of him as a man fascinated by violence—of war, bullfighting, hunting, and brawling. Above any such narrow point of view, Hemingway was a calm and a keen observer who first of all tried to see things as they were, not as he wanted them to be. Besides precise detail, what has he seen in this account of a hunt, taken from *Green Hills of Africa?* [3]

We all lay there on the hillside and watched the country carefully for rhino. Droopy was on the other side of the hilltop

[3] Ernest Hemingway, *Green Hills of Africa* (New York: Charles Scribner's Sons, 1935), pp. 49–51.

squatted on his heels, looking, and M'Cola sat below us. There was a cool breeze from the east and it blew the grass in waves on the hillsides. There were many large white clouds and the tall trees of the forest on the mountainside grew so closely and were so foliaged that it looked as though you could walk on their tops. Behind this mountain there was a gap and then another mountain and the far mountain was dark blue with forest in the distance.

Until five o'clock we did not see anything. Then, without the glasses, I saw something moving over the shoulder of one of the valleys toward a strip of the timber. In the glasses it was a rhino, showing very clear and minute at the distance, red-colored in the sun, moving with a quick waterbug-like motion across the hill. Then there were three more of them that came out of the forest, dark in the shadow, and two that fought, tinily, in the glasses, pushing head-on, fighting in front of a clump of bushes while we watched them and the light failed. It was too dark to get down the hill, across the valley and up the narrow slope of mountainside to them in time for a shot. So we went back to the camp, down the hill in the dark, edging down on our shoes and then feeling the trail smooth under foot, walking along that deep trail, that wound through the dark hills, until we saw the firelight in the trees.

We were excited that night because we had seen the three rhino and early the next morning while we were eating breakfast before starting out, Droopy came in to report a herd of buffalo he had found feeding at the edge of the forest not two miles from camp. We went there, still tasting coffee and kippers in the early morning heart-pounding of excitement, and the native Droopy had left watching them pointed where they had crossed a deep gulch and gone into an open patch of forest. He said there were two big bulls in a herd of a dozen or more. We followed them in, moving very quietly on the game trails, pushing the vines aside and seeing the tracks and the quantities of fresh dung, but though we went on into the forest where it was too thick to shoot and made a wide circle, we did not see or hear them. Once we heard the tick birds and saw them flying, but that was all. There were numbers of rhino trails there in the

woods and many strawy piles of dung, but we saw nothing but
the green wood-pigeons and some monkeys, and when we
came out we were wet to our waists from the dew and the sun
was quite high. The day was very hot, now before the wind had
gotten up, and we knew whatever rhino and buffalo had been
out would have gone back deep into the forest to rest out of the
heat.

Hemingway gives us the cycle of an evening and a morning but
he gives us only glimpses. He writes of what he sees as they hunt,
but he limits himself severely and skillfully. As he has informed us
in his comments on learning how to write, he is trying to put down
on paper the actual things which produced the sequence of motion and fact that created the hunters' intense excitement.

He could have tried to excite the reader with a more detailed
description of the rhinos fighting, or of the danger of descending
the dark trail, but this description is not about danger or about
rhinos. Hemingway does not try to borrow excitement from things
which are not a part of his real subject.

Notice the details he has chosen and ask yourself what they
convey to us about the hunt. Notice the sensuous descriptions and
carefully picked words—trees that look as though you can walk
through their tips, rhino red-colored in the sun, dew that wets the
hunters to their waists. Why do we see the rhinos looking, through
the glasses, like insects? In describing the second day, notice how
he gives us signs of the animals—never the animals, never the
hunters' expectations—only the detail which caused the hunters
to feel as they did.

QUESTIONS

1. What picture of man and nature is developed by the selection of
   detail?
2. Why doesn't Hemingway describe the hunters' feelings more
   fully?
3. Do you consider some of the detail, e.g., how their mouths tasted
   of coffee, too trivial?

In reading this description from *Cape Cod* by Henry David Thoreau, try to imagine it as it might have been told by the average citizen. By its very nature, the subject of shipwreck is interesting —as are all sudden and large accidents involving the loss of human life. Observers are fascinated by the detail, but few can make sense of what they see.

The brig St. John, from Galway, Ireland, laden with emigrants, was wrecked on Sunday morning; it was now Tuesday morning and the sea was still breaking violently on the rocks. There were eighteen or twenty of the same large boxes that I have mentioned, lying on a green hillside, a few rods from the water, and surrounded by a crowd. The bodies which had been recovered, twenty-seven or eight in all, had been collected there. Some were rapidly nailing down the lids, others were carting the boxes away, and others were lifting the lids, which were yet loose, and peeping under the cloths, for each body, with such rags as till adhered to it, was covered loosely with a white sheet. I witnessed no signs of grief but there was a sober dispatch of business which was affecting. One man was seeking to identify a particular body, and one undertaker or carpenter was calling to another to know in what box a certain child was put. I saw many marble feet and matted heads as the cloths were raised, and one livid, swollen, and mangled body of a drowned girl,—who probably had intended to go out to service in some American family,—to which some rags still adhered, with a string, half concealed by the flesh, about its swollen neck; the coiled-up wreck of a human hulk, gashed by the rocks or fishes, so that the bone and muscle were exposed, but quite bloodless,—merely red and white,—with wide-open and staring eyes, yet lustreless, dead-lights; or like the cabin windows of a stranded vessel, filled with sand. Sometimes there were two or more children, or a parent and child, in the same box, and on the lid would perhaps be written with red chalk, "Bridget such-a-one, and sister's child." The surrounding sward was covered with bits of sails and clothing. I have since heard, from one who lives by this beach, that a woman who had come over before, but had left her infant behind for her sister to bring, came and looked into these boxes, and saw in one—probably the same whose superscription I have quoted—her child in her sister's arms, as if the sister had meant to be found thus; and within three days after, the mother died from the effect of that sight.

Like Hemingway, Thoreau limits himself to observing, and records a sequence of sights that produce the emotion. He blocks away from his reader every sight except that of the row of corpses on the green hillside, then picks sensory details, a bone, a wide-open staring eye, a marble foot. And the trash on the ground, the torn sails, the bits of clothing, act as a frame for the central image of the bodies.

The method is deceptively simple, for what counts is not only what Thoreau puts into the passage but what he leaves out. What does he tell us about the crowd on the beach? About the hillside? About the ship that has gone down? What of the mother, who does not appear in the sketch at all? Why does he not show us the mother as she sees her dead sister and her dead child?

It is most important for us to understand what governs the detail he does put on paper. Here is the aftermath of the wreck of a ship full of emigrants, beaten to pieces on the shores of the "promised land." This is a description not only of a shipwreck, but of wrecked hope.

QUESTIONS

1. What words and phrases and images develop this theme of wrecked hope?
2. Why doesn't he simply write an essay on the fragility of human life and hope?
3. Find an example of public disaster in a newspaper or magazine. Imagine it treated in Thoreau's manner and in the manner of the ordinary, fascinated citizen.

Margaret Mead was one of the first Americans who dared to make sex a serious, scientific topic for both scientists and the public. Had she not been able to combine her talents as writer and scientist, she could not have reached the public successfully. Her anthropological work began in Samoa. Here, in the beginning of *Coming of Age in Samoa,* she introduces readers to a typical day in that country.[4] Where do the scientist and writer meet?

The life of the day begins at dawn, or if the moon has shown until daylight, the shouts of the young men may be heard before dawn from the hillside. Uneasy in the night, populous with ghosts, they shout lustily to one another as they hasten with their work. As the dawn begins to fall among the soft brown roofs and the slender palm trees stand out against a colourless, gleaming sea, lovers slip home from trysts beneath the palm trees or in the shadow of beached canoes, that the light may find each sleeper in his appointed place. Cocks crow, negligently, and a shrill-voiced bird cries from the breadfruit trees. The insistent roar of the reef seems muted to an undertone for the sounds of a waking village. Babies cry, a few short wails before sleepy mothers give them the breast. Restless little children roll out of their sheets and wander drowsily down to the beach to freshen their faces in the sea. Boys, bent upon an early fishing, start collecting their tackle and go to rouse their more laggard companions. Fires are lit, here and there, the white smoke hardly visible against the paleness of the dawn. The whole village, sheeted and frowsy, stirs, rubs its eyes, and stumbles towards the beach. "Talofa!" "Talofa!" "Will the journey start to-day?" "Is it bonito fishing your lordship is going?" Girls stop to giggle over some young ne'er-do-well who escaped during the night from an angry father's pursuit and to venture a shrewd guess that the daughter knew more about his presence than she told. The boy who is taunted by another, who has succeeded him in his sweetheart's favour, grapples with his rival, his foot slipping in the wet sand. From the other

[4] Margaret Mead, *Coming of Age in Samoa* (New York: William Morrow & Co., 1928), pp. 14–19.

end of the village comes a long drawn-out, piercing wail. A
messenger has just brought word of the death of some relative
in another village. Half-clad, unhurried women, with babies at
their breasts, or astride their hips, pause in their tale of Losa's
outraged departure from her father's house to the greater kindness in the home of her uncle, to wonder who is dead. Poor relatives whisper their requests to rich relatives, men make plans to
set a fish trap together, a woman begs a bit of yellow dye from a
kinswoman, and through the village sounds the rhythmic tattoo
which calls the young men together. They gather from all parts
of the village, digging sticks in hand, ready to start inland to
the plantation. The older men set off upon their more lonely
occupations, and each household, reassembled under its
peaked roof, settles down to the routine of the morning. Little
children, too hungry to wait for the late breakfast, beg lumps of
cold taro which they munch greedily. Women carry piles of
washing to the sea or to the spring at the far end of the village,
or set off inland after weaving materials. The older girls go
fishing on the reef, or perhaps set themselves to weaving a new
set of Venetian blinds.

In the houses, where the pebbly floors have been swept bare
with a stiff long-handled broom, the women great with child
and the nursing mothers sit and gossip with one another. Old
men sit apart, unceasingly twisting palm husk on their bare
thighs and muttering old tales under their breath. The carpen-
ters begin work on the new house, while the owner bustles
about trying to keep them in a good humour. Families who will
cook to-day are hard at work; the taro, yams and bananas have
already been brought from inland; the children are scuttling
back and forth, fetching sea water, or leaves to stuff the pig. As
the sun rises higher in the sky, the shadows deepen under the
thatched roofs, the sand is burning to the touch, the hibiscus
flowers wilt on the hedges, and little children bid the smaller
ones, "Come out of the sun." Those whose excursions have
been short return to the village, the women with strings of
crimson jelly fish, or baskets of shell fish, the men with cocoa-
nuts, carried in baskets slung on a shoulder pole. The women
and children eat their breakfasts, just hot from the oven, if this

is cook day, and the young men work swiftly in the midday heat, preparing the noon feast for their elders.

It is high noon. The sand burns the feet of the little children, who leave their palm leaf balls and their pin-wheels of frangipani blossoms to wither in the sun, as they creep into the shade of the houses. The women who must go abroad carry great banana leaves as sun-shades or wind wet cloths about their heads. Lowering a few blinds against the slanting sun, all who are left in the village wrap their heads in sheets and go to sleep. Only a few adventurous children may slip away for a swim in the shadow of a high rock, some industrious woman continue with her weaving, or a close little group of women bend anxiously over a woman in labour. The village is dazzling and dead; any sound seems oddly loud and out of place. Words have to cut through the solid heat slowly. And then the sun gradually sinks over the sea.

A second time, the sleeping people stir, roused perhaps by the cry of "a boat," resounding through the village. The fishermen beach their canoes, weary and spent from the heat, in spite of the slaked lime on their heads, with which they have sought to cool their brains and redden their hair. The brightly coloured fishes are spread out on the floor, or piled in front of the houses until the women pour water over them to free them from taboo. Regretfully, the young fishermen separate out the "Taboo fish," which must be sent to the chief, or proudly they pack the little palm leaf baskets with offerings of fish to take to their sweethearts. Men come home from the bush, grimy and heavy laden, shouting as they come, greeted in a sonorous rising cadence by those who have remained at home. They gather in the guest house for their evening kuva drinking. The soft clapping of hands, the highpitched intoning of the talking chief who serves the kuva echoes through the village. Girls gather flowers to weave into necklaces; children, lusty from their naps and bound to no particular task, play circular games in the half shade of the late afternoon. Finally the sun sets, in a flame which stretches from the mountain behind to the horizon on the sea, the last bather comes up from the beach, children straggle home, dark little figures etched against the sky; lights shine in the houses, and each household gathers for its evening meal. The suitor humbly presents his offering, the children have been summoned from their noisy play, perhaps there is an honoured guest who must be served first, after the soft, barbaric singing of Christian hymns and the brief and graceful evening prayer. In front of a house at the end of the village, a father cries out the birth of a son. In some family circles a face is missing, in others little runaways have found a haven! Again quiet settles upon the village, as first the head of the household, then the women and children, and last of all the patient boys, eat their supper.

After supper the old people and the little children are bundled off to bed. If the young people have guests the front of the house is yielded to them. For day is the time for the councils of old men and the labours of youth, and night is the time for lighter things. Two kinsmen, or a chief and his councillor, sit and gossip over the day's events or make plans for the morrow. Outside a crier goes through the village announcing that the communal breadfruit pit will be opened in the morning, or that the village will make a great fish trap. If it is moonlight, groups of young men, women by twos and threes, wander through the village, and crowds of children hunt for land crabs or chase each other among the breadfruit trees. Half the village may go fishing by torchlight and the curving reef will gleam with wavering lights and echo with shouts of triumph or disappointment, teasing words or smothered cries of outraged modesty. Or a group of youths may dance for the pleasure of some visiting maiden. Many of those who have retired to sleep, drawn by the merry music, will wrap their sheets about them and set out to find the dancing. A white-clad, ghostly throng will gather in a circle about the gaily lit house, a circle from which every now and then a few will detach themselves and wander away among the trees. Sometimes sleep will not descend upon the village until long past midnight; then at last there is only the mellow thunder of the reef and the whisper of lovers, as the village rests until dawn.

As an anthropologist, Margaret Mead chooses details which are important to her study of human behavior. Her description of a day in Samoa seems to be a simple compilation of random detail, structured only by the time dimensions morning, noon, and night. And, of course, she chooses detail which distinguishes life on Samoa from any other way of life.

If you look closely at the organization of Miss Mead's description, you will find more to it than chronology and vivid writing. It is a meticulously inclusive introduction to the principal human activity of Samoans. Each paragraph is a skillful weaving of the major economic, social, and religious activities of the people. What the reader has at the end of the essay is not merely quantity, but a sense of the way in which many human activities are interrelated.

Even the sequence of time is given special treatment. Time is not just hour after hour, but two cycles of activity, the first ending in the odd stillness of high noon, the second ending in the gay or romantic evening. You might say the structure of her writing is that of two circles within one larger circle.

QUESTIONS

1. Some writers have said that precise measurement is the foundation of all science. Perhaps so, but why do you think Miss Mead, a respected scientist, has chosen here to rely on language?
2. How would this description have been different if she had used statistical tables or graphs?
3. Having introduced her subject, where do you think Miss Mead will take the reader next?

Suppose you have a lot of facts and figures about a topic which is important to you as a scientist but boring to the general public. Usually you forget about the public and go on with your work, your specialty—in this case, dirt. In order to communicate with the public you would have to find some common ground. You would have to do as Peter Farb does in "The Hidden World of the Soil" from *Life* Nature Series Book *The Forest:* find a concrete pattern that is familiar to your reader and which can contain your scientific observations also.[5]

The dead leaves, needles, twigs and fallen branches that lie in heaps upon the forest floor appear at a casual glance to be a lifeless, rotting mass. Actually, they form the roof tops of the hidden world of the forest soil. The soil veneer shelters more life than can be found in any other stratum of the forest, or probably any other environment on earth, for that matter. The inhabitants exist in numbers that stagger the imagination. They carpet the grains of soil and weave passageways through them; they dig out burrows and tunnels and underground nests. The honeycombs of moles, the burrows of worms often form such a labyrinth in the forest floor that it has the springy feel of foam rubber. Some years ago, scientists blocked off a small section of forest soil in New York State and removed the top layer of earth to a depth of one inch. They made a careful count of the insects and other invertebrates found among the soil crumbs. In all, there was an average of 1,356 living creatures present in each square foot, including 865 mites, 265 springtails, 22 millepedes, 19 adult beetles and various numbers of 12 other forms. Had an estimate also been made of the microscopic population, it might have ranged up to two billion bacteria and many millions of fungi, protozoa and algae—in a mere *teaspoonful* of soil.

The forest floor is also a crossroads through which pass above ground forms that spend part of their lives in the subterranean darkness. About 95 percent of the nearly one million insect species invade the soil in either the egg, larval, pupal or adult stages; the longest-term tenant is a species of cicada which passes 17 years of its nymphal life in the soil and the remaining few weeks of its life as an adult sucking sap from the trees. Many animals spend their resting hours in burrows in the earth. And, of course, plants span both worlds of sunlight and darkness; there is a special place on the plant, called the crown, where the stem and roots meet.

[5] Peter Farb, "The Hidden World of the Soil," from *The Forest*, Time-Life Books (New York: Time Inc., 1961), pp. 131–132.

If this were a field report or a laboratory analysis the author would have included many more statistics, and his scientist reader would have formed his own vision of what the writer had revealed. However, in writing for both scientist and nonscientist, Peter Farb wants to present a unified picture of what soil is. Experimental data is the basis of his picture, not its purpose. He is thus trying to convey to the reader how that data has revealed a new concept of soil.

He starts with what soil *seems* to be—dead matter on the "floor" of the forest. He then takes this casual image of floor, turns it around and builds the larger image of the soil as a sheltered community with the forest floor as its roof tops. Notice how he chooses his diction to reinforce that image—shelters, inhabitants, carpet. Worm burrows are a labyrinth, a complex building. In the second paragraph he introduces the transient inhabitants, the tenants. Then he brings us above ground again, stopping to note that the meeting of sunlight and darkness are a special place, using the concrete image of the crown of the plant as a symbol of this special meeting.

Margaret Mead has said that imagery is a restructuring of experience in which inner feelings or perceptions are given recognizable concrete forms. We might also say an image is a likeness of something experienced or known.

QUESTIONS

1. Why do writers use images? How do images work on the mind?
2. What does the image of the community suggest besides size and complexity?
3. Choose something about which you have a lot of facts, gained by observation or measurement. What image might you use to present these to an uninformed reader?
4. When might the kind of imagery Farb uses be unnecessary or overelaborate?

Quite often we study metaphors and similes in poetry, because
poetry is noted for its figurative language. Sometimes the poem
itself contains few figures of speech. Instead the whole poem becomes an image of some idea or vision beyond its actual content.
Here Theodore Roethke looks at a florist's dump.[6]

FLOWER DUMP

Cannas shiny as slag,
Slug-soft stems,
Whole beds of bloom pitched on a pile,
Carnations, verbenas, cosmos,
Molds, weeds, dead leaves,
Turned-over roots
With bleached veins
Twined like fine hair,
Each clump in the shape of a pot;
Everything limp
but one tulip on top,
One swaggering head
Over the dying, the newly dead.

A dump for discarded flowers is an unlikely subject for a poem,
but a good poet, like a good scientist, does not limit himself to in-
vestigating the familiar. At first Roethke seems to be giving us little more than a pile of images and names. The careful reader will
see that from the very first line, the poem is more than simple description. The words work through their suggestiveness to build
an effect. Slag implies discarded and dead excess. Slug-soft suggests decay. In the third line the use of alliteration—repetition of
initial consonants—reflects in sound the piled quality of the
flowers. Then, the use of the words veins and hair, words common
to people and plants, remind us that this is a poem about death,
the same phenomenon that affects human life. Finally, the pile of

[6] Theodore Roethke, "Flower Dump" from *Words for the Wind* (New
York: Doubleday & Company, 1958), p. 51.

flowers and of words is crowned by one swaggering, bright tulip. We do not have to ask what this "means." The poem is an image; in it, Roethke has restructured his experience of a flower dump.

If you are awed by the height of a mountain or the violence of a mob, you do not ask what the height or the violence means. But you may be able to recreate their impressiveness in words. Does this tell you anything about the way language works?

QUESTIONS

1. How would a matter-of-fact prose description differ from Roethke's poem?
2. Look over the poem again. What words could you omit and still retain the sense of the poem?
3. Grammatically speaking, is this poem a complete sentence? Why is there no main verb and no object?
4. Look at your class-mates. Can you think of any description of them which would convey more than physical detail without explicitly stating your point of view?

When there is a lot to see, most of it unusual, as in the funeral of a President, a writer must be very careful not to overwhelm his reader with detail or personal impressions. This student writer has described President John Kennedy's funeral procession from a particular point of view. Is this point of view well tied to the observed event?

The lines were ten deep along the climbing walks of Connecticut Avenue. The tops of buildings were littered with spectators, television cameras and equipment, and the occasional pigeons that dared to land on the ledges that ran around the structures. Office windows were flung open as businessmen, secretaries and office boys crowded for a view with no regard for station or sex. Down on the streets, men of all service branches aligned themselves in front of the crowds to keep them from getting too curious. A skinny army lieutenant strutted here and there along the street marking "X's" with a piece of chalk. Members of the Washington Police Department stood in a disordered group as if waiting for some signal. Directly behind this group was an honor guard, all spit and polish, practicing with their swords before the signal was given for the final performance. Negro and White crowded together and looked with anxiety up the expanse of asphalt past the colorful bands, drums draped with black velvet, past the platoons from every branch of service, past the Special Forces group with their black berets, past the West Point cadets in gray and purple uniforms. A Negro sergeant ran back and forth shouting coded instructions into a walkie-talkie, "Red unit one to Mother hen, come in." In the background could be heard soft crying, muttered prayers, and the occasional cough. A small girl, maybe ten years old, no more than eleven, stood in the gutter with a small Kodak camera, anxiously wanting to take a picture. A whistle split the stillness, the bands and soldiers came to attention, a woman cried, then silence in the crowd. Again the whistle sounded and following it came a shuffle of feet, a blowing of trumpets, the roll of drums, and the parade moved forward, down the street, down past the soldiers and sailors that lined the sides of the street, down past the silent throngs of people. As group after group of soldiers, marines, and sailors moved past, the crowds pushed closer to the edge of the street. A woman fainted, a baby cried, far away in the sky puffs of smoke climbed upward and spread out into thick clouds. Planes roared overhead and disappeared over the tops of smut-white government buildings. The constant tromp of feet moved onward to be replaced by sparkling black limousines. Inside these beautiful machines, dressed in mourning black were grey-headed men, children, who unlike most, yet very like those that populated the crowds, did not wiggle and squirm. In the next car sat two young men, and between them a weeping young woman, her face covered with a black veil. The cars rolled slowly past followed by a black caisson which was pulled by six dappled-grey horses. Lying on the caisson was the flag of the United States of America. Completely identical to the others that flew over the city of Washington at half-mast with one exception, this particular flag covered a brilliant bronze coffin. There behind the caisson pranced a spirited, red-eyed, black stallion. On its back, a black English riding saddle. The stirrups were filled with black riding boots which were reversed. The horse reared and kicked as though he carried the departed spirit of the body that lay in the casket. The end of the procession passed; Connecticut Avenue was empty.

The student writer organized his piece by the method of enumerating, one after another, the multiple sights and sounds of the funeral procession of John F. Kennedy. Walt Whitman, in composing his poem on the death of Lincoln, used the lilac blooming in the dooryard and the great star in the west as the two central images of a nation's grief. This modern author, writing a few days after observing the cortege, simply registers, in sentence after sentence, the sights on Connecticut Avenue. The solemnity of the occasion is the centralizing thread of the theme.

The emphasis throughout is on the group scene, the spectator importance. In the theme's regular progression we are introduced to office workers, servicemen, and to police officers pushing back the spectators who actually seem, in this theme, to be *in* the procession. Everyone is presented as integral to the group. The widow of the dead President appears as a woman seen obliquely, a symbol behind a veil.

As for the writer himself, he never appears in the theme; rather he is an all-seeing eye, choosing what is to be reported but never revealing himself directly. He stays outside of his subject, concealing himself as "I" but revealing his responses by the method of piling sight on sight until at last the reader joins with him in responding to the grievous fanfare of the funeral.

QUESTIONS

1. Has the writer chosen details carefully or are they details anyone would have chosen?

2. Why do you think he does not pay more attention to the mourners in the black cars?
3. Why does he hold off in telling the reader the crowd is gathered for a funeral procession?

ASSIGNMENTS

1. Look at an object that is in your room or a classroom. Limit your observation of what you see to one paragraph. Whether your object is a pencil, a typewriter, a wall, a book, a bed, or a plant, try to give your description unity. Make your reader see what you see—not everything, not inches and feet—but the importance the object has for you.
2. When was the last time you watched a plane descend at an airport? What one aspect of the plane's motion impressed you most? Its speed? Its erratic course down the runway? Did you observe the plane the moment it came to a full stop? Write down the sequence of motion and your primary response to that motion. Limit your paper to four hundred words.
3. How does your town look early in the morning? Making yourself the "I," write freely of sights that impress you as you go from your home to your school. Throughout the paper keep yourself as the central viewer, showing what you see exactly as it appears to you, using the language that is most appropriate to your point of view.

CHAPTER 3

THE FUNCTION OF

READING

Were it not for the words we read and hear, most of the world would not exist for us. We would be like those ancient map makers who thought the Mediterranean Sea, southern Europe, and northern Africa were all that existed of the earth. There are even organs in our bodies whose presence we take for granted because we have read about them in credible books, or were told about them by someone whose knowledge we can trust.

This kind of secondhand or vicarious knowledge shapes our lives and our way of seeing the world as certainly as do experience and observation. This is as true of the writer's world as it is of anyone's. Often it is difficult or even impossible to know where firsthand experience stops and vicarious experience begins. But vicarious experience does exist, and in this chapter we are going to discuss the special ways that books can affect the work of a writer.

Of course books influence us whether or not we are studying the art of writing. But as writers, or students of writing, books affect us more acutely than they have done in the past. The most obvious demonstration of this is in the lives of professional writers. The man who chooses writing as the central activity of his life expects to remake the world in the shape of his own words, as he feels other writers have done before him.

The writer's personal experience of the world comes free through his own words, but he achieves this only after he encounters and absorbs the work of other writers. He plunges into a forest of books and clears a space of his own. Books are the main source of his intellectual life and through them he becomes himself, finds his own style, and writes his first book.

That is any writer's job when he begins—not to negate the work of other authors, but to find through that work a way of his own.

But how does one learn to use the books of others in his own creative process? James Joyce learned through a strict regime of study in a Jesuit school. Somerset Maugham first went to books as a boy because they were a refuge from the disagreeable realities of life. Your job, like that of Joyce and Maugham, is to learn to use the books of others in your own creative process. Your goal must not be to write like another writer. For as you can see from the following passages, in that way you learn to be not yourself but the man you imitate. Can you identify the origin of this student paper?

> But you never went to such places. Instead it was Bluebeard's or Capt'n Kidd's where the drinks were cheap and everybody all hot and sweaty dancing and you had to look at the wall real hard to keep the room from spinning around. Nights when you didn't know why you were there in the first place or who it was with you and not caring and not caring, but sometimes caring very much and all warm and soft and nice. Nights and then the days, days that were hot and bright; the nights always better than the days unless it was hard and clear and the water nice and no one to ask if you had seen Queen Anne's Stairway or the Governor's Palace, but always another night starting and how different were the nights . . .

How close is that paper to this, written by Hemingway:

I had gone to no cush place but to the smoke of cafes and nights when the room whirled and you needed to look at the wall to make it stop, nights in bed, drunk, when you knew that that was all there was, and the strange excitement of waking and not knowing who it was with you, and the world all unreal in the dark and so exciting that you must resume again unknowing and not caring. Suddenly to care very much and to sleep to wake with it sometimes morning and all that had been there gone and everything sharp and hard and clear and sometimes a dispute about the cost.[1]

The student's prose is at best imitation and at worst plagiarism. The writer has not tried to *use* Hemingway's techniques; he has tried to *be* Hemingway. In doing this he is defeating the real object of reading, which is not only enjoyment but discovery of self. When this self-finding comes in part from another writer, it has a double importance. First, when you absorb the work of another, that work changes for you as you absorb it. Then, the influence of the man whose books you have read actually becomes part of your own expression.

To use another writer's work does not mean you must sacrifice originality. Shakespeare is the most obvious example of a man who used stories from the public realm, bringing to them his own genius. Many modern writers show a debt to their predecessors and yet remain clearly original. Norman Mailer's war novel, *The Naked and the Dead,* borrows techniques from classical epic and drama. Jack Kerouac's *Doctor Sax* draws heavily on the material of comic books and comic book heroes. Science fiction writers readily admit their debt to Jules Verne, Edgar Rice Burroughs, and other pre-Space Age fantasy writers. But men like Ray Bradbury (*The Martian Chronicles*) have created a new kind of fiction of their own.

Your own goal is to project what is valuable to you through words, and there are a number of ways in which books may influence you in approaching this goal. Think back over the most

[1] Ernest Hemingway, *A Farewell to Arms* (New York: Charles Scribner's Sons, 1929), p. 13.

memorable books you have read. Some will be childhood whims and fads, others more permanently valuable. In all instances these books probably meant something to you because they opened the way to new experience, or because they gave substance and clarity to an idea or experience of your own.

Each book in its own measure, large or small, has probably shaped the way you feel about yourself and the rest of the world. A book itself may be an experience for you. It does not have to change the direction of your life, only bend or reinforce a feeling, or slow down or quicken your pace. Like one beam in a building, the book's influence is not easily seen, but it is there all the time, supporting its share.

When you sit down to your own writing you would not want to simply write out in paraphrase what another writer already has set down. But one of the ways in which a book may affect your own writing is to remind you of something in your own life that is important. In fact the book may even show you why that thing is important. In reading about an idea or experience similar to yours, you may find a method of exploring your own material. You see someone do something in his own house, and you think you know how to do the same kind of job in yours.

As for style, or your characteristic way of using words, you may be drawn to an author and want to imitate his use of language. Almost any writer will tell you there is much to be learned from trying to emulate someone who is better than you. You might begin by examining your choice of a model. Why do you choose this model? Rhythm? Vocabulary? Arrangement of sentences? In the larger sense of style, is this writer's philosophy what influences you? Before you begin your own work, ask yourself what you want to take from a writer you admire, and why.

There are many reasons why you might try to write in the manner of someone else. And good reasons. But again, the best writing for you will be that which is your own, because it grows out of your own way of thinking and being. No matter how close you feel to another writer, you must remember that, ultimately, all people are unique individuals and what will fit one will not fit the one who comes later. For what you know will be different from what anyone else knows.

In the matter of content, almost all writers stress working with a subject you know firsthand, although some, like Stephen Crane in his war novel, *The Red Badge of Courage*, have been able to create a fine book out of secondhand knowledge. The usual way of beginning is to choose a subject close to you. This way has two implications: you must decide how well you know your subject and how sound your knowledge is. It implies that a good writer is always questioning himself, always looking further into his subject, looking beneath his assumptions, trying to add to what he knows already.

It is here that our reading reenters the process. Books can help us determine how sound our knowledge is by providing supporting or contradicting evidence. Books which have basically the same themes as those in which we are interested may guide us to new associations and relationships. But whatever the role a book plays, the ultimate test of its value to you as a writer is not how pleasing, how profound, or how skillful it is but how effectively it helps you strengthen your own way of writing.

Selections

Some people think Thomas Wolfe's books are endless; others never want them to end. His most faithful followers feel that few if any other modern writers have had Wolfe's skill with language and emotion. Here, in *Look Homeward, Angel*, he tells about his own introduction to literature.[2]

Thus, pent in his dark soul, Eugene sat brooding on a fire-lit book, a stranger in a noisy inn. The gates of his life were closing him in from their knowledge, a vast aerial world of phantasy was erecting its fuming and insubstantial fabric. He steeped his soul in streaming imagery, rifling the bookshelves for pictures and finding there such treasures as *With Stanley in Africa*, rich in the mystery of the jungle, alive with combat, black battle, the

[2] Thomas Wolfe, *Look Homeward, Angel* (New York: Charles Scribner's Sons, 1929), pp. 86–87.

hurled spear, vast snake-rooted forests, thatched villages, gold
and ivory; or Stoddard's *Lectures*, on whose slick heavy pages
were stamped the most-visited scenes of Europe and Asia; a
Book of Wonder, with enchanting drawings of all the marvels
of the age—Santos Dumont in his balloon, liquid air poured
from a kettle, all the navies of the earth lifted two feet from the
water by an ounce of radium (Sir William Crookes), the building of the Eiffel Tower, the Flatiron Building, the stick-steered
automobile, the submarine. After the earthquake in San Francisco there was a book describing it, its cheap green cover lurid
with crumbling towers, shaken spires, toppling many-storied
houses plunging into the splitting flamejawed earth. And there
was another called *Palaces of Sin*, or *The Devil in Society*, pur-
porting to be the work of a pious millionaire, who had drained
his vast fortune in exposing the painted sores that blemish the
spotless-seeming hide of great position, and there were enticing pictures showing the author walking in a silk hat down a
street full of magnificent palaces of sin.

Out of this strange jumbled gallery of pictures the pieced-out
world was expanding under the brooding power of his imagination: the lost dark angels of the Doré "Milton" swooped into
cavernous Hell beyond this upper earth of soaring or toppling
spires, machine wonder, maced and mailed romance. And, as
he thought of his future liberation into this epic world, where
all the color of life blazed brightest far away from home, his
heart flooded his face with lakes of blood.

Wolfe fell under the spell of books and never was able to free
himself, nor wanted to get free. At the very last of his life, writing
to a man who had taken the place of the gaunt, poetry-crammed
father of his youth, Wolfe still thought in the literary frame of reference that had begun when he sat brooding on a firelit book
many years before. He wrote of Ecclesiastes, and in the manner of
the preacher. Here, in the above selection, recounting his early
life, he simply throws together a jumble of books that impressed
him. Out of this jumble his rich prose style emerged. As he writes
his language mirrors the language of the books, yet never de-
scends to their melodramatic level. It is a demonstration of what
he is writing about. You can truly say of Wolfe that for him, the

world of books, those he read and those he came to create, was as much an influence as the hill-girt land from which books liberated him.

QUESTIONS

1. Although Wolfe's language mirrors the language of the "lurid" books, why does it not share the faults—at least not to the same degree—of these sources?
2. How do you think Wolfe managed to transform these early influences into his own way of writing?
3. Apart from style, what might these books have done for Wolfe as a writer?

In these passages, the first an interview [3] the second a passage from *The Summing Up*,[4] two writers have their say about the men who influenced their work and about conscious or unconscious influence. The truth is that both Lawrence Durrell and the man he calls "old Maugham" (Somerset Maugham) are right. The important thing is not that these two authors differ in their approach to what books can do—and have done—for their own writing, but that each found what was best for him and used literature to strengthen his own talent.

INTERVIEWERS: Are you conscious of any specific influence in your writing?

DURRELL: You know, I'm not quite sure about the word, because I copy what I admire. I pinch. When you say "influences" it suggests an infiltration of someone else's material into yours, semiconsciously. But I read not only for pleasure, but as a journeyman, and where I see a good effect I study it, and try to reproduce it. So that I am probably the biggest thief imaginable. I

[3] Lawrence Durrell interview, *Writers at Work: The Paris Review Interviews*, Second Series (New York: The Viking Press, 1963).
[4] Somerset Maugham, *The Summing Up* (New York: Doubleday & Company, 1938), pp. 25-30.

steal from people—my seniors, I mean. And in fact, *Panic Spring*, which you said was a respectable book, seemed to me dreadful, because it was an anthology, you see, with five pages of Huxley, three pages of Aldington, two pages of Robert Graves, and so on—in fact all the writers I admire. But they didn't influence me. I pinched effects, I was learning the game. Like an actor will study a senior character and learn an effect of make-up or a particular slouchy walk for a role he's not thought of himself. He doesn't regard that as being particularly influenced by the actor, but as a trick of the trade which he owes it to himself to pick up.

INTERVIEWERS: It has been said that in your poetry you were considerably influenced by Auden.

DURRELL: Well, there again I pinched. Yes, of course. He is a great master of colloquial effects which no one before him dared to use.

INTERVIEWERS: Did you consciously develop your own style of writing, or did it just come naturally?

DURRELL: I don't think anyone can, you know, develop a style consciously. I read with amazement, for example, of old Maugham solemnly writing out a page of Swift every day when he was trying to learn the job, in order to give himself a stylistic purchase, as it were. It struck me as something I could never do. No. When you say "consciously" I think you're wrong. I mean, it's like "Do you consciously dream?" One doesn't know very much about these processes at all. I think the writing itself grows you up, and you grow the writing up, and finally you get an amalgam of everything you have pinched with a new kind of personality which is your own, and then you are able to pay back these socking debts with a tiny bit of interest, which is the only honorable thing for a writer to do—at least a writer who is a thief like me.

I studied Jeremy Taylor's *Holy Dying*. In order to assimilate his style I copied down passages and then tried to write them down from memory.

The first fruit of this labour was a little book about Andalusia called *The Land of the Blessed Virgin.* I had occasion to read parts of it the other day. I know Andalusia a great deal better now than I knew it then, and I have changed my mind about a good many things of which I wrote. Since it has continued in America to have a small sale it occurred to me that it might be worth while to revise it. I soon saw that this was impossible. The book was written by someone I have completely forgotten. It bored me to distraction. But what I am concerned with is the prose, for it was as an exercise in style that I wrote it. It is wistful, allusive and elaborate. It has neither ease nor spontaneity. It smells of hot-house plants and Sunday dinner like the air in the greenhouse that leads out of the dining-room of a big house in Bayswater. There are a great many melodious adjectives. The vocabulary is sentimental. It does not remind one of an Italian brocade, with its rich pattern of gold, but of a curtain material designed by Burne-Jones and reproduced by Morris.

I do not know whether it was a subconscious feeling that this sort of writing was contrary to my bent or a naturally methodical cast of mind that led me then to turn my attention to the writers of the Augustan Period. The prose of Swift enchanted me. I made up my mind that this was the perfect way to write and I started to work on him in the same way as I had done with Jeremy Taylor. I chose *The Tale of a Tub.* It is said that when the Dean re-read it in his old age he cried: "What genius I had then!" To my mind his genius was better shown in other works. It is a tiresome allegory and the irony is facile. But the style is admirable. I cannot imagine that English can be better written. Here are no flowery periods, fantastic turns of phrase or high-flown images. It is a civilized prose, natural, discreet and pointed. There is no attempt to surprise by an extravagant vocabulary. It looks as though Swift made do with the first word that came to hand, but since he had an acute and logical brain it was always the right one, and he put it in the right place. The strength and balance of his sentences are due to an exquisite taste. As I had done before I copied passages and then tried to write them out again from memory. I tried altering words or the order in which they were set. I found that the only possible words were those Swift had used and that the order in which he had placed them was the only possible order. It is an impeccable prose.

But perfection has one grave defect: it is apt to be dull. Swift's prose is like a French canal, bordered with poplars, that runs through a gracious and undulating country. Its tranquil charm fills you with satisfaction, but it neither excites the emotions nor stimulates the imagination. You go on and on and presently you are a trifle bored. So, much as you may admire Swift's wonderful lucidity, his terseness, his naturalness, his lack of affectation, you find your attention wandering after a while unless his matter peculiarly interests you. I think if I had my time over again I would give to the prose of Dryden the close study I gave to that of Swift. I did not come across it till I had lost the inclination to take so much pains. The prose of Dryden is delicious. It has not the perfection of Swift nor the easy elegance of Addison, but it has a springtime gaiety, a conversational ease, a blithe spontaneousness that are enchanting. Dryden was a very good poet, but it is not the general opinion that he had a lyrical quality; it is strange that it is just this that sings in his softly sparkling prose. Prose had never been written in England like that before; it has seldom been written like that since. Dryden flourished at a happy moment. He had in his bones the sonorous periods and the baroque massiveness of Jacobean language and under the influence of the nimble and well-bred felicity that he learnt from the French he turned it into an instrument that was fit not only for solemn themes but also to express the light thought of the passing moment. He was the first of the rococo artists. If Swift reminds you of a French canal Dryden recalls an English river winding its cheerful way round hills, through quietly busy towns and by nestling villages, pausing now in a noble reach and then running powerfully through a woodland country. It is alive, varied, windswept; and it has the pleasant open-air smell of England.

The work I did was certainly very good for me. I began to write better: I did not write well. I wrote stiffly and self-consciously. I tried to get a pattern into my sentences, but did not see that the pattern was evident. I took care how I placed my words, but did not reflect that an order that was natural at the beginning of the eighteenth century was most unnatural at the beginning of ours. My attempt to write in the manner of Swift made it impossible for me to achieve the effect of inevitable rightness that was just what I so much admired in him. I then wrote a number of plays and ceased to occupy myself with anything but dialogue. It was not till five years had passed that I set out again to write a novel. By then I no longer had any ambition to be a stylist; I put aside all thought of fine writing. I wanted to write without any frills of language, in as bare and unaffected a manner as I could. I had so much to say that I could afford to waste no words. I wanted merely to set down the facts. I began with the impossible aim of using no adjectives at all. I thought that if you could find the exact term a qualifying epithet could be dispensed with. As I saw it in my mind's eye my book would have the appearance of an immensely long telegram in which for economy's sake you had left out every word that was not necessary to make the sense clear. I have not read it since I corrected the proofs and do not know how near I came to doing what I tried. My impression is that it is written at least more naturally than anything I had written before; but I am sure that it is often slipshod and I daresay there are in it a good many mistakes in grammar.

Since then I have written many other books; and though ceasing my methodical study of the old masters (for though the spirit is willing, the flesh is weak), I have continued with increasing assiduity to try to write better. I discovered my limitations and it seemed to me that the only sensible thing was to aim at what excellence I could within them. I knew that I had no lyrical quality. I had a small vocabulary and no efforts that I could make to enlarge it much availed me. I had little gift of metaphor; the original and striking simile seldom occurred to me. Poetic flights and the great imaginative sweep were beyond my powers. I could admire them in others as I could admire their far-fetched tropes and the unusual but suggestive language in which they clothed their thoughts, but my own invention never presented me with such embellishments; and I was tired of trying to do what did not come easily to me. On the other hand, I had an acute power of observation and it seemed to me that I could see a great many things that other people missed. I could put down in clear terms what I saw. I had a logical sense, and if no great feeling for the richness and strangeness of words, at all events a lively appreciation of their sound. I knew that I should never write as well as I could wish, but I thought with pains I could arrive at writing as well as my natural defects allowed. On taking thought it seemed to me that I must aim at lucidity, simplicity and euphony. I have put these three qualities in the order of the importance I assigned to them.

Maugham set about deliberately developing a style. While the style that became his may not have been the one intended, he did finally decide what his style should consist of. Durrell says he could never do this, that he found his style developed more or less unconsciously as he "pinched" from other writers. There are different ways for different personalities. The important thing is that both writers were consciously studying other writers, and that their goal was not to be just like another writer but to be themselves.

If you are not quite sure of how Durrell's pinched effects became part of his own original style, think about some athletic skill, habit, or personal mannerism you first acquired by studying someone else. If it stayed with you any length of time, it probably became part of your overall personality or behavior. In the same way you can understand Maugham's process. Have you ever found that one of your copied skills or habits somehow didn't fit your life? Maybe in discovering this you moved closer to seeing what you were looking for, what you really could become.

Writing is part of life. It is a kind of behavior, part of personality. Learning writing is much like learning other skills.

QUESTIONS

1. What is the difference between Durrell's pinching and plagiarism?

2. What does Durrell mean when he says, "The writing itself grows you up, and you grow the writing up . . ." ?
3. Take a passage of some writer you admire very much and try changing words or word order.

Paul Green is well known for his outdoor dramas which recreate important eras of American history. He tries to work very close to the truth of his sources. For him, literature and life are very close. Here, in an excerpt from a speech, *The University in a Nuclear Age*, he explains something of how he first realized that connection.

I remember one lonely Sunday on the farm when I was a boy. From the peddler I mentioned I had got a copy of Shakespeare's *Hamlet*. And with the family gone off to church and the house silent and empty, I read the drama. And as I read, I grew more interested and filled with suspense as to the people and their fate in the story. And emotion became more and more packed up in me. And finally I came to the scene where poor piteous Ophelia enters with brains broken and mind deranged, speaking her little mad and anguished sayings—"there's rue for you, and here's some for me. We may call it herb of grace o' Sundays. O, you must wear your rue with a difference. There's a daisy. I would give you some violets, but they withered all when my father died. They say he made a good end." (Singing.) 'For bonny sweet Robin is all my joy.'" And the tears gushed from my eyes, my heart opened with a yearning deep and wide—

"O wert thou in the cauld blast,
On yonder lea, on yonder lea,
My plaidie to the angry airt,
I'd shelter thee, I'd shelter thee."

That day was a mark in my life. And because of that fresh, wild appreciation, untrammeled and unprepared for by any professional coaching as to influences and types and methods by which the play might have been derived to represent the Elizabethan age or something other than itself—because of that, *Hamlet* has stood solidly by me, a rich storehouse to draw from again and again through the years and has meant more to me than it otherwise could possibly have meant. And Ophelia has continued to live her sweet and piteous life in the chambers of my soul.

Another lonely hot Sunday on the farm, I was lying in my sweaty little shed room reading the Bible, when I came upon the twelfth chapter of Ecclesiastes. I suddenly sat up in delight at what I read—the beauty of it thrilled me and put a stuffiness in my throat. I hurried out of the room and down the side porch into the kitchen where my sister was getting lunch. "Listen," I said, "listen." And I read, " 'Or ever the silver cord be loosed, or the golden bowl be broken, or the pitcher be broken at the fountain or the wheel broken at the cistern.' "

"That's wonderful," she said. And she stood by the stove, holding a little piece of firewood balanced in her hand, her eyes wide and thoughtful as she went on hearing the words over a second time in her mind. "Read it again," she said. And I did, and for a while we shared the beauty and wonder of those lines and others in the chapter. And because of that experience, Ecclesiastes has always remained one of my favorite books. I thank my stars that I was not "prepared" for it by the usual teacher, say, of Comparative Literature who talked of a preceding Stoic philosophy and currents of Hebraic pessimism which brought the book to being—a resultant of clearly demarked and discernible scholarly laws and forces. For it would have been marred before I got to it—as so many of the great works of literature were marred for me in precisely that way.

And through the blue depths of the sky the bird flies, but the tips of its wings are never stained in it. Moreover it is written— that with faith a man thinks. Faithless he cannot think. And he who worships God as the great King milks heaven and drinks it day by day. His food is never exhausted . . . "And he shall be like a tree planted by the rivers of water, that bringeth forth his fruit in his season; his leaf also shall not wither, and whatsoever he doeth shall prosper."

Students and even teachers often complain that much good literature is ruined by being overanalyzed. As Wordsworth said, "We murder to dissect." An individual can encounter a book on his own terms if he wishes, which is true of few other modern forms of communication. Sometimes the result is frustration, but when real contact occurs two worlds become one. For Paul Green, this happened with Ecclesiastes and *Hamlet*. For him, this experience proves that there is no substitute for solitary, unguided reading. Only in this state does the connection between literature and life become real—not as a theory but as a fact, as experience. This kind of experience is invaluable to both readers and writers. Without it writers could not write, they would have no faith in their work.

QUESTIONS

1. How does the reading of Ecclesiastes transform not only literature but the writer's immediate world? Read the description of his sister. Why is she described in such detail?
2. What role would Paul Green assign to literary criticism?
3. What kinds of books have come alive for you in the way *Hamlet* and Ecclesiastes did for Paul Green? Are they still with you in any way?

A person who finds much of his emotional and intellectual life through books is always surprised that books fail to influence another person. Asked to write on the influence of books in his life, one student produced the following theme.

Concerning the assignment for this section, I can truthfully say that I have never read a book for style, and, by the same token, no book has ever affected or altered my personal style. For that matter, I don't believe that there is such a thing as *style*. Writing, at least as I see it, is not made great by some exact calculation of words in precise order, but by the ideas and emotions that can be transmitted most effectively through its medium of communication. In essence, *style* is very little more than expressing what you wish in such a way as to make it most effective; therefore, *style* must be flexible to meet any situation. This flexibility makes style an indefinable term, and I fail to see how something that no one can even explain can be affected to such great extents, especially by books. *Style,* like *realism,* is nothing more than a term used by critics to make books that say nothing sound good.

As far as the bit about books opening up new worlds and teaching one about life, I can only say that this is so much assorted crap. I would rather live life than read about it, and, by my standards, life is the only book worth reading. Some people are pages, some chapters, and some even volumes, but all are different and all are interesting, and all are worth reading. I doubt that the course of my yet young life will be altered too greatly by the books I do or do not read, but it will be by the people I do or do not meet.

By now I imagine you are wondering just what in the hell I am talking about, so I'll stop long enough in my exposition to tell you. . . . I can't really do the assignment as you would like, because no book has ever done for me what I am supposed to write about it doing.

Of course this writer places himself in direct opposition to many arguments in this textbook. We will not claim to be unbiased in calling his statements to question. First, the writer never tells us what books he has read, so we don't know if he might not just be hiding the influences both to himself and to the readers. We need to get a picture of what happens when he reads. And though style may be indefinable, at least to this author's knowledge or satisfaction, he admits there are different kinds of writing for different kinds of situations. And since writing is an invention, might we not learn how to meet different situations by studying how others have met them? Or does each person have within him all the possible useful writing inventions?

QUESTIONS

1. Are the words the author chooses in his writing the same as those he might use in "talking" his case? If not, where do you think he learned (consciously or unconsciously) the difference between talk and writing?
2. Does the use of the book metaphor to describe people subvert his own case? Why, or why not?

ASSIGNMENTS

1. Paul Green speaks of books being "marred" by teachers who prepare students for reading by employing a background of scholarly laws and theories to introduce a work of art. Write a paper in which you convey the influence of the books you *found for yourself* in your youth. You might want to limit your discussion to one book or one author.
2. In a paper of not less than 400 words, make a case for or against learning to write by close imitation of known authors. Use your own experience as a background for the paper.
3. Choose a science, economics, or sociology text that you feel is more than a collection of facts. How is the writer unifying his subject? Is there a particular "philosophy" underlying the facts? How might this "philosophy" influence your own view of the subject?
4. Write a theme titled "The Authors in Me," in which you talk about the way you think and write so as to reveal how authors and books have become a part of you.

PART TWO

PUTTING MATERIALS TOGETHER

Problems of Form and Order

FORM AND ORDER

No reader contracts with a writer to follow that writer's pages or book from beginning to end. Reading is a journey, and the reader expects to *go* somewhere when he starts reading. Not only that, he usually wants to know where he is going. Or at least he wants to feel sure he is going somewhere. He may wait at the starting gate a while and he may stand some delays, but if he begins to get the idea that he is not going anywhere after all, he will stop reading.

Order is the means by which writing moves the reader on his journey. Reading an essay or a book is not like looking at a picture or hearing an explosion. You cannot experience the whole thing at one time. Even if you could, your habit of using spoken language in an orderly way would make you aware of the order in written language. Technically, order is the most important business of writing. It is the business of choosing where to put things—commas, words, phrases, sentences, paragraphs, and chapters. It is the basis of style and of sense. Many of the choices are made before writing or in revision. The point is that they are choices, not accidents.

Although the act of writing can be discovery for the writer as

well as the reader, this does not mean the writer can pick a topic
and just start putting words on paper, waiting for the discovery.
This would be like an explorer suddenly leaping aboard ship and
setting sail, or a chemist mixing all the yellow chemicals or a
golfer picking a club blindfolded.

When you start writing you may not know all that will happen
along the way, but you should know why you are beginning where
you begin and how far you want to go before you finish. Some
writers say they are ready to write when they know the first and
last sentences of a work. If the first is full of direction and purpose
and the last full of resolution and finality, you can understand
what these writers mean.

Of course, these writers don't think only about first and last sentences before they begin. They know their themes and what the
boundaries of their work might be. They have a very clear idea
why their subject interests them. If you will excuse the comparison, we could say a hound dog doesn't race off baying just because
the woods are pretty. With a definite goal in mind the writer begins to create the order of words, sentences, and paragraphs
which will take him, and later the reader, through the complete
development of an idea or experience.

The most familiar order in our lives is time—on the clock, in
the cycle of night and day, in the change of seasons, and in
growing and aging. There is no absolute reason why we have to
be so aware of time. It is only our desire for order that makes
us see most events in the physical world in terms of time. Time
is a mathematical invention, a rigid order. Though one day seems
longer than the next, it never is longer. We are healthier at
some points than at others, but time measures only one direction—aging.

Time is also an easy order to use. A child telling about a trip, a
television show, or a book usually tells all he knows in almost the
order it first came to him. In grade school you were probably encouraged to write this way. You wrote an autobiography beginning with where and when you were born. Or, you described how
to put together an aquarium starting, "First you. . . ." Usually
you stopped the autobiography at the point it reached the present; or the aquarium process, when the fish tank was full of fish.

Ernest Hemingway said that the real end of all stories is death. But that was only true for the physical material, the flesh and blood of his stories. He did not always end with death. He was not just presenting all that happened to an interesting character. Even if he had had time, he would not have followed every character to death. Few writers write for the sake of telling you what time everything happened. Writers are not time clocks for every little event they observe. Writing is not reality. It is a means of communicating our awareness of reality. It is the use of symbols to convey not only sense perceptions but relationships, opinions, feelings, and even mysteries. Time provides a very obvious relationship between things in this world, but that relationship is not always the most important.

Writing cannot be reality. But it can reorder and reunite reality in meaningful ways. Writing has its own order, as deliberate and conscious as time, but much more flexible. Since writing is not reality, it requires no immediate physical reactions or verbal responses from a reader. An article containing the description of a runaway automobile does not require you to jump out of the way before you can take note of the car's color and driver. A description of a house does not have to start at the front door. Of course, the writer probably jumped out of the way or entered by the front door when he first gathered his material. Since then, he has contemplated that material and found something more significant in it than the raw data collected by his senses. This broader significance is something which happened in the writer's mind. In writing, he has tried to transfer this significance to the reader's mind. Therefore, the order of all writing is dictated by the minds of the reader and writer.

Even the smallest act of writing is an act of imposing order on the world around us. Every phrase and every sentence imposes order of some kind. This is why Aristotle was so interested in grammar. Some modern students of language—anthropologists, linguists, psychologists, philosophers—say that the language a person speaks determines the possible ways in which he can think about his world. Similarly, within your own language the more possible orders you are aware of, the greater will be your ability to think about the world you perceive.

Look at the two paragraphs that follow and try to rearrange
words, sentences, and the entire paragraph, asking yourself in
each case why the author chose the order he did. The first paragraph is the opening one in Reynolds Price's novel *A Long and
Happy Life.*

Just with his body and from inside like a snake, leaning that
black motorcycle side to side, cutting in and out of the slow line
of cars to get there first, staring due-north through goggles towards Mount Moriah and switching coon tails in everybody's
face was Wesley Beavers, and laid against his back like sleep,
spraddle-legged on the sheepskin seat behind him was Rosacoke Mustian who was maybe his girl and who had given up
looking into the wind and trying to nod at every sad car in the
line, and when he even speeded up and passed the truck (lent
for the afternoon by Mr. Isaac Alston and driven by Sammy his
man, hauling one pine box and one black boy dressed in all he
could borrow, set up in a ladder-back chair with flowers
banked around him and a foot on the box to steady it)—when
he passed that, Rosacoke said once into his back "Don't" and
rested in humiliation, not thinking but with her hands on his
hips for dear life and her white blouse blown out behind her
like a banner in defeat.[1]

You probably won't be writing prose as intricate as this, but you
can see here the effect a keen sense of order can build. The second
paragraph is from *The War Lords of Washington* by Bruce Catton, a writer and formerly a reporter and member of several government agencies active in World War II. The book is about the
struggle to maintain democracy under wartime conditions.

They were often admitted to be the ablest men in the nation
and they were very high up in the Defense Effort, and the best
was none too good for them. If, collectively, they were neither
as beautiful nor as terrible as an army with banners, individu-
ally they were very impressive. Their faces had that indefinable
but unmistakable gloss which comes to faces that are photo-

[1] Reynolds Price, *A Long and Happy Life* (New York: Atheneum Publishers, 1962), p. 3.

graphed a great deal (good food, right living, and the proper kind of publicity can do much for a man) and if the North Lounge of the Carlton had been set aside for the party it was only fitting and proper.[2]

Did these two paragraphs give you any idea of what the entire books were like? If so you were forming an idea of *form*. Form is simply the total of all the choices of order an author has had to make. The most common forms of writing are familiar to all of us: the novel, story, poem, and essay. But these are only general labels for forms. There are lyric and narrative poems, sonnets, epics, limericks, and sestinas. There are formal and informal essays. A novel can be an autobiographical *bildungs roman* or a complex weaving of different points of view, place, and time. The names for forms are more help to you as a critic than as a writer. As a writer your interest begins with your material, not with your form. You don't sit down and say, "I want to write a play. What's a good situation?" This can be done, but the result is usually not very effective.

You start with the subject or with what the subject means to you. You try to see the kinds of choices you will have to make and you try to see how they can all be part of one form. All of your smaller choices of order have their own meanings. When you look for a form you are looking for a way of uniting all the small choices you'll make into a consistent and meaningful whole. You don't worry whether your form can be fit with a neat label. In other words, form grows out of subject and purpose. But this does not mean form grows while you actually write. First you study your subject, find your goal. This is how Edgar Allen Poe approached the short story:

A skilful artist has constructed a tale. He has not fashioned his thoughts to accommodate his incidents, but having deliberately conceived a certain *single effect* to be wrought, he then invents such incidents, he then combines such events, and discusses them in such tone as may best serve him in establishing

[2] Bruce Catton, *The War Lords of Washington* (New York: Harcourt, Brace & World, 1948), p. 1.

this preconceived effect. If his very first sentence tend not to the outbringing of this effect, then in his very first step has he committed a blunder. In the whole composition there should be no word written of which the tendency, direct or indirect, is not to the one pre-established design. And by such means, with such care and skill, a picture is at length painted which leaves in the mind of him who contemplates it with a kindred art, a sense of the fullest satisfaction.

As you begin each assignment in the following chapters, use the guides below to help you get a good idea of order and form before you start writing. If you can answer all of these questions clearly and logically about each paper, you will have a lot in your favor before you begin writing.

1. What is my subject?
2. Is it small enough to be specific and interesting without boring the reader with excess detail?
3. What is my personal interest in this subject? Be specific.
4. In one to five words, what is my specific theme or thesis?
5. What details are relevant and necessary to illustrate and develop theme?
6. How can I start in an interesting way that will indicate subject, theme, and direction?
7. How will the reader's mind keep a sense of direction or goal as I enter each new aspect of my subject?
8. What should happen to the reader's mind between the first word and the last?
9. What is the essence of my first paragraph and my last?

If you are in doubt as to just how writers use form and order, try the following exercises.

1. Choose several fiction and nonfiction magazine articles. Read the first and last paragraphs. What is the theme of each? Do they reveal what movement the work as a whole took? (Caution: Not every piece you choose will be appropriate.)

2. Look at several poems you like or can read easily. Try to rearrange words or omit lines. What is the effect?
3. Find what you think is a well-written essay that does not follow a
   chronological order. How would it be different if presented
   chronologically?
4. Pick a certain period in your life. How would you tell it in some
   way other than the way it happened?
5. Read a very emotional piece of writing and single out individual sentences you feel are very powerful. Try to rearrange the
   order of words.

CHAPTER 4

WHAT IS A PLACE?

When someone writes, "There's no place like home," he is not telling us very much. If we think he likes home, we are only guessing that he is like most people who use the phrase. We know nothing about "home," only about the author's probable attitude.

Above all, places are physical. You (or somebody) can be there, touch things, stand on solid footing. If the place is imaginary or unreachable, as is the sun or the setting for science fiction or a vanished Biblical city, then you can at least think yourself into the place. Of course, "home" is a place, and you can probably visualize it. You may even agree that there's no place like it, but the place you visualize is *your* idea of home, not the writer's actual home.

Physical description of a place is necessary to make a place seem real to the reader, but it is not nearly enough. In the following selection, a student has given a clear picture of a park. We get the layout and size, but is there anything else?

Cranston Park is a green rectangle, 100 by 150 yards. Crossing it diagonally is a gravel path about ten feet wide. On one side of the path is a baseball diamond with a big wire backstop and a well-kept infield. On the other side of the path is a picnic area with five wooden tables, each with benches on both sides and a wire trash basket nearby. On all four sides of the park are large pine and maple trees between the park and the sidewalk. Cranston Park is used for recreation by individuals and groups from our town.

This is one of those paragraphs that could easily be a list. Why? How could the writer have made this a more coherent description? Of course, you may say he was only interested in listing important features. Perhaps so, but it doesn't make good reading, does it? Below, in a passage from *Lotus and the Robot,* Arthur Koestler describes a place.

The sewers of Bombay had been opened by mistake, I was told, before the tide had come in. The damp heat, impregnated by their stench, invaded the air-conditioned cabin the moment the door of the Viscount was opened. As we descended the steps I had the sensation that a wet, smelly diaper was being wrapped around my head by some abominable joker. This was December; the previous day I had been slithering over the frozen snow in the mountains of Austria. Yet, by the time we had crossed the reclaimed marshes of the seven islands on which Bombay is built, I had accepted the heat and was no longer aware of the smell.

An hour after leaving the aircraft, I was ushered into another air-conditioned environment: my hotel room. Its windows and shutters were hermetically closed against the outer atmosphere, its curtains drawn tight against the outer light. It was the peaceful interior of a bathyscope suspended in the sea. After a while I got accustomed to that too, and found it quite natural to live in an artificial atmosphere with artificial light, while the sun was blazing outside. However, each time I left my bathyscope and was hit by the steaming air with its heavy blend of smells, I felt the same shocked surprise as on the first occasion.

Late at night, on the day after my arrival, I opened the curtains, blinds and shutters, and walked out to the balcony. At this hour there were no pedestrians. My first impression of the deserted street was that a firing squad had passed through it, leaving the pavements strewn with corpses. The lifeless heaps of rags and bones, naked except for a loin-cloth, seemed to be lying in the position in which they had fallen when the bullets struck them. They were lying on the pavement amidst the red spittle, the dogs' excrement, the undefinable filth. But the idea of the firing squad did not really fit, for there was no atmosphere of heroism in the street; it had a look of resignation, rather like etchings of mediaeval towns in the grip of the Plague. I had read that out of the total population of three and a half million in Bombay, seven hundred thousand slept on the pavements—but these were abstract figures, and statistics neither bleed nor smell.

During my first week in Bombay, I was haunted by the corpse-like sleepers along the kerbs, on the stairs and passages of dilapidated Indo-Victorian houses. One late evening, visiting a friend, I actually stumbled over one of the lifeless shapes lying in the hallway. It did not stir. I lit a match and saw that there were actually five of them: their skins nearly black, their ribs sticking out like Christ's on the Cross.

The next day, I had an appointment with a physician working at a clinic. I went early in the morning before surgery hours: the gateway and courtyard of the clinic were a camp of human castaways—men, old women, children like twisted skeletons, sleeping among the refuse in the company of several pie dogs. Whenever, late at night, I tried to go for a stroll, I felt that I was walking over a battlefield combined with a refuse heap. Nobody in Bombay walks through the streets at night, except for some compelling reason.

My Indian acquaintances were puzzled by my obsession with the seven hundred thousand street-campers. It had always been like that, they explained, but perhaps with progressive industrialization under the third Five Year Plan . . . In actual fact, the third Five Year Plan does not even pretend to be concerned with the problem. As far as one can foretell, the situation, instead of improving, will get worse: the population increases at the rate of six or seven million a year; in the next ten years a figure larger than the total population of Great Britain will be added to its numbers. My Indian friends shrugged; after a while I stopped harassing them with questions. After another week, I took the huddled corpses for granted and actually no longer saw them—just as I was no longer aware of the beggars, cripples and legless deformities dragging themselves on naked buttocks along the pavement amidst the milling crowd.

Though I had read about it in books, the din and noise and profanity in Indian places of worship came as another shock. I found that there is more peace to be had in Manhattan than in any Indian town or village, temple or shrine. If the temple was an historic monument, the atmosphere was that of Brighton pier; if it was a modest local shrine, the scene was that of a family picnic. The voices were shrill and unrestrained; children would caper all over the place with mothers and sisters yelling after them; obeisance was shown to the idol, but no reverence; the feeling of sanctity was completely absent. I began to suspect that I had never encountered a people as un-contemplative as the nation of Yogis. At the same time I also suspected that something essential was escaping me, and that I must be mistaken.

But above all I felt that I had fallen into a chaotic antheap of ants of my size; gentle ants, mindlessly milling in all directions, falling over each other in the hot dust, some crippled, some starving, some hanging in grapes from ant-sized tramcars and liable to panic at any moment.

When it became too much, there was always an escape. I would retire to my air-conditioned bathyscope, close the shutters, and the ant-town would cease to exist. Instead, I would feel that I was sinking through an unreal world towards the bottom of the sea. My heart was sinking, my morale was sinking. I had almost forgotten what I had come for. It must have been some abstract, air-conditioned idea about spiritual values.[1]

[1] Arthur Koestler, *The Lotus and the Robot* (New York: The Macmillan Company, 1960).

Think of people you know in school. What themes would each use if he were describing the school? The themes probably vary widely, but this only means individual points of view are working. Things are what they are, but language is the human mind making symbols for things. As minds vary, so does language. No one person's observation of the external world can be 100 percent complete, so he must organize his experience, and personality will influence the order he creates from his perceptions.

Not everybody will be personally involved with every place. If involvement is shallow or absent, a writer will resort to tricks and he will write badly. Sometimes you will feel very strongly about some place, but your writing will sound like everyone else's quick descriptions. This may be because your feeling is produced by other people's feelings, and not by the place itself. Yet you will think you are reacting to the place.

When you choose a place (or any subject) to write about, you must be willing and able to look long and hard. If you are unable to do this, perhaps you should be reading about the place rather than writing about it.

When you do look you may discover historical ties, social patterns, economic vitality, ethnic character, or perhaps some kind of mystery. If you were writing a book on the place, you could make many discoveries. But long or short, your writing must do more than present colors, sizes, and sounds. Few readers are intrinsically interested in random places, although they might be interested in what you discover.

All we have said so far concerns writing whose sole purpose is to describe a particular place. Such descriptions are common and valuable, but often we are interested in a place as the location for something else. Then we call it a scene or a setting.

The beginning writer often makes the mistake of thinking that the more fully described a setting is, the better the writing. This hypothesis does not stand up in practice. The reason you have a setting is not simply because the reader expects one or because you want "atmosphere." You describe setting because that place (as reflected in its own theme) is important to what you are writing. The English novelist Elizabeth Bowen has said that scene is justified only when it acts on character and has dramatic use.

What is true for fiction is true in almost all writing. The scene or setting must be carried in the reader's mind and be constantly at work. Therefore, you must be careful to use only what is necessary to establish the setting and its relation to the larger themes. In some cases the bare minimum will do.

> Just as a writer cannot give the total past in his exposition, so he cannot give the total present in his scene. His problem is to select the relevant details, the items which will suggest the whole scene, and in certain cases give clues to character situation, and theme. Chekhov once told a writer to cut out his long passage describing the moonlight in a scene and give simply the glint of the moon on a piece of broken bottle. Such a perception might do more to give the sense of a scene than would a full rendering, because more vivid, more sharply focused, more stimulating to the imagination.[2]

If Chekhov's friend took the advice, he may have had to scrap some fine writing about moonlight.

As you begin writing your own settings, you too will have to pass up things which interest you. Save them if you wish, but remember that writing is not a stage entertainment; it is communication. You must know what your sense of place communicates, either by itself or as part of a larger work.

The selections that follow will give you an idea of the many uses of place in writing. As you read them, ask yourself how the writer as an individual has made his work distinct. Why is he interested in this place? After all, even readers sitting in armchairs or lying in bed cannot be expected to journey any old place for the sake of looking around.

SELECTIONS

Nathaniel Hawthorne's description of a colonial prison is a good example of place being developed as part of a larger subject. If

[2] Cleanth Brooks, Jr. and Robert Penn Warren, *Understanding Fiction* (New York: Appleton-Century-Crofts, 1943), p. 576.

you read carefully, you will see that this description, taken from *The Scarlet Letter,* tells much about the author's approach to the rest of the story.

A throng of bearded men, in sad-colored garments, and gray, steeple-crowned hats, intermixed with women, some wearing hoods and others bareheaded, was assembled in front of a wooden edifice, the door of which was heavily timbered with oak, and studded with iron spikes.

The founders of a new colony, whatever Utopia of human virtue and happiness they might originally project, have invariably recognized it among their earliest practical necessities to allot a portion of the virgin soil as a cemetery, and another portion as the site of a prison. In accordance with this rule, it may safely be assumed that the forefathers of Boston had built the first prison-house somewhere in the vicinity of Cornhill, almost as seasonably as they marked out the first burial-ground, on Isaac Johnson's lot, and round about his grave, which subsequently became the nucleus of all the congregated sepulchres in the old churchyard of King's Chapel. Certain it is, that some fifteen or twenty years after the settlement of the town, the wooden jail was already marked with weather-stains and other indications of age, which gave a yet darker aspect to its beetle-browed and gloomy front. The rust on the ponderous iron-work of its oaken door looked more antique than anything else in the New World. Like all that pertains to crime, it seemed never to have known a youthful era. Before this ugly edifice, and between it and the wheel-track of the street, was a grass-plot, much overgrown with burdock, pigweed, apple-peru, and such unsightly vegetation, which evidently found something congenial in the soil that had so early borne the black flower of civilized society, a prison. But, on one side of the portal, and rooted almost at the threshold, was a wild rose-bush, covered, in this month of June, with its delicate gems, which might be imagined to offer their fragrance and fragile beauty to the prisoner as he went in, and to the condemned criminal as he came forth to his doom, in token that the deep heart of Nature could pity and be kind to him.

This rose-bush, by a strange chance, has been kept alive in history; but whether it had merely survived out of the stern old wilderness, so long after the fall of the gigantic pines and oaks that originally overshadowed it,—or whether, as there is fair authority for believing, it had sprung up under the footsteps of the sainted Anne Hutchinson, as she entered the prison-door,—we shall not take upon us to determine. Finding it so directly on the threshold of our narrative, which is now about to issue from that inauspicious portal, we could hardly do otherwise than pluck one of its flowers, and present it to the reader. It may serve, let us hope, to symbolize some sweet moral blossom, that may be found along the track, or relieve the darkening close of a tale of human frailty and sorrow.

The writer might have begun his description by saying right out, "The prison was an ugly building." Many people would consider this a good "topic sentence" which could be supported by detail in the rest of the paragraph. That kind of opening has its place, but at best it means opening with the author telling the reader how to think.

Hawthorne gets his reader well into his scene physically before he ever uses the epithet "ugly." His opening establishes the prison as the center of this piece of narrative. The description of the door and the people suggests the rigid and severe Puritan attitude toward punishment. The background of the settlement seems a mild digression, but in fact it works toward establishing the prison's place in the society.

In paragraph three we return to the door, the prisoner about to emerge onto the stage just set. Because of the description, the person who emerges will be more than a face and body. The prisoner's specific crime is not known, but the community's attitude toward crime is at least implied by the setting. That attitude is the real human center of the story.

QUESTIONS

1. How does Hawthorne move smoothly from the history of the colony to physical description of the prison?

2. Why does he give the specific names of weeds rather than just calling them a lot of weeds?
3. What do you expect the crowd's attitude toward the prisoner will be?

The Palace in San Francisco was one of America's first big luxury hotels. Here is a description of it from the book *Bonanza Inn*, by sociologist Oscar Lewis and reporter Carroll Hall.[3]

By the spring of 1875, construction had reached a point where it was possible for visitors to visualize the future wonders of the place. On Saturday afternoons Superintendent King piloted groups of citizens through the spacious chambers of the ground floor. The sightseers looked with wonder at the grand court, its seven tiers of galleries rising to the lofty dome, and passed on to other rooms: a marble-flagged office 65 by 55 feet, with a 25-foot ceiling; a ballroom of the same dimensions as the office; ladies' and men's reception rooms, each 40 by 40; billiard room, barber shop, and bar (all on the Jessie Street side) of the same generous proportions; and a main dining-room 150 feet long, incomparably the largest in the West.

Features new in hotel design were not lacking. On the Montgomery and Market Street sides provision had been made for eighteen retail stores. Each had two entrances and two sets of show-windows, one facing on the streets, the other on long galleries within the building; guests would thus enjoy the luxury of doing their shopping—or of merely admiring the displays—without the inconvenience of stepping outdoors.

Inventors were then putting electricity to a variety of clever uses, and many of the devices were installed for the convenience of the Palace's guests. A hundred and twenty-five miles of wires permitted the functioning of electric call buttons in each room, of telegraphic instruments providing communication between the service pantries on each floor and the main

[3] Oscar Lewis and Carroll Hall, *Bonanza Inn* (New York: Alfred A. Knopf, 1939), pp. 24–29.

office or dining-room, and of what was perhaps the greatest novelty of all: electrically operated clocks—". . . sixteen large and handsome time dials, running in perfect unison, and controlled by Field's patent electric regulator." Telephones and electric lights were still too crude for practical operation (both were installed a few years later), but gas fixtures were modern as well as elaborate, with burners of an improved design, and in the public rooms they were so arranged that a hundred jets might be regulated by the turning of a single master key.

Other interesting gadgets charmed a mechanically minded generation. Each floor had its own "tubular conductor" to carry outgoing mail direct to a central box in the office. Another system of pneumatic tubes conveyed incoming letters, messages, or even small parcels, to a score of stations, requiring only a few seconds to reach the most distant parts of the building. Each of the 755 water closets—made by Maddock & Sons, Burslem—boasted "an arrangement by which the water is carried off without producing the horrid noise one usually hears." Bathtubs and wash-stands had devices that prevented overflowing should faucets be carelessly left running. There was even a primitive air-conditioning system, with more than two thousand vents connecting with each room, closet, and bathroom, and thirty-three ventilating boxes. "Hot coils placed in these boxes rarefy the air, drawing all the foul air out and admitting fresh air at will."

Five hydraulic elevators provided access to the acres of upstairs rooms. The elevators were described as luxurious and spacious, with mirror-faced walls, and seats upon which passengers might recline at ease while being whisked noiselessly to the dizzy height of seven stories. The upper floors contained 755 rooms, with accommodations for 1,200 guests. By modern standards the rooms were large. Most of them were twenty feet square and none was less than sixteen by sixteen. Ceilings were uniformly fifteen feet high. Hallways and the arcades fronting on the main court were on a like scale. The arrangement of the rooms about short, lateral hallways, and a system of intercommunicating doors, permitted a wide variety of grouping. "The connections and approaches are such that an individual, a family, or a party of any size can have a suite of any number of rooms, combining the seculusion of the most elegant private residence, with its own private toilet, ample clothes-closet and fire-grate."

When rough construction was completed and hundreds of workmen began installing the interior fittings, new wonders greeted the Saturday afternoon crowds of visitors. So great was the amount of marble used that contracts had to be made with fifteen different firms, for 804 mantels, 900 wash-stands, 40,000 square feet of pavement. Finishing woods came from many parts of the world: mahogany, East India teak, primavera from Mexico, rosewood, ebony. Much of it was elaborately hand-carved, all was highly polished. Painters applied finishing coats to walls, inside and out. The color of the public rooms was a delicate pink, "somewhat resembling the peach blossom"—a shade described as "showy in the highest degree, but not at all offensive. . . ." The exterior was even more striking; it emerged from behind the scaffolding a dazzling white, with gold trim, sparingly used. Some observers were reminded of a gigantic wedding-cake. But San Francisco's staple fuel was then a low-quality California coal, which gave off as much soot as heat. Within a few months the hotel's snowy walls were visible only in memory.

Most of the furnishings were locally made. This was in line with Ralston's policy of encouraging manufacturing on the Coast. A factory was bought specially for the purpose—a typical Ralston gesture. It was one example of the banker's way of doing things on a big scale. There were others. Because a considerable amount of oak flooring would be needed for the hotel, he purchased a large ranch in the Sierra foothills, near Grass Valley. The ranch contained hundreds of oak trees. Not until after the deal was made did he discover that they were not the variety of oaks from which flooring could be made. Such feats presently caused misgivings even among Ralston's empire-building friends. William Sharon was one of those who protested: "I said to him: 'If you are going to buy a foundry for a nail, a ranch for a plank, and a manufactory to build furniture, where is this going to end?' He said: 'It does look ridiculous to you?' 'Yes,' I said, '. . . it looks pretty bad.' "

Nonetheless, Ralston went ahead with his furniture project. As usual everything had to be done in a hurry. His factory was presently humming with activity, filling in the short space of a hundred and twenty days "the largest contract ever undertaken by any furniture manufactory." New machinery had to be installed and new men trained, but that was the sort of thing Ralston liked best. For four months two hundred and fifty men worked from seven in the morning until ten thirty at night—but skeptics were confounded and the contract was filled on time, down to the last table and chair. The furniture was of the "East Lake" style, then at the height of its vogue. It was made of natural finished woods—primavera, golden mahogany, and tomano—with austere decorations consisting chiefly of parallel grooves, gilded, extending vertically along the head and footboards of beds, on the legs of chairs and bureaus.

This was for the regular guest chambers; the public rooms and de luxe suites were on a grander scale. For the downstairs chambers there were huge rugs specially woven in France, fragile and befringed French furniture of the ladies' reception room, leather-upholstered chairs for more masculine chambers, and for the parlors two grand pianos "ornamented with inlaid foreign woods." California's school of landscape painters enjoyed a period of unprecedented prosperity, and scores of views of Yosemite, Lake Tahoe, the Golden Gate at sunset, and clipper ships under full sail, ornamented the twenty-five-foot-high walls of the ground floor.

As midsummer approached and furniture and equipment were installed, San Francisco papers printed new columns of statistics. Of dishes there were enough to supply an army, although they were not of army quality: 9,000 plates, 8,800 "side" and 8,000 "vegetable" dishes, 4,000 cups and saucers. These had been made, on special order, by C. F. Haviland, France. There were also 9,000 cuspidors, maker unspecified; 2,000 knives (silver plated, with ivory handles); forks, spoons, tea and coffee jugs, cruets, silver serving dishes in quantity. The catalogue of Irish linens was so lengthy that "the Belfast warehouses must have been stripped as bare as Mother Hubbard's cupboard," and to supply and install the acres of carpets the firm of W. & J. Sloane, of New York, established a local store and so went permanently into business in San Francisco.

On careless reading this seems like an attempt to influence by mere number and measure. It is that and much more. The reader is conducted through the new building as were the early visitors, though the authors are not naïve enough to think the modern reader will identify in all ways with the visitor of 1875. The reader not only sees the structure of the hotel in deliberate order, but also the progress of construction. The conclusion is the table setting for guests. By then the reader knows who the guests will be, what they'll be like, and how they'll live. *Place* has told us all that.

QUESTIONS

1. What is the order in which the new hotel is described?
2. Why are the quotations included?
3. What themes influence the selection of detail?
4. How is numerical detail kept from becoming like the list of items on a bill of sale?

Often a writer's interest in a place will be very specialized. Andalusia is, for most outsiders, one of Spain's many tourist areas. For British writer John Stewart it is vulture country. Here is the beginning of his essay by that title.[4]

Spain is the stronghold of the vultures. There are four listed species in Europe, two common and two rare; if they are anywhere, they are in Spain. The bearded vulture and the black survive there, the Egyptian flourishes, and the great griffon swarms. The further south you go the more numerous they be-

[4] John Stewart, "Vulture Country," *Atlantic Monthly* (April 1959).

come, until you reach the hot grazing plains of Andalusia. There, summer and winter through, they hang in hordes in the roofless sky, for Andalusia is the vulture country.

There are three essential qualities for vulture country: a rich supply of unburied corpses, high mountains, a strong sun. Spain has the first of these, for in this sparsely populated and stony land it is not customary, or necessary, to bury dead animals. Where there are vultures in action such burial would be a self-evident waste of labor, with inferior sanitary results. Spain has mountains, too, in no part far to seek; and the summer sun is hot throughout the country. But it is hottest in Andalusia, and that is the decisive factor.

The sun, to the vulture, is not just something which makes life easier and pleasanter, a mere matter of preference. His mode of life is impossible without it. Here in Andalusia the summer sun dries up every pond and lake and almost every river. It drives the desperate frogs deep into the mud cracks and forces the storks to feed on locusts. It kills the food plants and wilts the fig trees over the heads of the panting flocks. Andalusia becomes like that part of ancient Greece, "a land where men fight for the shade of an ass."

All animals, both tame and wild, weaken in these circumstances, and the weakest go to the wall and die. The unpitying sun glares down on the corpses and speeds their putrefaction, rotting the hide and softening the sinews and the meat, to the vulture's advantage. But the sun plays a still greater part in his life. Its main and vital function, for him, is the creation of thermal currents in the atmosphere, for without these he would be helpless.

The vulture must fly high—high enough to command a wide territory, for, except at times of catastrophe, dead animals are never thick on the ground. His task is to soar to ten thousand feet, more or less, two or three times in a day, and to hang there and keep constant survey. A male griffon weighs up to sixteen pounds, so that to hoist himself up to that necessary viewpoint would call for fifty-three thousand calories, the equivalent of fifty pounds of meat. To find and eat three times his own weight in a day is clearly impossible; a short cut must be made. In the dawn of any day, in Andalusia, you may see the vulture discovering that short cut.

The eagles, buzzards, kites, and falcons are already on the wing, quartering the plain fast and low, seeking reptiles and small game. But the vulture sits on a crag and waits. He sees the sun bound up out of the sierra, and still he waits. He waits until the sun-struck rocks and the hard earth heat up and the thermal currents begin to rise. When the upstream is strong enough, he leaps out from the cliff, twists into it, and without one laborious wingbeat, spirals and soars.

By the time the vulture reaches his station, a half hour later and maybe more, the sun is blazing down on the plain and betraying every detail to his telescopic eye, and the updraft is strengthening as the day approaches its zenith. His ceiling for this day is fixed by two factors. One is the strength and buoyancy of his chosen thermal, which will vary with the strength of the sun and the behavior of the upper winds. But the more important factor, for it fixes his horizontal bearings as well, is the distribution of neighboring vultures in the sky, his colleagues and competitors.

He cocks his head from side to side and checks their various positions. There they hang, dotted across the clear sky at intervals of a mile or so—at the corners of one-mile squares. Height and lateral distances all adjusted, the vulture settles, circling slowly on his invisible support, and begins his long and lonely vigil.

John Stewart knew his subject would be novel for many readers, but he did not feel the need to apologize for or to explain his choice. He was not simply out to surprise his readers with an unusual topic. In the pattern of the vulture's life he sensed the fantastic intricacy of natural adaptation. He set out to turn the reader's revulsion or ignorance into respectful awe. Rather than draw attention to himself by playing up his unusual knowledge, he relies on the material and the writing to interest the reader.

The simple first sentence turns the reader away from the usual image of Spain. Whatever else Spain is, it is the "stronghold of vultures." The word *stronghold* implies not only large numbers but dominance and endurance. On the surface the essence of place can be presented simply. There are four kinds of vultures, and they need three essential elements in their environment. Now the reader has the necessary introduction, and if his reflex disgust for vultures is not too strong, he wants to read on. In answering why the vulture needs the three essential elements, the author begins to reveal the great intricacies of nature. He develops unexpected ties between the vulture and a seemingly barren and hostile environment. Soon the reader sees that a country so brutal to man is life itself to the vulture.

Through a sense of place, the writer moves man's mind beyond the borders of man's own life. In this situation only a coward or someone very dull would be devoid of wonder.

QUESTIONS

1. What are the most important details in establishing this land as belonging naturally to the vultures?
2. How does the element of time provide a meaningful as well as logical principle of organization?
3. How is the last paragraph a fitting conclusion to the description of this scene?

Writing about your own home town involves many of the problems you have studied in the selections of this chapter. However, you probably have some definite interest and knowledge to start with. Perhaps you have strong feelings, such as did the student who wrote the following theme.

Our town is a housing development, but it's not one of those ritzy places like Cedar Woods and Nottingham Forest Park. There are three kinds of houses in our place—porch on the right, porch on the left and porch in the middle. Maybe they didn't have any imagination just after the war when they built the place. They just cut down all the trees (nothing is bigger than one story houses) and put up boxes with porches. Then they painted them different colors and sold them to war veterans like my father. I don't know why he bought here. Maybe I don't understand what it was like because I was only a year old. Anyway, like Robert Frost said, "Home is a place that when you go there they have to take you in." They'd take me in if I went back, but now I'm away, I'm staying away.

This theme begins with the ironic title "Our Town," the title of Thornton Wilder's play about the human qualities of a typical nondevelopment American town. The theme ends with the same kind of irony in which the writer declares that "Our Town" is not *his* town. This is good as a large structure, but in between the writer has not been disciplined enough. Though the language is simple and forceful and much is suggested through small specific detail, the development of the piece is more by personal association than consideration of purpose and audience. We can make some guesses as to why the writer dislikes the town, but we are not given any glimpse of life. One principle of organization might have been to start with the kind of place the father bought, characterize its effect on the family's life, then conclude the theme with some concrete act of repudiation. Perhaps a short scene involving the actual moment of departure would make the Frost quote a more integral part of the theme.

QUESTIONS

1. How much more description of the town do you think is necessary?
2. How does the tone (kind of language) add to or subtract from the theme's effectiveness?
3. How would the paper be different if the author had described the town from the point of view of an artist?

ASSIGNMENTS

1. Describe a building or park in such a way that its role in the community is clear. Do *not* explain that role in abstract terms.

2. Choose a place about which you have much factual information of the kind Lewis and Hall used in *Bonanza Inn*. Organize and edit that information into a description that develops a central theme.
3. Describe a landscape (or a "townscape") from the point of view of a particular occupation or way of life.

CHAPTER 5

REVEALING

PERSONALITIES

Writing about people could start with two axioms: Every human being is different from every other human being; all human beings are alike in some ways. As a writer, your interest may be in the likeness, the difference, or both. Your particular interest will determine how you write about a person, be he real or fictional.

Before you think about characters in general, think about yourself a moment. Overall, what themes are most evident in your life? What decisions have you made and what controlled them? Even if you say chance or parents controlled your decisions, that in itself suggests a theme. For examples of writers seeing themes in their own lives, refer to David Ogilvy and James Agee in Chapter 1.

What is true of themes in your life is true of people you will want to write about. Usually you write about a person because he has some relation to your life, your work, or your personal interests. Whatever the case, you want to make some sense, some order out of your subject's life.

Begin by asking yourself how and why this person interests you.

In your mind or on paper make a list of his characteristics, being sure you recognize the difference between your own impressions and inferences and the record of actual observation. When the list is long enough, look at it closely and strike out the items that are irrelevant to your interest. (Be sure you don't simply strike out items that conflict with a preconceived image of the person.)

A list is not a life. Before you begin turning your list into an essay or story, make the person come to life in your mind. See him, hear him, watch him move. You will never know all there is and you will not want to put in writing all you do know. But in order to feel confident of your writing, every detail must issue from a strong sense of character.

As you plan the actual writing, keep in mind the reason why this person interests you. If your main interest is in his likeness to other people, you are probably drawing what in fiction is called a "flat" character. If you are interested in the character's uniqueness, you are drawing a "round" character. (Combinations and exceptions are also common.) E. M. Forster's definitions of flat and round characters can be of help in all kinds of writing.

Flat characters were called "humours" in the seventeenth century, and are sometimes called types, and sometimes caricatures. In their purest form, they are constructed round a single idea or quality: when there is more than one factor in them, we get the beginning of the curve towards the round. The really flat character can be expressed in one sentence such as "I never will desert Mr. Micawber." There is Mrs. Micawber—she says she won't desert Mr. Micawber, she doesn't, and there she is. Or: "I must conceal, even by subterfuges, the poverty of my master's house." There is Caleb Balderstone in *The Bride of Lammermoor*. He does not use the actual phrase, but it completely describes him; he has no existence outside it, no pleasures, none of the private lusts and aches that must complicate the most consistent of servitors.

One great advantage of flat characters is that they are easily recognized whenever they come in—recognized by the reader's emotional eye, not by the visual eye, which merely notes the recurrence of a proper name. . . . It is a convenience for an author when he can strike with his full force at once, and flat characters are very useful to him, since they never need reintroducing, never run away, have not to be watched for development, and provide their own atmosphere—little luminous disks of a pre-arranged size, pushed hither and thither like counters across the void or between the stars; most satisfactory.

A second advantage is that they are easily remembered by the reader afterwards. They remain in his mind as unalterable for the reason that they were not changed by circumstances; they moved through circumstances, which gives them in retrospect a comforting quality, and preserves them when the book that produced them may decay.

The test of a *round character* is whether it is capable of surprising in a convincing way. If it never surprises, it is flat. If it does not convince, it is a flat pretending to be round. It has the incalculability of life about it—life within the pages of a book. And by using it sometimes alone, more often in combination with the other kind, the novelist achieves his task of acclimatization and harmonizes the human race with the other aspects of his work.[1]

What is most important is that you know when a character is flat and when he is round. If you intend a character to be flat, be sure his consistency is not boring. A day-by-day psychological study of a woman who did nothing but rock in a chair all day would be very boring.

Another reason flat characters are often unsuccessful is because we unwittingly create them out of the stereotypes on which society thrives. The most obvious examples appear in the literature of prejudice. Rather than see individual cases, bigots invariably use clichés to think and talk about other people: kike, spic, commie, capitalist, egghead, nigger, Chink, hayseed, and even bigot. Less obvious words used this way are politician, big wheel, swinger, hippie, teeny-bopper, beatnik, aristocrat, brain, demagogue, square, and grind. Similar to these epithets are stock phrases and descriptions which we lazily pick up and use instead of taking

[1] E. M. Forster, *Aspects of the Novel* (New York: Harcourt, Brace & World, 1927), pp. 103–106, 118.

time to be accurate. What are some of these stock descriptions for students, teachers, and administrators?

Whether your character is round or flat, you should be very wary of using words, phrases, and ideas that are from the vast warehouse of popular description. When you draw on these resources to form your concepts, you are admitting that your concepts are inherited rather than being made by your own mind. You are being a human tape recorder playing back the automatic language of your culture.

In his book *White Collar*, sociologist C. Wright Mills was consciously trying to form an image of a new kind of "typical" American. He was aware that the public has its own cherished images but felt that they were no longer accurate.

> Images of American types have not been built carefully by piecing together live experience. Here, as elsewhere, they have been made up out of tradition and schoolbook and the early, easy drift of the unalerted mind. And they have been reinforced and even created, especially in white-collar times, by the editorial machinery of popular amusement and mass communications.
>
> Manipulations by professional image-makers are effective because their audiences do not or cannot know personally all the people they want to talk about or be like, and because they have an unconscious need to believe in certain types. In their need and inexperience, such audiences snatch and hold to the glimpses of types that are frozen into the language with which they see the world. Even when they meet the people behind the types face to face, previous images, linked deeply with feeling, blind them to what stands before them. Experience is trapped by false images, even as reality itself sometimes seems to imitate the soap opera and the publicity release.
>
> Perhaps the most cherished national images are sentimental versions of historical types that no longer exist, if indeed they ever did. Underpinning many standard images of The American is the myth, in the words of the eminent historian, A. M. Schlesinger, Sr., of the 'long tutelage to the soil' which, as 'the chief formative influence,' results in 'courage, creative energy

and resourcefulness . . .' According to this idea, which clearly bears a nineteenth-century trademark, The American possesses magical independence, homely ingenuity, great capacity for work, all of which virtues he attained while struggling to subdue the vast continent.

One hundred years ago, when three-fourths of the people were farmers, there may have been some justification for engraving such an image and calling it The American. But since then, farmers have declined to scarcely more than one-tenth of the occupied populace, and new classes of salaried employees and wage-workers have risen. Deep-going historic changes resulting in wide diversities have long challenged the nationalistic historian who would cling to The American as a single type of ingenious farmer-artisan. In so far as universals can be found in life and character in America, they are due less to any common tutelage of the soil than to the leveling influences of urban civilization, and above all, to the standardization of the big technology and of the media of mass communication.

America is neither the nation of horse-traders and master builders of economic theory, nor the nation of go-getting, claim-jumping, cattle-rustling pioneers of frontier mythology. Nor have the traits rightly or wrongly associated with such historic types carried over into the contemporary population to any noticeable degree. Only a fraction of this population consists of free private enterprisers in any economic sense; there are now four times as many wage-workers and salary workers as independent entrepreneurs. 'The struggle for life,' William Dean Howells wrote in the 'nineties, 'has changed from a free fight to an encounter of disciplined forces, and the free fighters that are left get ground to pieces . . .'

If it is assumed that white-collar employees represent some sort of continuity with the old middle class of entrepreneurs, then it may be said that for the last hundred years the middle classes have been facing the slow expropriation of their holdings, and that for the last twenty years they have faced the spectre of unemployment. Both assertions rest on facts, but the facts have not been experienced by the middle class as a *double* crisis. The property question is not an issue to the new middle class of the present generation. That was fought out, and lost, before World War I, by the old middle class. The centralization of small properties is a development that has affected each generation back to our great-grandfathers, reaching its climax in the Progressive Era. It has been a secular trend of too slow a tempo to be felt as a continuing crisis by middle-class men and women, who often seem to have become more commodity-minded than property-minded. Yet history is not always enacted consciously; if expropriation is not felt as crisis, still it is a basic fact in the ways of life and the aspirations of the new middle class; and the facts of unemployment *are* felt as fears, hanging over the white-collar world.

By examining white-collar life, it is possible to learn something about what is becoming more typically 'American' than the frontier character probably ever was. What must be grasped is the picture of society as a great salesroom, an enormous file, an incorporated brain, a new universe of management and manipulation. By understanding these diverse white-collar worlds, one can also understand better the shape and meaning of modern society as a whole, as well as the simple hopes and complex anxieties that grip all the people who are sweating it out in the middle of the twentieth century.[2]

Mills' white-collar man is essentially a flat character, but as a scholar Mills based his character on careful observation—interviews, statistics, experiments, and experience. He did not simply sit back and say, "Now let's see, what do I think a typical white-collar man would be like?"

In a flat character you must discover the likeness for yourself. You must discover it in his own life—*his* looks, *his* actions, *his* words. Don't decide he is a flat character and then dress him in the ready-made clothes of his class. You must choose details which suggest the likeness or consistency while retaining the sense of the character as a human being.

In a round character you must avoid another kind of cliché— the cliché of the individualist. Because it is difficult to describe

[2] C. Wright Mills, *White Collar* (London: Oxford University Press, 1953), pp. xiii–xv.

uniqueness, too often the writer is tempted to *tell* the reader a person is unique. In doing so, a set of "uniqueness" terms is used: *indescribable, unforgettable, amazing, extraordinary, different from the others, perfect,* and, of course, *unique.*

Your style will affect your subject matter. If you write about people in automatic language, it means you are either willfully removing the identity of your subject or that you are lazy. Probably it means you often think of other people as *things* and groups of things. This is the kind of thinking you find in the literature of bigotry and totalitarianism.

When writing about people, remember you are also a person. If you forget about others, you may be forgetting about yourself.

In each of the following selections, the author was personally interested in his subject. Ask yourself what the nature of this interest was, and how the author succeeded or failed to keep the subject alive and interesting for you.

SELECTIONS

We have recommended that before you start the actual writing about a person, you explore your own interest and make some notes about the subject. Below Andrew Turnbull, one of F. Scott Fitzgerald's biographers, talks about Fitzgerald's interest in certain characters.[3] Following this is a set of notes from *The Crack-Up*, which Fitzgerald made for a character named Becky.[4]

The Great Gatsby was indeed a more conscious work of art than Fitzgerald's first two novels, just as its hero was less obviously an autobiographical projection than either Amory Blaine or Anthony Patch. Gatsby had been created, Fitzgerald said later, on the image of some Minnesota farm type, known and forgotten and associated with a sense of romance. With Gatsby

---

[3] Andrew Turnbull, *Scott Fitzgerald* (New York: Charles Scribner's Sons, 1962), pp. 149–150.

[4] F. Scott Fitzgerald, *The Crack-Up* (New York: New Directions, 1945), pp. 132–133.

in mind he had studied bootleggers of his acquaintance, and Gatsby's financial intrigues were perhaps modeled on the Fuller-McGee case which had filled the papers in 1922. The essential Gatsby, however—he of the heightened sensitivity to the promises of life, of the extraordinary gift for hope and the romantic readiness—was Fitzgerald himself. In the figure of Gatsby, he had been able to objectify and poetize his early feelings about the rich: that they were a race apart with a better seat in life's grandstand, that their existence was somehow more beautiful and intense than that of ordinary mortals. Barricaded behind their fortunes, they had seemed to him almost like royalty. Fitzgerald's snobbery was romantic—graced and to some extent redeemed by the imagination in a way that is peculiarly Irish. One finds the same point of view in Yeats or Oscar Wilde.

But also Fitzgerald sensed a corruption in the rich and mistrusted their might. "That was always my experience," he wrote near the end of his life, "—a poor boy in a rich town; a poor boy in a rich boy's school; a poor boy in a rich man's club at Princeton. . . . I have never been able to forgive the rich for being rich, and it has colored my entire life and works." He told a friend that "the whole idea of Gatsby is the unfairness of a poor young man not being able to marry a girl with money. This theme comes up again and again because I lived it."

(She was the dark Gunther—dark and shining and driven.

(He had not realized that flashing fairness could last so far into the twenties.

(Nevertheless, the bright little apples of her cheeks, the blue of the Zuyder Zee in her eyes, the braided strands of golden corn on the wide forehead, testified to the purity of her origin. She was the school beauty.

(Her beauty was as poised and secure as a flower on a strong stem; her voice was cool and sure, with no wayward instruments in it that played on his emotions.

(She was not more than eighteen—a dark little beauty with the fine crystal gloss over her that, in brunettes, takes the place of a blond's bright glow.

(Becky was nineteen, a startling little beauty, with her head set upon her figure as though it had been made separately and then placed there with the utmost precision. Her body was sturdy, athletic; her head was a bright, happy composition of curves and shadows and vivid color, with that final kinetic jolt, the element that is eventually sexual in effect, which made strangers stare at her. (Who has not had the excitement of seeing an apparent beauty from afar; then, after a moment, seeing that same face grow mobile and watching the beauty disappear moment by moment, as if a lovely statue had begun to walk with the meager joints of a paper doll?) Becky's beauty was the opposite of that. The facial muscles pulled her expressions into lovely smiles and frowns, disdains, gratifications and encouragements; her beauty was articulated, and expressed vividly whatever it wanted to express.

(Anyone looking at her then, at her mouth which was simply a kiss seen very close up, at her head that was a gorgeous detail escaped from the corner of a painting, not mere formal beauty but the beholder's unique discovery, so that it evoked different dreams to every man, of the mother, of the nurse, of the lost childish sweetheart or whatever had formed his first conception of beauty—anyone looking at her would have conceded her a bisque on her last remark.

(She was a stalk of ripe corn, but bound not as cereals are but as a rare first edition, with all the binder's art. She was lovely and expensive, and about nineteen.

(A lovely dress, soft and gentle in cut, but in color a hard, bright, metallic powder blue.

(An exquisite, romanticized little ballerina.

(He imagined Kay and Arthur Busch progressing through the afternoon. Kay would cry a great deal and the situation would seem harsh and unexpected to them at first, but the tender closing of the day would draw them together. They would turn inevitably toward each other and he would slip more and more into the position of the enemy outside.

(Her face, flushed with cold and then warmed again with the dance, was a riot of lovely, delicate pinks, like many carnations, rising in many shades from the white of her nose to the high spot of her cheeks. Her breathing was very young as she came close to him—young and eager and exciting.

(The intimacy of the car, its four walls whisking them along toward a new adventure, had drawn them together.

(A beauty that had reached the point where it seemed to contain in itself the secret of its own growth, as if it would go on increasing forever.

(Her body was so assertively adequate that someone remarked that she always looked as if she had nothing on underneath her dress, but it was probably wrong.

In the notes Fitzgerald was trying out his character, getting to know her so that he would know when his words about her were true and when they were false. He is also testing her out on other characters. A character that cannot interact with other characters or a reader is not alive.

Although there is frequent use of abstractions like *beauty*, there is also a strong concrete presence. Some of the concreteness is in the form of direct observation of physical observation, some is metaphor and simile. With the direct and the figurative description, he both describes and suggests what the girl is like.

These notes are not a first-rate, finished delineation of character. Professionals and students alike have to fight the battle of concreteness and particularity. No one sits down at the typewriter and creates a finished character in one try. In Fitzgerald's notes he was working on the first stage of giving the *idea* of a character a sense of life. This is your struggle too.

Questions

1. How is Becky's beauty made concrete?
2. Why is there so much figurative language in the notes?
3. Can you make any connection between Turnbull's comments and Fitzgerald's notes?
4. Is there anything in your life that would color your description of certain characters?

As a reporter assigned by the National Broadcasting Company to the United Nations, Pauline Fredericks has observed closely both events and personalities. Below she describes former Secretary-General Dag Hammarskjold for the January 5, 1960, program *NBC Emphasis*.[5]

On a frigid December day I saw four men striding hatless and coatless under the wintry branches of the cherry trees in the garden below my UN office. A trim blond was a pace ahead of the others—Secretary-General Dag Hammarskjold. After him, a little breathless, came Executive Secretary Andrew Cordier, Under Secretary Ralph Bunche, and a body guard.

"He always has to be out in front," a watcher murmured. "No one can keep up with his stride," said another. The sight was symbolic. The fifty-four-year-old S.G., as he has been called, has become a lonely eminence striding into crises where others hesitate to tread. His winter walk was part of rugged discipline that keeps him fit for a monumental amount of work (his whole life) which leaves associates breathless.

Since his boyhood in Sweden, Hammarskjold has hiked and climbed mountains, so he now misses the good earth under his feet in concrete-clad New York. The garden is a small substitute until he can indulge in a weekend of pacing the fields at his

[5] Pauline Fredericks, "January 5, 1960" from *The Best of NBC Emphasis* (Glen Rock, N.J.: Newman Press, 1962), pp. 81–83.

country home upstate where he also has been known to chop a hole in the ice for a mid-winter dip.

His aides are always braced for the aftermath of such a weekend. Hammarskjold is not only refreshed physically, but his restless and agile mind has been spinning out new ways to deal with deadlocks and crises. Pretty soon, subtly worded statements from his office will have the Assembly and Security Council concurring. And that usually means giving him a free hand to deal with a situation.

One story going around the UN is that endless debate could be curbed if there were agreement to skip discussion of any issue on which the S.G. could foresee the outcome. At the height of the Laos crisis he was privately saying it would taper off. The solution would be a representative of the Secretary-General going to the troublesome scene. It happened after he went through the motions of calling the Security Council.

His name is a household word, yet he is a man few people know. It is largely his own fault. He wraps himself in a cloak of privacy. He was annoyed with reporters until he decided to make their encounters a game.

A former Assembly President, Sir Leslie Munro, likens the Secretary-General's asceticism to a pope's or a priest's. He has been called intellectually arrogant, yet he is at home with Bach and Bracque and the best of literature in four languages. He can talk Chinese porcelain in Peking, exotic flora and fauna in Australia, ancient religions in Jerusalem and New Delhi, economics in London, and philosophy in European centers of learning.

He has been called cold and inhuman, but he has entertained the UN maintenance workers and their wives at picnics at his country home, when he did the barbecuing and serving.

He has never married. But friends see significance in the fact that he calls the UN "This House"—and the employees, "The Family."

In a short sketch like this, the writer has to tell a great amount in few words. Pauline Fredericks works with a tight structure as well as well-chosen detail. She starts from the outsider's point of view and in some five hundred words arrives at a portrait that makes Hammarskjold a real individual yet maintains a sense of the unknowable depth for which others admire him.

The underlying purpose of the sketch is to convey to the outsider an accurate sense of a person much talked about but little known. She works through two principal methods. First, her paragraphs are filled with concrete language and events that are specific, yet typical. Second, the details are not only relevant in themselves, but they *suggest* more. His vitality on a frigid December day reminds knowledgeable readers of his Scandinavian origins. It also suggests he possesses the kind of spirit that is not daunted by the unavoidable course of events, whether that course is a change of seasons or political tensions.

QUESTIONS

1. Can you see any pattern in the order of the subjects treated?
2. Pick out several small details whose suggestiveness is later echoed in more important passages.
3. Where did Miss Fredericks get her details?
4. Think of some specific but insignificant action in the life of someone you know. How is it typical of an important theme in his life?

As a psychologist, Bruno Bettelheim is interested in patterns of behavior. But the patterns are only meaningful to him as they relate to real individuals. Read the case below, "Joey: A 'Mechanical Boy,'" and see how the writer has made his subject interesting, both as a psychological case and as an individual.[6]

Joey, when we began our work with him, was a mechanical boy. He functioned as if by remote control, run by machines of his own powerfully creative fantasy. Not only did he himself be-

---

[6] Bruno Bettelheim, "Joey; A Mechanical Boy," *Scientific American* (March 1959).

lieve that he was a machine but, more remarkably, he created this impression in others. Even while he performed actions that are intrinsically human, they never appeared to be other than machine-started and executed. On the other hand, when the machine was not working we had to concentrate on recollecting his presence, for he seemed not to exist. A human body that functions as if it were a machine and a machine that duplicates human functions are equally fascinating and frightening. Perhaps they are so uncanny because they remind us that the human body can operate without a human spirit, that body can exist without soul. And Joey was a child who had been robbed of his humanity.

Not every child who possesses a fantasy world is possessed by it. Normal children may retreat into realms of imaginary glory or magic powers, but they are easily recalled from these excursions. Disturbed children are not always able to make the return trip; they remain withdrawn, prisoners of the inner world of delusion and fantasy. In many ways Joey presented a classic example of this state of infantile autism. In any age, when the individual has escaped into a delusional world, he has usually fashioned it from bits and pieces of the world at hand. Joey, in his time and world, chose the machine and froze himself in its image. His story has a general relevance to the understanding of emotional development in a machine age.

Joey's delusion is not uncommon among schizophrenic children today. He wanted to be rid of his unbearable humanity, to become completely automatic. He so nearly succeeded in attaining this goal that he could almost convince others, as well as himself, of his mechanical character. The descriptions of autistic children in the literature take for their point of departure and comparison the normal or abnormal human being. To do justice to Joey I would have to compare him simultaneously to a most inept infant and a highly complex piece of machinery. Often we had to force ourselves by a conscious act of will to realize that Joey was a child. Again and again his acting-out of his delusions froze our own ability to respond as human beings.

During Joey's first weeks with us we would watch absorbedly as this at once fragile-looking and imperious nine-year-old went about his mechanical existence. Entering the dining room, for example, he would string an imaginary wire from his "energy source"—an imaginary electric outlet—to the table. There he "insulated" himself with paper napkins and finally plugged himself in. Only then could Joey eat, for he firmly believed that the "current" ran his ingestive apparatus. So skillful was the pantomime that one had to look twice to be sure there was neither wire nor outlet nor plug. Children and members of our staff spontaneously avoided stepping on the "wires" for fear of interrupting what seemed the source of his very life.

For long periods of time, when his "machinery" was idle, he would sit so quietly that he would disappear from the focus of the most conscientious observation. Yet in the next moment he might be "working" and the center of our captivated attention. Many times a day he would turn himself on and shift noisily through a sequence of higher and higher gears until he "exploded," screaming "Crash, crash!" and hurling items from his ever present apparatus—radio tubes, light bulbs, even motors or, lacking these, any handy breakable object. (Joey had an astonishing knack for snatching bulbs and tubes unobserved.) As soon as the object thrown had shattered, he would cease his screaming and wild jumping and retire to mute, motionless nonexistence.

Our maids, inured to difficult children, were exceptionally attentive to Joey; they were apparently moved by his extreme infantile fragility, so strangely coupled with megalomaniacal superiority. Occasionally some of the apparatus he fixed to his bed to "live him" during his sleep would fall down in disarray. This machinery he contrived from masking tape, cardboard, wire and other paraphernalia. Usually the maids would pick up such things and leave them on a table for the children to find, or disregard them entirely. But Joey's machine they carefully restored: "Joey must have the carburetor so he can breathe." Similarily they were on the alert to pick up and preserve the motors that ran him during the day and the exhaust pipes through which he exhaled.

How had Joey become a human machine? From intensive interviews with his parents we learned that the process had be-

gun even before birth. Schizophrenia often results from paren-
tal rejection, sometimes combined ambivalently with love.
Joey, on the other hand, had been completely ignored.

"I never knew I was pregnant," his mother said, meaning
that she had already excluded Joey from her consciousness. His
birth, she said, "did not make any difference." Joey's father, a
rootless draftee in the wartime civilian army, was equally un-
ready for parenthood. So, of course, are many young couples.
Fortunately most such parents lose their indifference upon the
baby's birth. But not Joey's parents. "I did not want to see or
nurse him," his mother declared. "I had no feeling of actual dislike—I simply didn't want to take care of him." For the first
three months of his life Joey "cried most of the time." A colicky
baby, he was kept on a rigid four-hour feeding schedule, was
not touched unless necessary and was never cuddled or played
with. The mother, preoccupied with herself, usually left Joey
alone in the crib or playpen during the day. The father discharged his frustrations by punishing Joey when the child
cried at night.

Soon the father left for overseas duty, and the mother took
Joey, now a year and a half old, to live with her at her parents'
home. On his arrival the grandparents noticed that ominous
changes had occurred in the child. Strong and healthy at birth,
he had become frail and irritable; a responsive baby, he had
become remote and inaccessible. When he began to master
speech, he talked only to himself. At an early date he became
preoccupied with machinery, including an old electric fan
which he could take apart and put together again with surprising deftness.

Joey's mother impressed us with a fey quality that expressed
her insecurity, her detachment from the world and her low
physical vitality. We were struck especially by her total indifference as she talked about Joey. This seemed much more remarkable than the actual mistakes she made in handling him.
Certainly he was left to cry for hours when hungry, because she
fed him on a rigid schedule; he was toilet-trained with great
rigidity so that he would give no trouble. These things happen
to many children. But Joey's existence never registered with

his mother. In her recollections he was fused at one moment with one event or person; at another, with something or somebody else. When she told us about his birth and infancy, it was as if she were talking about some vague acquaintance, and soon her thoughts would wander off to another person or to herself.

When Joey was not yet four, his nursery school suggested that he enter a special school for disturbed children. At the new school his autism was immediately recognized. During his three years there he experienced a slow improvement. Unfortunately a subsequent two years in a parochial school destroyed this progress. He began to develop compulsive defenses, which he called his "preventions." He could not drink, for example, except through elaborate piping systems built of straws. Liquids had to be "pumped" into him, in his fantasy, or he could not suck. Eventually his behavior became so upsetting that he could not be kept in the parochial school. At home things did not improve. Three months before entering the Orthogenic School he made a serious attempt at suicide.

To us Joey's pathological behavior seemed the external expression of an overwhelming effort to remain almost nonexistent as a person. For weeks Joey's only reply when addressed was "Bam." Unless he thus neutralized whatever we said, there would be an explosion, for Joey plainly wished to close off every form of contact not mediated by machinery. Even when he was bathed he rocked back and forth with mute, engine-like regularity, flooding the bathroom. If he stopped rocking, he did this like a machine too; suddenly he went completely rigid. Only once, after months of being lifted from his bath and carried to bed, did a small expression of puzzled pleasure appear on his face as he said very softly: "They even carry you to your bed here."

For a long time after he began to talk he would never refer to anyone by name, but only as "that person" or "the little person" or "the big person." He was unable to designate by its true name anything to which he attached feelings. Nor could he name his anxieties except through neologisms or word contaminations. For a long time he spoke about "master paintings" and "a master painting room" (*i.e.*, masturbating and masturbating room). One of his machines, the "criticizer," prevented him from "saying words which have unpleasant feelings." Yet he gave personal names to the tubes and motors in his collection of machinery. Moreover, these dead things had feelings; the tubes bled when hurt and sometimes got sick. He consistently maintained this reversal between animate and inanimate objects.

In Joey's machine world everything, on pain of instant destruction, obeyed inhibitory laws much more stringent than those of physics. When we came to know him better, it was plain that in his moments of silent withdrawal, with his machine switched off, Joey was absorbed in pondering the compulsive laws of his private universe. His preoccupation with machinery made it difficult to establish even practical contacts with him. If he wanted to do something with a counselor, such as play with a toy that had caught his vague attention, he could not do so: "I'd like this very much, but first I have to turn off the machine." But by the time he had fulfilled all the requirements of his preventions, he had lost interest. When a toy was offered to him, he could not touch it because his motors and his tubes did not leave him a hand free. Even certain colors were dangerous and had to be strictly avoided in toys and clothing, because "some colors turn off the current, and I can't touch them because I can't live without the current."

Joey was convinced that machines were better than people. Once when he bumped into one of the pipes on our jungle gym he kicked it so violently that his teacher had to restrain him to keep him from injuring himself. When she explained that the pipe was much harder than his foot, Joey replied: "That proves it. Machines are better than the body. They don't break; they're much harder and stronger." If he lost or forgot something, it merely proved that his brain ought to be thrown away and replaced by machinery. If he spilled something his arm should be broken and twisted off because it did not work properly. When his head or arm failed to work as it should, he tried to punish it by hitting it. Even Joey's feelings were mechanical.

Much later in his therapy, when he had formed a timid attachment to another child and had been rebuffed, Joey cried: "He
broke my feelings."

Gradually we began to understand what had seemed to be
contradictory in Joey's behavior—why he held on to the motors and tubes, then suddenly destroyed them in a fury, then set
out immediately and urgently to equip himself with new and
larger tubes. Joey had created these machines to run his body
and mind because it was too painful to be human. But again
and again he became dissatisfied with their failure to meet his
need and rebellious at the way they frustrated his will. In a re-
current frenzy he "exploded" his light bulbs and tubes, and for
a moment became a human being—for one crowning instant
he came alive. But as soon as he had asserted his dominance
through the self-created explosion, he felt his life ebbing away.
To keep on existing he had immediately to restore his machines
and replenish the electricity that supplied his life energy.

What deep-seated fears and needs underlay Joey's delusional system? We were long in finding out, for Joey's preventions effectively concealed the secret of his autistic behavior. In
the meantime we dealt with his peripheral problems one by
one.

During his first year with us Joey's most trying problem was
toilet behavior. This surprised us, for Joey's personality was not
"anal" in the Freudian sense; his original personality damage
had antedated the period of his toilet-training. Rigid and early
toilet-training, however, had certainly contributed to his anxieties. It was our effort to help Joey with this problem that led to
his first recognition of us as human beings.

Going to the toilet, like everything else in Joey's life, was surrounded by elaborate preventions. We had to accompany him;
he had to take off all his clothes; he could only squat, not sit, on
the toilet seat; he had to touch the wall with one hand, in which
he also clutched frantically the vacuum tubes that powered his
elimination. He was terrified lest his whole body be sucked
down.

To counteract this fear we gave him a metal wastebasket in
lieu of a toilet. Eventually, when eliminating into the waste-

basket, he no longer needed to take off all his clothes, nor to hold on to the wall. He still needed the tubes and motors which, he believed, moved his bowels for him. But here again the all-important machinery was itself a source of new terrors. In Joey's world the gadgets had to move their bowels, too. He was terribly concerned that they should, but since they were so much more powerful than men, he was also terrified that if his tubes moved their bowels, their feces would fill all of space and leave him no room to live. He was thus always caught in some fearful contradiction.

Our readiness to accept his toilet habits, which obviously entailed some hardship for his counselors, gave Joey the confidence to express his obsessions in drawings. Drawing these fantasies was a first step toward letting us in, however distantly, to what concerned him most deeply. It was the first step in a year-long process of externalizing his anal preoccupations. As a result he began seeing feces everywhere; the whole world became to him a mire of excrement. At the same time he began to eliminate freely wherever he happened to be. But with this release from his infantile imprisonment in compulsive rules, the toilet and the whole process of elimination became less dangerous. Thus far it had been beyond Joey's comprehension that anybody could possibly move his bowels without mechanical aid. Now Joey took a further step forward; defecation became the first physiological process he could perform without the help of vacuum tubes. It must not be thought that he was proud of this ability. Taking pride in an achievement presupposes that one accomplishes it of one's own free will. He still did not feel himself an autonomous person who could do things on his own. To Joey defecation still seemed enslaved to some incomprehensible but utterly binding cosmic law, perhaps the law his parents had imposed on him when he was being toilet-trained.

It was not simply that his parents had subjected him to rigid, early training. Many children are so trained. But in most cases the parents have a deep emotional investment in the child's performance. The child's response in turn makes training an occasion for interaction between them and for the building of genuine relationships. Joey's parents had no emotional invest-

ment in him. His obedience gave them no satisfaction and won
him no affection or approval. As a toilet-trained child he saved
his mother labor, just as household machines saved her labor.
As a machine he was not loved for his performance, nor could
he love himself.

So it had been with all other aspects of Joey's existence with
his parents. Their reactions to his eating or noneating, sleeping
or wakening, urinating or defecating, being dressed or un-
dressed, washed or bathed did not flow from any unitary interest in him, deeply embedded in their personalities. By treating
him mechanically his parents made him a machine. The various
functions of life—even the parts of his body—bore no integrat-
ing relationship to one another or to any sense of self that was
acknowledged and confirmed by others. Though he had acquired mastery over some functions, such as toilet-training and
speech, he had acquired them separately and kept them isolated from each other. Toilet-training had thus not gained him
a pleasant feeling of body mastery; speech had not led to communication of thought or feeling. On the contrary, each
achievement only steered him away from self-mastery and integration. Toilet-training had enslaved him. Speech left him
talking in neologisms that obstructed his and our ability to relate to each other. In Joey's development the normal process of
growth had been made to run backward. Whatever he had
learned put him not at the end of his infantile development toward integration but, on the contrary, farther behind than he
was at its very beginning. Had we understood this sooner, his
first years with us would have been less baffling.

It is unlikely that Joey's calamity could befall a child in any
time and culture but our own. He suffered no physical depriva-
tion; he starved for human contact. Just to be taken care of is
not enough for relating. It is a necessary but not a sufficient
condition. At the extreme where utter scarcity reigns, the forming of relationships is certainly hampered. But our society of
mechanized plenty often makes for equal difficulties in a child's
learning to relate. Where parents can provide the simple
creature-comforts for their children only at the cost of significant effort, it is likely that they will feel pleasure in being able

to provide for them; it is this, the parents' pleasure, that gives children a sense of personal worth and sets the process of relating in motion. But if comfort is so readily available that the parents feel no particular pleasure in winning it for their children, then the children cannot develop the feeling of being worthwhile around the satisfaction of their basic needs. Of course parents and children can and do develop relationships around other situations. But matters are then no longer so simple and direct. The child must be on the receiving end of care and concern given with pleasure and without the exaction of return if he is to feel loved and worthy of respect and consideration. This feeling gives him the ability to trust; he can entrust his well-being to persons to whom he is so important. Out of such trust the child learns to form close and stable relationships.

For Joey relationship with his parents was empty of pleasure in comfort-giving as in all other situations. His was an extreme instance of a plight that sends many schizophrenic children to our clinics and hospitals. Many months passed before he could relate to us; his despair that anybody could like him made contact impossible.

When Joey could finally trust us enough to let himself become more infantile, he began to play at being a papoose. There was a corresponding change in his fantasies. He drew endless pictures of himself as an electrical papoose. Totally enclosed, suspended in empty space, he is run by unknown, unseen powers through wireless electricity.

As we eventually came to understand, the heart of Joey's delusional system was the artificial, mechanical womb he had created and into which he had locked himself. In his papoose fantasies lay the wish to be entirely reborn in a womb. His new experiences in the school suggested that life, after all, might be worth living. Now he was searching for a way to be reborn in a better way. Since machines were better than men, what was more natural than to try rebirth through them? This was the deeper meaning of his electrical papoose.

As Joey made progress, his pictures of himself became more dominant in his drawings. Though still machine-operated, he has grown in self-importance. Another great step forward is rep-

resented in a picture in which he has acquired hands that do
something, and he has had the courage to make a picture of the
machine that runs him. Later still the papoose became a person, rather than a robot encased in glass.

Eventually Joey began to create an imaginary family at the
school: the "Carr" family. Why the Carr family? In the car he
was enclosed as he had been in his papoose, but at least the car
was not stationary; it could move. More important, in a car one
was not only driven but also could drive. The Carr family was
Joey's way of exploring the possibility of leaving the school, of
living with a good family in a safe, protecting car.

Joey at last broke through his prison. In this brief account it
has not been possible to trace the painfully slow process of his
first true relations with other human beings. Suffice it to say
that he ceased to be a mechanical boy and became a human
child. This newborn child was, however, nearly 12 years old.
To recover the lost time is a tremendous task. That work has
occupied Joey and us ever since. Sometimes he sets to it with a
will; at other times the difficulty of real life makes him regret
that he ever came out of his shell. But he has never wanted to
return to his mechanical life.

One last detail and this fragment of Joey's story has been
told. When Joey was 12, he made a float for our Memorial Day
parade. It carried the slogan: "Feelings are more important
than anything under the sun." Feelings, Joey had learned, are
what make for humanity; their absence, for a mechanical existence. With this knowledge Joey entered the human condition.

The portrait of Joey begins immediately with the boy, his problem, and the observers. Joey is a human being, so before we go
into history of the problem we get a vivid picture of Joey as Bettelheim first saw him. Though Joey is certainly unusual, he is not
merely a freak case, a curiosity. Throughout the portrait, we see
Joey through Bettelheim's sensibility. Without this, Joey would
not seem as human.

The two major themes of the story are mechanization and feeling. While the theme of mechanization is developed in Joey,

feeling is unstated but constantly present in the author's point of view. The interaction of these two themes, through carefully selected detail and exposition, carry the story and provide a meaningful end.

QUESTIONS

1. Restate a portion of Joey's portrait in impersonal and general terms. How is this better or worse than the original?
2. Do the adults intrude on Joey's portrait? Why or why not?
3. Could this essay have a surprise ending? How? What would the effect be?
4. Why does Bettelheim feel it unnecessary to tell the progress of Joey's "first true relations with other human beings?"

While at Oxford University, English novelist Reynolds Price found himself suddenly reminded of an old man who used to work for his family. He wrote a long memoir about the man, entitled "Uncle Grant." [7] Before you read the first part of that memoir, stop and think of some older person you know and how you would attempt to cross the gap in years to an understanding.

Supposing he could know I have thought of him all this week. Supposing I was not three thousand miles from northeast North Carolina and supposing he had not been dead six years and I could find him and say, "I have thought of you all this week"— then he would be happy. Supposing though he was alive and I was still here in England—in Oxford whose light and color and trees and even grass would be strange to him as the moon (as they are to me)—and supposing he heard I had thought of him. It would go more or less like this. He would be in my aunt's kitchen in a straight black chair near the stove, having

[7] Reynolds Price, "Uncle Grant," *Names and Faces of Heroes* (New York: Atheneum Publishers, 1963), pp. 110–113.

finished his breakfast. My aunt would have finished before he started and by then would be spreading beds or sweeping the porch, in her nightdress still. So he would be alone—his natural way, the way he had spent, say, sixty per cent of his life, counting sleep. His back would be straight as the chair, but his body would lean to the left, resting. The way he rested was to feel out the table beside him with his left elbow (an apple-green table with red oilcloth for a cover) and finding a spot press down and then lay his head, his *face*, in his hand. His long right arm would lie on his hollow flank, the fingers hinged on the knee, and his legs would be clasped, uncrossed not to wrinkle the starched khaki trousers and ending in high-top shoes that, winter or summer, would be slashed into airy patterns, clean as the day they were bought, just ventilated with a razor blade. His white suspenders would rise from his waist to his shoulders, crossing the starched gray shirt (never with a tie but always buttoned at the neck and when he was dressed, pinned with a dull gold bar), but his face would be covered, his eyes. Only the shape of his skull would be clear—narrow and long, pointed at the chin, domed at the top—and the color of the skin that covered it, unbroken by a single hair except sparse brows, the color of a penny polished down by years of thumbs till Lincoln's face is a featureless shadow but with red life running beneath. That way he would be resting—not waiting, just resting as if he had worked when all he had done was wake at six and reach to his radio and lie on till seven, hearing music and thinking, then shaving and dressing and spreading his bed and stepping through the yard to the kitchen to eat what my aunt cooked (after she fired the stove if it was winter)—and he would rest till half-past eight when the cook would come and say towards him "Mr. Grant" (they were not good friends) and towards my aunt down the hall, "Miss Ida, here's you a letter," having stopped at the post office on her way. My aunt would come and stand by the stove and read with lips moving silent and then say, "Look, Uncle Grant. Here's a letter from Reynolds." He would look up squinting while she read out something like, " 'Tell Uncle Grant I am thinking about him this week,' " but before she could read any more, he would slap his flank and spring to his feet, rocking in his lacework shoes, opening and shutting his five-foot-ten like a bellows, and flicking at his ears—"Great God A-mighty! Where *is* Reynolds?" When she said "England" he would say, "Over yonder with them Hitalians and he been thinking about Grant? Great God A-mighty!" and then trail off into laughing and then for a long time to come into smiling. He would be happy that whole day and it is a fact—there is no one alive or dead I could have made happier with eight or ten words.

But he is dead and the reason I have thought of him these few days is strange—not because I remembered some joke on him and certainly not from seeing his likeness in the blue-black Negroes of the Oxford streets but because I went in a store to buy postcards and saw a card from the Berlin Museum—on a black background an Egyptian head, the tall narrow skull rocked back on the stalky neck, the chin offered out like a flickering tongue, the waving lips set in above (separate as if they were carved by a better man), the ears with their heavy lobes pinned close to the skull, and the black-rimmed sockets holding no eyes at all. I looked on, not knowing why, and turned the card over. The head was Amenhotep IV, pharaoh of Egypt in the eighteenth dynasty who canceled the worship of bestial gods and changed his name to Akhnaton, "it pleases Aton," the one true god, the streaming disc, the sun. I bought the card and left the shop and walked ten yards and said to myself in the street what I suddenly knew, "It's the one picture left of Uncle Grant."

The sketch starts with "supposing," a way of bringing the dead man momentarily on stage without having to use some clever trick. Also it suggests that Uncle Grant's death was felt by the author. The "supposing" works entirely through concrete detail, never attempting to enter the old man's mind. We see him and hear him so vividly that through a sense of pure physical presence he comes alive.

The second part of the sketch goes beyond the physical man, beyond his death into what he has become to the author. He is more than a funny man of another race. The physical picture of the first paragraph is transformed into the more timeless and pro-found image of Akhnaton. At this point, we know the author is be-ginning to realize that in a simple, unpretending life there was a regal dignity. The reader is ready for the closer look that follows.

QUESTIONS

1. Why does the author tell us the meaning of the name Akhnaton?
2. How are the physical descriptions of Uncle Grant and Akhnaton similar and how are they different? How do you account for the differences?
3. Rephrase part of paragraph one as it might be written if it were a typical sentimental portrait of a likable old man.

Below, is a student's description of a high school Latin teacher, entitled "Bonville's Roman Mother." Which techniques of the professional writers does the student use and which should have been used?

It is known in Bonville that when a child reaches high school, he will probably be adopted by Miss Wilkins, the Latin teacher. Although she has been an old maid for about 40 years, she has more children she can call her own than any mother in town. Students can tell by looking at her that she is under-standing. She is a large woman but has a small face and soft gray and white streaked hair. Her eyes, small and sparkling, ex-press her enthusiasm as she teaches Latin.

Miss Wilkins is much like her favorite orator, Cicero. She is warm-hearted and emotional when a student's ideas are far from what she feels is right. She is fond of books and art, and like Cicero has her own collection, a special gallery for her children. Unlike Cicero she is very modest and declines any honor or memorial for the future. Like Caesar she has a forgiv-ing spirit.

These qualities make Miss Wilkins a kind, understanding

person, but a mother must also have discipline. In class she controls her children like a Roman guard. Her sophomores memorize their lessons perfectly for fear of her glaring stare. She lets juniors relax a little, and they study hard to prove to her that they are worthy of her efforts. Seniors are her cohorts. They work together in common interest and enjoyment.

Her family of children finds its home in the Latin Club, the largest and most active club in school. The student consul takes charge and twice a month a group from the club provides Roman entertainment. Miss Wilkins never speaks in the meetings, but her silent presence in the back of the room urges everyone to do his best.

In class Miss Wilkins has the power to become momentarily the old Roman writer himself as she is reading his work. While studying the Catilinarian Conspiracy she shows the good and bad sides of the conspirators. Under her guidance the students can put themselves in the conspirators' place to understand their feelings. Miss Wilkins even finds merit in the conceit of Cicero after he has crushed the conspiracy. Her understanding of human nature startles her students and awakens in them new thoughts and feelings. She brings Latin writing out of the book into the lives of her students.

Miss Wilkins' philosophies were absorbed by her students. As a Romantic she shares with them her love of the mountains, trees, and the cool air around Bonville. She is an Epicurean trying to find pleasant thoughts and avoiding depressing ones. Miss Wilkins may like the happy side of life, but that does not mean that she doesn't take life seriously. Her faith in the honesty of her students, their patriotism, morals, and religion is so strong that its bond on her children is hard for them to break.

Miss Wilkins' children always do well in their lives. She has prepared them to think for themselves and has given them some sound basis upon which to base these thoughts.

Miss Wilkins will soon leave her home in the Bonville High School. Age is slowing her down and making her cheerfulness an increasingly harder task. It is no longer an unusual sight to see her eating crackers and milk in class for her ulcers or walking slowly and unsteadily down the hall. Yet there is still a sparkle in her eyes for she will never stop enjoying life. In her retirement she will read books, paint, and do all the things she has wanted to do all the years that she has been raising her children. Miss Wilkins gave forty years of her life to them, and they will multiply her gift by many generations.

The title suggests the two themes of the sketch—Miss Wilkins' identity with her subject and her role as a kind of family leader. These two themes constantly control selection of detail and words, but at times the writer overemphasizes the maternal role. This idea, once established, could be better sustained by more concrete detail and less repetition of "mother" and "children." However, the sense of theme is specific and the paper moves to an end that works in terms of both subject and theme. There is the skeleton of a good paper here.

Questions

1. Where could the writer use more specific detail, such as scenes or dialogue?
2. Identify and replace clichés that weaken the author's purpose.
3. What would you do to improve the organization of the paper?

Assignments

1. Using the third-person point of view, describe someone you know or have a lot of information about (a historical or public figure). Your aim is to convey, in 300 to 600 words, some sense of why this person is worth writing about. Do not in any way *state* your reasons.
2. Choose a group of people in school or one person with whom you have worked. As Mills set out to do with the much larger group in *White Collar*, describe a typical member of the group, based on your close observation and careful recall.

3. In 600 words or less, describe a person eating, walking, talking, or doing some other small, ordinary action. Make this simple action reveal him as a person you might use in a fiction or nonfiction story. He may be "round" or "flat."

CHAPTER 6

HOW TO MAKE
THINGS HAPPEN

Ask a friend how he liked a certain book or movie. "Great," he says. Ask him why. He may well say it had a good story, a lot of suspense, or fast-moving action. He is talking about *narrative*, the element of writing that first captures most readers' attention.

Narrative is not always fiction. Lawyers, doctors, mechanics, and cooks all use narrative. Anyone who describes something that happens uses narrative. Anyone who has told a joke has tried his skill at narrative. As you know, few people are really effective joke-tellers or storytellers. Think of someone, maybe yourself, who has trouble telling jokes well. What is wrong with the joke technique? What would make the jokes better?

If you want to discover the key to narrative, try telling about the simplest action without mentioning a place, using only the verb *to be,* and calling your character "a man." The reason good narrative grips our attention is because it is concrete and because specific things happen. The reader is *in* the action because the action is so concrete it has the feeling of reality. The two sentences below illustrate this difference.

1. Suddenly it was very windy and rainy.
2. With an explosive rush of wind the rain crashed against the house like stone.

Sentence 2 replaces the overworked adverbs *suddenly* and *very*. The meaningless "it" is scrapped. The key elements, wind and rain, are changed from adjectives modifying "it" to nouns which act through a strong verb.

Good narrative is concrete because it must let the reader know where he is and where he is going. A vague narrative is like looking at the world through wax-paper glasses. If you put these glasses on your reader, you cannot expect him to follow you through your writing. Action means change, and when things around us are changing, we want to see exactly what is happening.

This does not mean you must start at the end and tell the reader what is going to happen before he will be willing to follow your narrative. Whether you do this or not depends on theme and purpose. Sometimes knowing the end in advance makes the reader more interested in the preliminary causes and events. At other times a writer suggests two or more ends. Very rarely is the reader kept entirely ignorant of the narrative's conclusion.

Most narrative writing "tells" as it moves. The action embodies what the author wants the reader to know. Catherine Drinker Bowen said that there were two ways to write history—critical and narrative.

You see, then, that in the critical style, our reader knows at once what the author thinks, and more importantly, knows what he, the reader, is supposed to think. The narrative form has no such prop to lean upon—and we have already declared an intention to use the narrative form in our biography. The choice lays upon us then, an extra burden, an extra technical procedure: we must make our book three dimensional instead of two. To our task of researcher and annalist is added a third task: the artist's task of creating characters in the round—

characters known to the reader not through criticism but through straight narration, action, their speech upon the printed page. Teachers of creative writing have a phrase for this. "Don't tell 'em, show 'em!"—they say. The narrative method is the method of parable; it is fable rather than exposition. Again, an Example:

Our narrative does not permit us to make the straight statement that young John Adams was shy, nor even to quote a reminiscent Adams's acquaintance in proof of his shyness. How, then, can we convey to our reader the fact that John was shy? There is only one way; we must show him being shy. From John's *Autobiography*, written fifty years after the event, we learn briefly of that fateful day when, at sixteen, he journeyed the ten miles from Braintree to take his examinations for Harvard College. Quite obviously those were, for John, fearful hours. How then, shall we convey it? We must travel to Cambridge with John, walk invisible beside his pony, trudge with him across Harvard Yard and up the steps to face his four examiners and that large, handsome, distinguished and terrifying individual, President Holyoke of Harvard College. It is not for us to write, "*We can therefore image* John's feelings as he confronted the President of Harvard." We must do more than that. We must ourselves stand with John before that polished desk; with John, we must answer questions put in Latin, with John freeze to paralysis when we cannot recall the Latin word for *morality*.

And in our method is no deception. The reader knows we are not God, knows we cannot actually be inside John's mind—and knows also, by now, that behind our narrative is historical source and historical evidence without which we would not presume to take young John Adams to Harvard Hall or anywhere else.[1]

The narrative Miss Bowen makes for John Adams' life is, of course a complexity of techniques and materials and themes. The

---

[1] Catherine Drinker Bowen, *Writing Biography* (Boston: The Writer, Inc., 1951), pp. 16–17.

simplest kind of narrative is what E. M. Forster calls a "story." Most writers aim for what he calls a "plot."

Let us define a plot. We have defined a story as a narrative of events arranged in their time-sequence. A plot is also a narrative of events, the emphasis falling on causality. "The king died and then the queen died," is a story. "The king died, and then the queen died of grief" is a plot. The time-sequence is preserved, but the sense of causality overshadows it. Or again: "The queen died, no one knew why, until it was discovered that it was through grief at the death of the king." This is a plot with a mystery in it, a form capable of high development. It suspends the time-sequence, it moves as far away from the story as its limitations will allow. Consider the death of the queen. If it is in a story we say "and then?" If it is in a plot we ask "why?" That is the fundamental difference between these two aspects of the novel. A plot cannot be told to a gaping audience of cave men or to a tyrannical sultan or to their modern descendant the movie-public. They can only be kept awake by "and then— and then—" They can only supply curiosity. But a plot demands intelligence and memory also.

Curiosity is one of the lowest of the human faculties. You will have noticed in daily life that when people are inquisitive they nearly always have bad memories and are usually stupid at bottom. The man who begins by asking you how many brothers and sisters you have, is never a sympathetic character, and if you meet him in a year's time he will probably ask you how many brothers and sisters you have, his mouth again sagging open, his eyes still bulging from his head. It is difficult to be friends with such a man, and for two inquisitive people to be friends must be impossible. Curiosity by itself takes us a very little way, nor does it take us far into the novel—only as far as the story. If we would grasp the plot we must add intelligence and memory.[2]

[2] E. M. Forster, *Aspects of the Novel* (New York: Harcourt, Brace & World, 1927), pp. 130–131.

The beginning writer is too often tempted to gain the reader's interest by story alone. He holds up the end and tries to keep the reader asking "—and then?—and then?" Failure to reach a real conclusion this way often results in "trick endings" or sudden "twists," which actually are surprises rather than suspense or drama. Trick endings are often used as consolation prizes at the end of poorly told stories. They are convenient and often seem clever. In most cases the reader either guesses the trick too early and signs off or he becomes absorbed in the cleverness of the trick and forgets the real significance of the writing—if there is any.

Unless you are simply playing with your reader, suspense and twists and trick endings should reflect tension or conflict in the ideas, emotions, themes, or values of your material. The following student theme, titled "Man in the Park," is about a girl's very real problem. What effect is this writer working for and how does the conclusion work for or against this effect?

My mother, like most mothers, told me not to talk to strange men. However, at thirteen I was getting a little too old to let Mom make all my decisions, and besides I was lonely.

We lived in the city and I had two or three girlfriends right in our apartment house. There were just certain days I wanted to be away from the usual people. I guess I knew them too well to tell them anything really personal—like how I was going to be a jazz singer. I mean I knew they would laugh.

To get away I used to go to the park and find a clean spot of grass to lie on and look at the sky. One afternoon when dreaming and humming I kept thinking someone was watching me. I looked around, and across a path a big man in a heavy overcoat sat smiling very faintly, but not moving. He had been watching all the time.

Just to show I was not embarrassed I waved to him. He didn't move, but the smile seemed to grow more definite. I walked over to him and said hello and asked did he think I was crazy.

"No, just happy," he said.

I told him I was happy enough, and he kept smiling. "What makes you happy?" he asked.

A good question which I should have asked myself long before. "I sing," I told him. I knew from his smile he was waiting to hear something. So for the first time ever in that park I sang right out loud—that old song Billie Holliday sang, "What a Little Moonlight Can Do."

It seems very sudden and impulsive for a young girl to sing for an old man who's only said a few words. But he just sat smiling and listening. I'm glad I was corny enough to do that, because as soon as I finished I began to cry. After all I was thirteen and lonely, and he was an old man in an overcoat, and he had been smiling so long in that one place his bronze face was almost dusty green.

"Man in the Park" has the right kind of economy and concreteness a good narrative requires, but its total effect is controlled by the final paragraph. What other endings would have worked? Can you think of circumstances when a surprise ending would be useful?

As with many jokes, surprise endings entertain, but in most writing, narrative or action includes more than entertainment. People, places, and ideas are like water in the reader's swimming pool. Narrative makes him swim. If nothing ever *happened* in the world, it would be an easy, a boring, and a safe place. So when you start your material in motion, remember your reader may be in there, too. To play with an old slogan, move carefully, be alert; the writing you save may be your own.

SELECTIONS

Economist John Kenneth Galbraith was an adviser to President Kennedy and Ambassador to India. His study of economics is not limited to numbers and graphs. For him economics is a very human study. In debunking the "conventional wisdom" about wartime economics, he used this brief narrative about strategic bomb-

ing, entitled "The Illusion of National Security," from the book
The Affluent Society.[3] What makes it different from other wartime
narratives?

On three nights late in July and at the beginning of August
1943, the heavy planes of the R.A.F. Bomber Command droned
in from the North Sea and subjected the city of Hamburg to an
ordeal such as Germans had not experienced since the Thirty
Years War. A third of the city was reduced to a wasteland. At
least 60,000 and perhaps as many as 100,000 people were
killed—about as many as at Hiroshima. A large number of
these were lost one night when a ghastly 'fire storm', which literally burned the asphalt pavements, swept a part of the city
and swept everything into itself. Adolf Hitler heard the details
of the attack and for the only known time during the war said it
might be necessary to sue for peace. Hermann Goering visited
the city with a retinue to survey the damage and was accorded
so disconcerting a reception that he deemed it discreet to retire.

Yet this terrible event taught a lesson about the economics of
war which very few have learned and some, indeed, may have
found it convenient to forget. The industrial plants of Hamburg
were around the edge of the city or, as in the case of the submarine pens, on the harbour. They were not greatly damaged by
the raids; these struck the centre of the city and the working-
class residential areas and suburbs. In the days immediately
following the raids production faltered; in the first weeks it was
down by as much as 20 or 25 per cent. But thereafter it returned
to normal. By then the workers had scanned the ruins of their
former homes, satisfied themselves that their possessions and
sometimes their families were irretrievable, had found some
rude clothes and the shelter of a room or part of a room in a still
habitable house, and had returned to work. On these three
nights of terror their standard of living, measured by house-
room, furnishings, clothing, food and drink, recreation, schools,
and social and cultural opportunities, had been reduced to a

[3] John Kenneth Galbraith, *The Affluent Society* (New York: Houghton
Mifflin, 1958), pp. 161–163.

fraction of what it had been before. But the efficiency of the worker as a worker was unimpaired by this loss. After a slight period of readjustment, he laboured as diligently and as skilfully as before.

There is a further chapter to the story. Before the attacks, there had been a labour shortage in Hamburg. Afterwards, despite the number killed and the number now engaged on indispensable repairs, there was no shortage. For, as a result of the attacks, thousands who were waiters in restaurants and cafés, attendants in garages, clerks in banks, salesmen in stores, shopkeepers, janitors, ticket takers, and employees in handicraft industries (which, being small and traditional, were more likely to be in the centre of town) lost their places of employment. They had previously contributed nothing to war production. Their contribution to the standard of living proved dispensable. Now they turned to the war industries as the most plausible places to find employment.

Even in the presumably austere and dedicated world of the Third Reich, in the third year of a disastrous war, the average citizen had access to a wide range of comforts and amenities which habit had made to seem essential.° And because they were believed to be essential they were essential. On such matters governments, even dictatorships, must bow to the convictions of the people even if—the exceptional case—they do not share them. The German standard of living was far above what was physically necessary for survival and efficiency. The R.A.F. broke through the psychological encrustation and brought living standards down somewhere nearer to the physical minimum. In doing so it forced a wholesale conversion of Ger-

---

° In fact, in 1943 the Germans were not concentrating their energies with particular severity on war production. In this respect they were almost certainly behind the British at the time. Until not long before there had been a heady mood of victory with, inevitably, some relaxation. Quite a few of the Nazi leaders were sybarites and were thus somewhat handicapped in imposing austerities which they would not practise themselves. A dictatorship which does not quite trust its people is likely to be hesitant in imposing hardships. Finally, the strategy of industrial mobilization was poorly understood in Germany and this strategy assumed a short war. This failure of understanding was most important of all and might be a lesson.

many's scarcest resource, that of manpower, to war production.

In reducing, as nothing else could, the consumption of non-essentials and the employment of men in their supply, there is a distinct possibility that the attacks on Hamburg increased Germany's output of war material and thus her military effectiveness.°

Obviously this is no blood and thunder war story. It is a narrative written to examine an economic theory of warfare—strategic bombing.

Rather than start with theory, Galbraith starts with the action itself. The events are what we expect from intensive bombing. Then, still using concrete detail, we see the somewhat unexpected results of bombing. This is the simple structure of the story. The author now goes back and reorganizes the detail from the point of view of economics—employment, unemployment, luxury, necessity, standard of living.

The narrative follows the simple action–result pattern, but to serve the author's purpose there are two parallel narratives. The conclusion has a double strength.

QUESTIONS

1. Show at least two instances in the first paragraph in which the author's vocabulary is chosen to guide the reader's expectation away from the real results. Why is this done? (Remember the author is debunking conventional wisdom.) Is this a trick ending?
2. What would be the effect of putting the second narrative first?
3. What would be missing if this narrative were turned into pages of graphs and columns of numbers? What does that suggest about the nature of language?

° These details are based on studies made in 1945 by the United States Strategic Bombing Survey (of which I was a director) which included detailed investigation of the effect of the Hamburg raids. The Germans had an understandable pride in the speed of Hamburg's industrial recovery and kept detailed records which much facilitated the investigation.

When people look at each other they usually look at faces. We take the existence of faces for granted, but if life starts at conception, then man does not always have a face. In *Biography of the Unborn* Margaret Shea Gilbert tells how man acquires a face in the second month of life.[4] Remember in reading it that this is only part of a larger chapter from a technical book. Compare the writing here to narratives you have read in other science texts.

From tadpole to man: So one might characterize the changes that occur during the second month of life. True, the embryo is not a tadpole at the beginning of the month, but it looks not unlike one. The tailed, bulbous creature, with its enormous drooping head, fish-like gill-slits, and formless stubs for arms and legs, bears little resemblance to an acceptable human form. By the end of the second month, however, the embryo has a distinctly human character and would be recognized by anyone as a promising example of *Homo sapiens.* He possesses an unmistakable although rather grotesque human face, a smooth neck proudly supporting his still large head, arms and legs possessing fingers and toes, elbows and knees, and an elongated trunk whose smoothly modeled belly and muscular back no longer show the contours of the organs within.

During the second month several of the internal organs take on the functions which will be theirs throughout life, and at this time the first movements of the embryo's body occur. The sex becomes apparent not only in the specific sex glands (testes and ovary) but also in the appearance of the external sex organs. At first the external sex organs are similar in the male and female, but by the end of the second month there are enough sexual differences to make possible the correct prognosis of sex, at least in 65% of the cases. Bones and muscles, developing between the skin and the internal organs, round out the contours of the body. It is now that the human tail reaches its greatest development and then undergoes regression. Accompanying these complex changes in form there occurs the steady growth that

[4] Margaret Shea Gilbert, *Biography of the Unborn* (Baltimore: Williams and Wilkins Co., 1963), pp. 32–37.

characterizes the entire developmental period. In this month the human embryo increases six-fold in length (from 6 mm. to 35 mm.) and approximately five hundred times in weight.

The developing face and neck are perhaps the main features which give to the two month embryo its human appearance. At the beginning of the month the head of the embryo consists almost entirely of the expanding bulbous brain whose contours mold the thin skin of the head. Below the brain the growing eyes bulge out from the sides of the head, and the shallow nasal pits overlie the front end of the brain. Between the overhanging brain and the protruding heart lies the wide mouth-cavity. Behind the eyes occur the series of clefts which were likened to the gill-slits of lower forms. Between successive clefts lie compact columns of tissue which are called 'branchial arches;' these arches are 'evolutionary hang-overs' from the gill-bars of lower animals and, like other evolutionary remnants, they are utilized to form new and different structures.

It is around the eyes, nose and ears, and especially around the wide gaping mouth, that the face is now built. The lower ends of the first branchial arches fuse below the mouth to form the lower jaw. At the angles of the mouth buds of tissue appear, which grow forward above the mouth cavity and fuse to form the upper jaw. The mouth, thus bounded by upper and lower jaws, is a very wide slit which is gradually reduced in size by the partial fusion of the two jaws at the angles of the mouth. The fused material then forms the cheeks.

At the same time the nasal-sacs gradually move closer together so that, by the time the upper jaw has been formed, the two nasal sacs lie side by side, incorporated by a wide ridge of tissue into a single, broad nose. The eyes, which at first lie on the sides of the head, are shifted around to the front where, by the end of the second month, the two eyes may gaze more or less on the same field. During the last week of the month eyelids develop as folds of skin above the eyes; shortly afterwards the eyelids close down over the eyes and seal them shut for the following three months.

The external ears develop from the fusion of a series of nodules formed from parts of the first and second branchial arches.

By the end of the second month the embryo has a decently human ear. The only odd thing about this ear is that it lies rather low on the side of the head.

At the close of the second month, the lower jaw is still small, and the chin is poorly defined; seen in profile the embryo looks almost chinless. The nose is broad and flat, with the nostrils opening forward rather than downward. The eyes are far apart. The forehead is prominent and bulging, giving the embryo a very 'brainy' appearance. In fact, it is interesting to note that the embryo is truly 'brainy' in the sense that the brain forms by far the largest part of the head. It will take the face many years to overcome this early dominance of the brain and to reach the relative size the face has in the adult.

The writer begins with an image which sums up in ordinary terms the scope of her narrative. It also suggests her attitude. The changes she is relating are almost magical.

Choosing vocabulary to carry through the unifying idea of the initial image, Miss Gilbert builds an orderly narrative. The details are very full, as in a text, but they are more than just a list of biological transformations. As the author writes, she changes her description from the frog-like, one-month embryo into the shape of man.

QUESTIONS

1. How would this piece be changed by omitting paragraph one? Paragraphs one and two?
2. Show an instance of how the author's vocabulary changes to mirror the changes in the embryo.
3. How would you revise this selection to be a self-contained essay for a less science-minded audience?
4. How does the initial image help bridge the gap between the author and less knowledgeable people?

René Dubos is a well-known medical scientist who does not believe disease can be conquered simply by killing off germs which cause disease. In his book *The Mirage of Health* he uses narrative to help demonstrate his thesis that there are many causes of disease other than germs.[5] Here he tells the story of a Central American fungus that affected the destiny of the Irish people.

As far as is known, the potato originated in the Andes, where it still grows wild, yielding tubers so small as to be hardly fit for human use. In its native habitat the plant is infected with the parasitic fungus *Phytophthora infestans* but suffers little, if at all, from its presence. Through evolutionary adaptation, the fungus and the wild potato have obviously achieved a state of ecological equilibrium which permits the survival of both. Eventually the potato was improved for human consumption, and it became one of the most important sources of food in the Western world after the eighteenth century. While the fungus phytophthora has followed the potato wherever the plant has been taken, the relationship between the two has changed, the improved varieties of potatoes selected for large yields being much more susceptible to infection than are the wild varieties. Fortunately, it is possible by proper techniques of farming to arrange that most of the potato crop escapes destruction by the parasite. Now and then, however, the weather conditions upset the best farming practices, the fungus multiplies more rapidly and abundantly than usual, and kills the plant.

The potato blight broke out on a disastrous scale in Europe and particularly in Ireland around 1845. For two years in succession the blight not only killed the foliage but rotted the tubers in the ground and in storage. Because the impact of the disaster was so varied and so great, it is worth recording in some detail the constellation of circumstances under which it occurred and the scientific debates to which it gave rise.

Weather had been very unpleasant shortly before the blight broke out. For several weeks the atmosphere had been one of continued gloom, with a succession of chilling rains and fog,

[5] Rene Dubos, *The Mirage of Health* (New York: Harper & Row, 1959), pp. 87–91.

the sun scarcely ever visible, the temperature several degrees below the average for the previous nineteen years. The botanist John Lindley held the theory that bad weather had caused the potato plants to become saturated with water. They had grown rapidly during the good weather, then had absorbed moisture with avidity when the fog and the rain came. As absence of sunshine had checked transpiration, wrote Dr. Lindley, the plants had been unable to get rid of their excess of water and in consequence had contracted a kind of dropsy. Putrefaction was the result of this physiological disease. The Rev. Miles Berkeley, a naturalist with much knowledge of the habits of fungi, held a different theory and connected the potato disease with the prevalance of a species of mold on the affected tissues. To this Lindley replied that Berkeley was attaching too much importance to a little growth of mold on the diseased potato plants. He added that "as soon as living matter lost its force, as soon as diminishing vitality took the place of the customary vigour, all sorts of parasites would acquire power and contend for its destruction. It was so with all plants, and all animals, even man himself. First came feebleness, next incipient decay, then sprang up myriads of creatures whose life could only be maintained by the decomposing bodies of their neighbours. Cold and wet, acting upon the potato when it was enervated by excessive and sudden growth, would cause a rapid diminution of vitality; portions would die and decay, and so prepare the field in which mouldiness could establish itself."

Thus, the professional plant pathologists, represented by Lindley, believed that the fungus could become established on the potato plant only after the latter had been debilitated by unhealthy conditions, whereas Berkeley saw the fungus as the primary cause of the disease, with fog and rain as circumstances which favored its spread and growth. In this manner the controversies which were to bring Pasteur in conflict with the official world of the French Academy of Medicine in the 1880's were rehearsed three decades earlier in the pages of the English *Gardener's Chronicle.*

It must be emphasized that the destruction of the crop in 1845 was not the result of a new infection by *Phytophthora in-*

festans. The fungus had been present on the potato plant since its introduction from Central America, but it took unusual weather conditions to render the plant highly susceptible to infection. Although the fungus persisted in Ireland after the Great Blight, it was only during occasional years that the weather was propitious for its proliferation, so that potato culture recovered progressively.

The two years of the blight, however, had been sufficient to ruin the economy of Ireland. Following the introduction of the potato during the eighteenth century, the Irish population had much increased, as is always the case when a new source of food becomes available. From 3.5 million around 1700 it had reached approximately 8 million in 1840. The potato blight caused an acute food shortage, with the result that a million persons died of outright starvation. Furthermore, many of those who escaped death became more susceptible to a variety of infectious diseases. Thus began a great epidemic of tuberculosis which after a century is only now beginning to abate. Also, lack of food and economic misery forced a large percentage of the Irish population to emigrate, particularly to America. Even today the population of Ireland is only half what it was before the potato famine.

In America the Irish immigrants found work in the mushrooming industries of the Atlantic seaboard. But they found also crowded and unhealthy living conditions. Coming from rural environments they suddenly experienced the worst aspects of slum existence. The profound upheaval in their way of life made them ready victims to all sorts of infection. The sudden and dramatic increase of tuberculosis mortality in the Philadelphia, New York, and Boston areas around 1850 can be traced in large part to the Irish immigrants who settled in these cities at that time.

Thus, all sorts of accidents played their part in linking tuberculosis—the Great White Plague of the nineteenth century—to a fungus living on the wild potato in Central America. The change in ecological relationship between fungus and potato that occurred when the latter was removed from its native habitat and was "improved" for human consumption; the disturbance in the internal physiology of the potato caused at a critical time by unusual weather conditions; the biological and cultural urges which brought about the rapid increase in the Irish population during the first part of the nineteenth century—all these forces and many social factors that cannot be discussed here played an essential part in transforming Pat the Irish pig-tender into a New York City cop. If ever a writer succeeds in making a popular story of the potato blight, he may conclude, as Tolstoy did for Napoleon's invasion of Russia, that its determinism is beyond human analytical power. In fact, it is perhaps just an illusion of science to believe that the vagaries of the relations between the potato and a microscopic fungus, inadequate farming practices, and the weather conditions in the 1840's were the real factors that led the adventurous spirit of man to establish on the American continent the wit of the Irish, their Catholic faith, and their political genius.

This narrative could be said to follow the pattern of "out of the wilderness into the modern world." Before he began writing, Dubos knew how this pattern fitted his theme. His theory was that epidemics of disease are not explained simply by saying that such and such made a germ spread. He saw many coincidences contributing to each epidemic. He began his narrative with one of the smallest coincidences—the fact that wild potatoes are not as susceptible to a Central American fungus disease as domestic ones. Because of this fact climate and the area of planting are also important. At this point Dubos presents his specific situation. While he seems to be explaining easily, he is also introducing new complexity at every turn. He has traced a path of accidents, and having done so, he concludes his argument as well as the narrative. Accident, not eternally true cause and effect, determines the course of disease. In fact the writer yields to his own argument and admits his explanation is also subject to doubt: The cause of disease is so complex perhaps even his complex writing has not explained it.

Questions

1. What is the purpose of introducing the Lindley–Berkeley debate?
2. How does the author's final doubt contribute to his thesis?
3. What might have been included in this narrative that was not?

The extreme of passivity is being dead, and dead men usually are not the subjects of narrative. By uniting theme, action, and fantasy in his story "The Autopsy," German writer Georg Heym turns a routine autopsy into a short, swift narrative.[6]

> The dead man lay naked and alone on a white table in the great theater, in the oppressive whiteness, the cruel sobriety of the operating theater that seemed to be vibrating still with the screams of unending torment.
>
> The noon sun covered him and caused the livid spots on his forehead to awaken; it conjured up a bright green out of his naked belly and made it swell like a great sack filled with water.
>
> His body was like the brilliant calyx of a giant flower, a mysterious plant from the Indian jungles which someone had shyly laid down at the altar of death.
>
> Splendid shades of red and blue grew along his loins, and the great wound below his navel, which emitted a terrible odor, split open slowly in the heat like a great red furrow.
>
> The doctors entered. A few kindly men in white coats, with duelling scars and gold pince-nez.
>
> They went up to the dead man and looked at him with interest and professional comments.
>
> They took their dissecting instruments out of white cupboards, white boxes full of hammers, bonesaws with strong

[6] Georg Heym, "The Autopsy," trans. Michael Hamburger, from *Great German Short Stories*, ed. Stephen Spender (New York: Dell Books, 1960).

teeth, files, horrible batteries of tweezers, little cases full of enormous needles that seemed to cry out incessantly for flesh like the curved beaks of vultures.

They commenced their gruesome work, They were like terrible torturers. The blood flowed over their hands which they plunged ever more deeply into the cold corpse, pulling out its contents, like white cooks drawing a goose.

The intestines coiled around their arms, greenish-yellow snakes, and the excrement dripped on their coats, a warm, putrid fluid. They punctured the bladder. Cold urine glittered inside it like a yellow wine. They poured it into large bowls; it had a sharp and caustic stench like ammonia. But the dead man slept. Patiently he suffered them to tug him this way and that, to pull at his hair. He slept.

And while the blows of the hammer resounded on his head, a dream, the remnant of love in him, awoke like a torch shining into his night.

In front of the large window a great wide sky opened, full of small white clouds that floated in the light, in the afternoon quiet, like small white gods. And the swallows traveled high up in the blue, trembling in the warm July sun.

The dead man's black blood trickled over the blue putrescence of his forehead. It condensed in the heat to a terrible cloud, and the decay of death crept over him with its brightly colored talons. His skin began to flow apart, his belly grew white as an eel's under the greedy fingers of the doctors, who were bathing their arms up to the elbows in his moist flesh.

Decay pulled the dead man's mouth apart. He seemed to smile. He dreamed of a blissful star, of a fragrant summer evening. His dissolving lips quivered as though under a light kiss.

How I love you. I loved you so much. Shall I tell you how much I loved you? When you walked through the poppy fields, yourself a fragrant poppy flame, you had drawn the whole evening into yourself. And your dress that blew about your ankles was like a wave of fire in the glow of the setting sun. But you inclined your head in the light, and your hair still burned and flamed with all my kisses.

So you walked away, looking back at me all the time. And the lamp in your hand swayed like a glowing rose in the dusk long after you had gone.

I shall see you again tomorrow. Here, under the chapel window; here, where the candlelight pours through and changes your hair into a golden forest; here, where the narcissi cling to your ankles, tender as tender kisses.

I shall see you again every night at the hour of dusk. We shall never leave each other. How I love you! Shall I tell you how much I love you?

And the dead man trembled softly with bliss on his white mortuary table, while the iron chisel in the doctor's hand broke open the bones of his temple.

In contemplating the brutal inhumanity of the autopsy, Georg Heym also thought about the nature of human life. We cannot know what went through his mind, but we can see how he used narrative to turn the grotesque detail of an autopsy into an image that reaches much farther into our human emotions.

The story starts with the vivid and repulsive details of the autopsy. It follows the order of dissection from the point of view of a fascinated observer. Because the detail is very concrete and vivid, we seem to see everything. However, the narrative moves quickly, almost skimming from image to image. There is none of the amateurish, Halloween-show lingering on horror. Nevertheless, for a while the author seems intent only on shocking us. However, the careful reader, having read the whole story, can look back and see that from the first sentence the physical narrative is controlled by a deeper theme. This theme surfaces in the story of the dead man's love. Within the last sentence the physical destruction and the spiritual longing are made one story.

QUESTIONS

1. Mark the adjectives and adverbs in the first eight paragraphs. How do they function in the overall story?

2. How could the autopsy part be rewritten so it would not be controlled by the larger theme?
3. Do you think Heym overplays the gruesomeness of the autopsy?

"Landing" is a student theme describing an actual incident. The author was obviously excited when he witnessed the action. In evaluating this piece decide what its strong and weak points are, and pick out specific words, phrases, and sentences that you would change. Can you make any generalization about the paper's most important weakness?

With growing frustration, we tried to stare through the ground fog that was billowing in off the swamps. Squinting and straining for a glimpse of the jet's lights had turned us into an edgy group. Somewhere above the air traffic control tower a circling jet was low on fuel and long on strip length requirements. An aircraft of this size had never condescended to land on our modest air field. The pilot had originally intended to put down at New Orleans, but prevailing weather conditions in Louisiana forced him to change his flight plan and head for Florida.

When radar control picked up an unscheduled aircraft heading our way, we tried to make contact but got no results. Finally, at the five mile check point, the pilot began to boom in loud and clear. By the time he and the tower operator came to an agreement over procedures, the jet was out over the Gulf and had to relocate the field.

Getting the jet down safely without ruining the strip was like trying to water-ski in an irrigation ditch. After almost crashing into the tower on the first try, the pilot maneuvered around for another attempt. He came in low and fast right between the twinkling rows of lights and cut down his power. Too late, he realized that the swirling shrouds of fog had tricked him into believing that he was much closer to the ground. Interminable moments ticked by before the jet slammed down on the runway. It struck with such force that three tires blew and it bounced one-hundred feet back into the air. When our unexpected guest came to rest amidst tons of crash foam, it had blown five tires, awakened everyone within ten miles, and demolished about two-thousand dollars' worth of landing lights.

New tires were flown in, and by working all night, the mechanics had the jet ready for take-off early the next morning. We all held our breath and then slowly expelled it as the jet took every inch of available runway to get airborne, crept up over the top of the trees and disappeared from sight.

The author tries to be concrete but never attains the really strong sense impressions the story needs to put the reader in the scene. He is too concerned with telling *what* happened and pays too little attention to *how* it happened. For this reason too, the narrative is what Forster calls a "story." In effect the author says "and then, and then, and then. . . ." One suspects in this kind of writing that the author is more interested in boasting about what he has seen than in letting the reader see for himself.

Questions

1. Rewrite the sentence in paragraph three that begins, "After almost crashing into the tower. . . ."
2. Why did the author place himself in the story?
3. What themes might be developed to make this narrative more interesting?

Assignments

1. Describe a small incident in someone's life that moves to its conclusion through several steps or phases. First decide what your theme is; then be sure each step moves both physical narrative and theme along.
2. Describe an event you witnessed, intentionally or unintentionally. This may be a laboratory experiment, part of an athletic event, or a car accident. Use theme as in assignment 1.

PART THREE

UNITING IDEA
AND EMOTION

Problems of Control

FROM ABSTRACT
TO CONCRETE

Problems of Control over Subjective and Emotional Expression

Probably all the important human emotions found their way into literature very soon after the written word was invented. Through thousands of years the best writers of every age have written about anger, delight, sorrow, mirth, fear, and courage. Where does this put you? Last with the least? Not by any means, not if you feel you have any worth as an individual.

When you find a way of stating your own point of view, of conveying your own particular feeling about a particular subject, you will not be sounding like anyone except yourself. Learning to express a personal relationship between your own emotions and something else in the world is not easy, but a good way to begin is by funneling an emotion into concrete form so that other people will feel in turn what you have felt. This concrete form is the only way an emotion becomes yours. Everybody uses the same names for emotions. Grandma says she loves Grandpa, Baby Sister says she loves her dog, you say you love the blonde in Dorm Five. Maybe both you and your roommate love the blonde. The names of emotions provide a general category for the emotion; they don't convey its power. They don't convey individual human realities.

In writing, the problem of emotion is a problem of control. It is difficult to have your emotion and write about it too, at least at first. This is why people so often say, "Emotion's inside you, don't try to explain it." Or, "It's something you just can't put in words. It's in your heart, not your mind." We try to escape writing about emotion, not because writing about it is impossible, but because in writing about it we must experience the emotion more fully. In some ways we have to become detached; in other ways we have to plunge ourselves beyond the easily recognizable symptoms.

All this is very abstract. But emotion can be conveyed without being killed; you have seen it done in the movies and experienced it in books. Do you think the man who infected you with the emotion was some kind of scheming robot because he could write about it? In the following chapters you will be asked to write out of your own emotions. Don't be afraid to examine them, question them. Only then will you be sure of their depth. And perhaps you will obtain both more control and the ability to lead a fuller emotional life.

CHAPTER 7

ANGER AND JEALOUSY: CONTROLLING THE DESTRUCTIVE FORCE

Of all the emotions, anger and jealousy are certainly among the most destructive and the most distorting. They are seen in the lover's quarrel or the passions of international war. When the passions have died, what is left is seldom better than what we had before. Anger and jealousy possess us so completely that we often lose part or all of our power to create anything rational or worthwhile out of our experience.

If writing is the mind working on chaos to create order, then anger and jealousy work to create disorder—or at least false order.

Most of us at one time or another have become so angry we have physically flailed out at someone else. You could hardly call the flailing rational or even "well fought." Whatever our method of fighting, anger gives our aggression strength but not effectiveness. The same is true of writing.

Any writing is difficult enough, but writing when you are angry is most difficult of all. There is no writing more obviously bad than that of anger. You can probably recall many newspaper editorials or anonymous criticisms in which the anger of the writer was clear but his reasons either weakly stated or not present at all. Perhaps we see this most often in political campaigns, especially in anonymous broadsheets or pamphlets issued more to destroy one candidate than to build another. In politics we call this propaganda. We know at what or at whom the author is angry, but not how his anger was incurred. So, unless we are interested in the author personally, his writing will fail. This kind of failure is common in all writing—book reviews, essays, fiction, poetry, and drama.

As much as it may help your own state of mind to give someone a written "punch in the nose," it will be very boring or even distasteful to the reader if he cannot understand your situation, the relationship between you and the object of your anger. The strongest temptation to an angry writer is to write in strong, abstract language that draws attention to the degree of anger rather than to the subject itself. This writing abounds in words like *disgusting, horrible, rotten, cowardly, immoral, stupid, tyrannical, cruel,* and *despotic.* The semanticist Hayakawa calls these "snarl words" because like a dog's snarl, they tell the reader how the writer feels but they *show* nothing. What these abstract words do is label things. Think of them as labels on a bottle of something to drink. They do not tell what the liquid inside tastes like or exactly what it will do to you. They only say "rotten stuff."

Some people argue that an emotion—say love or fear—cannot be captured in words. Of course if you limit your idea of emotion to just what goes on in the electrical circuits of the brain and in the protoplasm of the body, then no matter who you are, an emotion can only be biological, physical, or chemical. But when you use the words *love* or *fear,* you are not thinking of the inside of a brain. You are thinking of external realities, of certain combinations of *things* that let you label the unseen process in the brain with the name of an emotion. For most people an emotion is a state of mind or even health produced by both external and internal circumstances.

You might still object and say that even externally emotions are the same for everyone. What you probably mean is that the obvious external symptoms are similar: Angry people shout, clench their fists, brood, fight. If you think the experience is the same for all, you are not using your powers of thought and observation acutely or you have had few intense emotions. Go back to the Hemingway paragraph in the chapter on observation. You have to know what you really felt and what the "actual things were which produced the emotion." For instance you may say you are angry at your school administration. What kind of anger is it? Is it hatred, frustration, prejudice, revenge, spite, disgust? And exactly how did *you* become angry? Like a skillful lawyer try to establish the exact process. Don't hang your emotion on the accepted clichés—the administration is tyrannical, ignorant, incompetent, blind, or patronizing. What does the administration mean in terms of the actual substance of your life or someone else's? Does it mean lumpy beds, short dates, crowded classrooms?

Accepting clichés and vague abstractions can destroy our ability to have intense feelings. Clichés screen us from recognizing real emotion. Abstraction reduces the source and experience of emotion to intellectual trivia. Brainwashing uses these techniques to break down bonds built on experience, on actual living. By learning to write well about emotion, you are not destroying it. You are testing its reality. You may also be making yourself a fuller human being.

The first problem in writing out of anger is to choose a form that will express your emotion. The best form for you will depend on your own personality and circumstances—how you react to anger or jealousy and what the object of your emotion means to you. If you are writing out of anger, for instance, you may choose a short, almost unrhymed, harsh-sounding way of expressing resentment, as did Randall Jarrell in "The Death of the Ball Turret Gunner," a famous poem about war. But in his poem it is at once apparent that the writer has his material under control. The poem mirrors emotion, shows concretely the terrible waste of war. Yet each word, each image, each syllable, even, is a result of careful selection.

From my mother's sleep I fell into the State,
And I hunched in its belly till my wet fur froze.

Six miles from earth, loosed from its dream of life,
I woke to black flak and the nightmare fighters.
When I died they washed me out of the turret with a hose.[1]

Notice the difference in the sharpness of the imagery in the Jarrell
poem and in "Go Everybody," the student poem that follows. The
student, like Jarrell, was angry. He used a poem to show his anger
and he tried to give us a clue by speaking of a choir that is paid for
singing. But is it a real clue? And what of the statement at the end
of the poem?

Call to worship
A hymn saying
Holy Holy Holy
And prayers thanking God
For the blessings bestowed upon us
And our daily bread
And a fancy sounding anthem
Sung by people who get paid
For singing it.

The sermon was
About repentance
And
How good it makes you feel when
God's on your side.

Invitation to Christian discipleship.
That's when the chance was given
For people to join
The church
And please the minister.

And that's when
I saw an old man

[1] Randall Jarrell, "The Death of the Ball Turret Gunner," *Little
Friend, Little Friend* (New York: Dial Press, 1945), p. 58.

Struggle up and hobble down the aisle
With his cane.
His mouth was trembling
And little drops of water
Were coming from his eyes
And he said he had finally found God
And he wanted the preacher man
To join him to the church.

Right then and there
The man in the black robe
Who had been preaching
Goodness
And mercy
And loving your fellowman
Actually stood before everybody
And asked that all of those
Who were in favor
Of letting the man into the church
Raise their right hands.

It made me want to vomit.

You may choose to write in the form of a poem, an essay, a cool reserved humorous anecdote, a sermon, a short story, or even a play. Whatever form you choose, whether it is dramatic and impersonal or as personal as a letter to a lover, you will have to master certain disciplines. First of all, you need to have a point of view. This point of view determines whether you use plain language or imagery, where you begin, where you end, and also the internal structure of the poem, essay, or play with which you are working. Point of view is where you begin to separate your anger from the vague feeling people think of when anyone says the word anger.

The following selections show how writers have handled many different points of view in writing out of anger or jealousy. The discussion of each selection is centered around a particular technique—irony, characterization, reiteration for emphasis. In reading each selection ask yourself why the author chose his particular technique and what the emotion was like before it was given written form.

SELECTIONS

In looking back on her family life, the French writer Colette saw quite clearly how certain emotions—specifically, jealousy— ruled her parents and herself. Without ever explaining or giving long history, she conveys that situation within the frame of one day, in a chapter from her book *My Mother's House*.[2]

"There's nothing for dinner to-night. Tricotet hadn't yet killed this morning. He was going to kill at noon. I'm going myself to the butcher's, just as I am. What a nuisance! Why should one have to eat? And what shall we eat this evening?"

My mother stands, utterly discouraged, by the window. She is wearing her house frock of spotted sateen, her silver brooch with twin angels encircling the portrait of a child, her spectacles on a chain and her lorgnette suspended from a black silk cord that catches on every door key, breaks on every drawer handle, and has been reknotted a score of times. She looks at each of us in turn, hopelessly. She is well aware that not one of us will make a useful suggestion. If appealed to, my father will reply, "Raw tomatoes with plenty of pepper."

"Red cabbage and vinegar," would have been the contribution of my elder brother, Achille, whose medical studies keep him in Paris.

My second brother, Léo, will ask for "A big bowl of chocolate!" and I, bounding into the air because I so often forget that I am past fifteen, will clamour for "Fried potatoes! Fried potatoes! And walnuts with cheese!"

It appears, however, that fried potatoes, chocolate, tomatoes and red cabbage do not constitute "a dinner."

---

[2] Colette, "Jealousy," *My Mother's House* (New York: Farrar, Straus and Young, 1953), pp. 15–20.

"But why, mother?"

"Don't ask foolish questions!"

She is absorbed in her problem. She has already seized hold of the black cane basket with a double lid and is about to set forth, just as she is, wearing her wide-brimmed garden hat, scorched by three summers, its little crown banded with a dark brown ruche, and her gardening apron, in one pocket of which the curved beak of her secateur has poked a hole. Some dry love-in-the-mist seeds in a twist of paper in the bottom of the other pocket make a sound like rain and finger-nails scratching silk as she walks.

In my vanity on her behalf, I cry out after her, "Mother, do take off your apron!"

Without stopping, she turns toward me that face, framed by its bands of hair, which looks its full fifty-five years when she is sad and when she is gay would still pass for thirty.

"Why on earth? I'm only going to the Rue de la Roche."

"Can't you leave your mother alone?" grumbles my father into his beard. "By the way, where is she going?"

"To Léonore's, for the dinner."

"Aren't you going with her?"

"No. I don't feel like it to-day."

There are days when Léonore's shop, with its knives, its hatchet, and its bulging bullocks' lungs, pink as the pulpy flesh of a begonia, iridescent as they sway in the breeze, delight me as much as would a confectioner's. Léonore cuts me a slice of salted bacon and hands me the transparent rasher between the tips of her cold fingers. In the butcher's garden, Marie Tricotet, though born on the same day as myself, still derives amusement from pricking the unemptied bladders of pigs or calves and treading on them to "make a fountain." The horrid sound of skin being torn from newly killed flesh, the roundness of kidneys—brown fruit nestling in immaculate padding of rosy lard—arouse in me a complicated repugnance that attracts me while I do my best to hide it. But the delicate fat that remains in the hollow of the little cloven pig's trotter when the heat of the fire bursts it open, that I eat as a wholesome delicacy! No matter. To-day, I have no wish to follow my mother.

My father does not insist, but hoists himself nimbly on to his one leg, grasps his crutch and his stick, and goes upstairs to the library. Before going, he meticulously folds the newspaper, *Le Temps*, hides it under the cushion of his armchair, and thrusts the bright blue-covered *La Nature* into the pocket of his long overcoat. His small Cossack eye, gleaming beneath an eyebrow of hempen grey, rakes the table for printed provender which will vanish to the library and be seen no more. But we, well trained in this little game, have left him nothing to take.

"You've not seen the *Mercure de France?*"

"No, father."

"Nor the *Revue Bleue?*"

"No, father."

He glares at his children with the eyes of an inquisitor.

"I should like to know who it is, in this house, who . . ."

He relieves his feelings in gloomy and impersonal conjecture, embellished with venomous expletives. His house has become *this* house, a domain of disorder, wherein *these* "base-born" children profess contempt for the written word, encouraged, moreover, by *that* woman. . . .

"Which reminds me, where is that woman now?"

"Why, she's gone to Léonore's, father."

"Again?"

"But she's only just started. . . ."

He pulls out his watch, consults it as though he were going to bed and, for want of anything better, grabs a two-day-old copy of *L'Office de Publicité* before going up to the library. With his right hand he keeps a firm grip on the cross-piece of the crutch that acts as a prop for his right armpit: in his other he has only a stick. As it dies away, I listen to that firm, regular rhythm of two sticks and a single foot, which has soothed me all my childhood. But suddenly, to-day, a new uneasiness assails me, because for the first time I have noticed the prominent veins and wrinkles on my father's strikingly white hands, and how the fringe of thick hair at the nape of his neck has faded just lately. Can it really be true that he will soon be sixty years old?

It is cool and melancholy on the front steps, where I wait for my mother's return. At last I hear the sound of her neat little footsteps in the Rue de la Roche, and I am surprised at how happy it makes me feel. She comes round the corner and down the hill towards me, preceded by the dog—the horror from Patason's—and she is in a hurry.

"Let me pass, darling! If I don't give this shoulder of mutton to Henrietta to roast at once, we shall dine off shoe-leather. Where's your father?"

I follow her, vaguely disturbed for the first time that she should be worrying about my father. Since she left him only half an hour ago and he scarcely ever goes out, she knows perfectly well where he is. There would have been more sense, for instance, had she said to me, "Minet-Chéri, you're looking pale. Minet-Chéri, what's the matter?"

Without replying, I watch her throw off her old garden hat with a youthful gesture that reveals her grey hair and her face, fresh coloured, but marked here and there with ineffaceable lines. Is it possible—why, yes, after all, I am the youngest of us four—is it possible that my mother is nearly fifty-four? I never think about it. I should like to forget it.

Here comes the man on whom her thoughts are centred. Here he comes, bristling, his beard tilted aggressively. He has been listening for the bang of the closing front door, he has come down from his eyrie.

"There you are! You've taken your time about it."

She turns on him, quick as a cat.

"Taken my time? Are you trying to be funny? I've simply been there and come straight back."

"Back from where? From Léonore's?"

"Of course not. I had to go to Corneau's for . . ."

"For his sheep's eyes? And his comments on the weather?"

"Don't be tiresome! Then I had to go and get the black-currant tea at Cholet's."

The small Cossack eye darts a piercing look.

"Ah, ha! At Cholet's!"

My father throws his head back and runs his hand through his thick hair that is almost white.

"Ah, ha! At Cholet's! And did you happen to notice that he's losing his hair and that you can see his pate?"

"No. I didn't notice it."

"You didn't notice it? No, of course not! You were far too busy making eyes at the popinjays having a drink at the café opposite, and at Mabilat's two sons!"

"Oh! This is too much! I, I making eyes at Mabilat's sons! Upon my word, I don't know how you dare! I swear to you I didn't even turn my head in the direction of his place. And the proof of that is . . ."

Indignantly my mother folds her hands, pretty still though ageing and weatherbeaten, over a bosom held up by gusseted stays. Blushing beneath the bands of her greying hair, her chin trembling with resentment, this little elderly lady is charming when she defends herself without so much as a smile against the accusations of a jealous sexagenarian. Nor does he smile either, as he goes on to accuse her now of "gallivanting." But I can still smile at their quarrels because I am only fifteen, and have not yet divined the ferocity of love beneath his veteran eyebrow, and the blushes of adolescence upon her fading cheeks.

Here is a young girl caught in the long unpleasantness of family disintegration. Controlled by jealousy and a sense of inadequacy, the father is tyrannizing the mother and the child is losing those things which in the past have bound her closely and happily to her parents. What would be your own reactions and feelings in this kind of situation? Would you be capable of organizing them into a coherent, clearly expressed piece of writing? Probably not, and neither could the girl in the sketch at the time the action takes place.

The story is told by a mature writer looking back through time. First she looks back to the girl she used to be. The story is told as the writer sees things through her younger self. The details of the mother's appearance, the spectacles, lorgnette, frock, and brooch quite probably did not register on the child's consciousness when she saw her mother at the window. They were always with her mother. Yet the mature writer, looking back, realizes these details were a part of the woman, just as her voice and eyes and build were part of her, and they all add up to the way the girl sees her mother.

Had the girl told the story at the age of fifteen she would not have told it as taking place in one afternoon. The writer, however, chooses a particular afternoon to reveal what is happening just as she chooses particular details to characterize the people. By focusing her story in these ways, she makes the jealousy of the father and of the girl concrete and remote. Notice how at the end the girl begins to talk of "this little elderly lady" and "a jealous sexagenerian." Earlier she has indicated disapproval and despair because her father speaks in the same terms, "this house" and "that woman." The sketch does not cry out for compassion or sympathy from the reader.

Colette's largest achievement has been to see her earlier self objectively and to refrain from making the child a device to call forth our sympathy. She lets the situation, the day, the dialogue create a picture of a family being eroded by jealousy. This is what we must try to do as writers; let our facts and images speak to the reader by themselves and without our telling the reader what he is supposed to feel and see.

Questions

1. Look at several places where the lines of dialogue are short and simple. Why isn't this paraphrased or omitted?
2. Pick out several instances of physical description of a person and relate these to the general effect of the writing.
3. Why is the present tense used?
4. Why did the author choose to write about this particular day?

"Laugh it off!" Such advice is commonly given to people overcome by anger. The advice is also difficult to put into practice. It takes great control to produce laughter when you are angry. Satire is one way of doing this in writing, but in satire the author makes the reader laugh while seeming matter-of-fact himself. Irish writer Jonathan Swift felt very strongly about the plight of the poor, but he did not write his "Modest Proposal" for them. He aims at the real object of his anger—the Establishment of his day —using their language, their terms, and seeming to be on their side.

A MODEST PROPOSAL

For Preventing the Children of Poor People From
Being A Burthen to Their Parents or Country,
and for Making Them Beneficial to the Public.

It is a melancholy object to those who walk through this great town, or travel in the country, when they see the streets, the roads, and cabin-doors crowded with beggars of the female sex, followed by three, four, or six children, all in rags, and importuning every passenger for an alms. These mothers, instead of being able to work for their honest livelihood, are forced to employ all their time in strolling, to beg sustenance for their helpless infants, who, as they grow up, either turn thieves for want of work, or leave their dear Native Country to fight for the Pretender in Spain, or sell themselves to the Barbadoes.

I think it is agreed by all parties that this prodigious number of children, in the arms, or on the backs, or at the heels of their mothers, and frequently of their fathers, is in the present deplorable state of the kingdom a very great additional grievance; and therefore whoever could find out a fair, cheap, and easy method of making these children sound useful members of the commonwealth would deserve so well of the public as to have his statue set up for a preserver of the nation.

But my intention is very far from being confined to provide only for the children of professed beggars; it is of a much greater extent, and shall take in the whole number of infants at a certain age who are born of parents in effect as little able to support them as those who demand our charity in the streets.

As to my own part, having turned my thoughts, for many years, upon this important subject, and maturely weighed the several schemes of other projectors, I have always found them grossly mistaken in their computation. It is true a child, just dropped from its dam, may be supported by her milk for a solar year with little other nourishment, at most not above the value of two shillings, which the mother may certainly get, or the value in scraps, by her lawful occupation of begging, and it is exactly at one year old that I propose to provide for them, in such a manner as, instead of being a charge upon their parents, or the parish, or wanting food and raiment for the rest of their lives, they shall, on the contrary, contribute to the feeding and partly to the clothing of many thousands.

There is likewise another great advantage in my scheme, that it will prevent those voluntary abortions, and that horrid practice of women murdering their bastard children, alas, too frequent among us, sacrificing the poor innocent babes, I doubt, more to avoid the expense than the shame, which would move tears and pity in the most savage and inhuman breast.

The number of souls in this kingdom being usually reckoned one million and a half, of these I calculate there may be about two hundred thousand couple whose wives are breeders, from which number I subtract thirty thousand couple who are able to maintain their own children, although I apprehend there cannot be so many under the present distresses of the kingdom, but this being granted, there will remain an hundred and seventy thousand breeders. I again subtract fifty thousand for those women who miscarry, or whose children die by accident or disease within the year. There only remain an hundred and twenty thousand children of poor parents annually born: The question therefore is, how this number shall be reared, and provided for, which, as I have already said, under the present situation of affairs, is utterly impossible by all the methods hitherto proposed, for we can neither employ them in handicraft, or agriculture; we neither build houses (I mean in the country), nor cultivate land: they can very seldom pick up a livelihood by stealing till they arrive at six years old, except where they are of towardly parts, although I confess they learn the rudiments much earlier, during which time they can however be properly looked upon only as probationers, as I have been informed by a principal gentleman in the County of Cavan, who protested to me that he never knew above one or two instances under the age of six, even in a part of the kingdom so renowned for the quickest proficiency in that art.

I am assured by our merchants that a boy or a girl, before twelve years old, is no saleable commodity, and even when they come to this age, they will not yield above three pounds, or three pounds and a half-a-crown at most on the Exchange, which cannot turn to account either to the parents of the kingdom, the charge of nutriment and rags having been at least four times that value.

I shall now therefore humbly propose my own thoughts, which I hope will not be liable to the least objection.

I have been assured by a very knowing American of my acquaintance in London, that a young healthy child well nursed is at a year old a most delicious, nourishing, and wholesome food, whether stewed, roasted, baked, or boiled, and I make no doubt that it will equally serve in a fricassee, or a ragout.

I do therefore humbly offer it to public consideration, that of the hundred and twenty thousand children already computed, twenty thousand may be reserved for breed, whereof only one fourth part to be males, which is more than we allow to sheep, black-cattle, or swine, and my reason is that these children are seldom the fruits of marriage, a circumstance not much regarded by our savages, therefore one male will be sufficient to serve four females. That the remaining hundred thousand may at a year old be offered in sale to the persons of quality, and fortune, through the kingdom, always advising the mother to let them suck plentifully in the last month, so as to render them plump, and fat for a good table. A child will make two dishes at an entertainment for friends, and when the family dines alone, the fore or hind quarters will make a reasonable dish, and seasoned with a little pepper or salt will be very good boiled on the fourth day, especially in winter.

I have reckoned upon a medium, that a child just born will weigh 12 pounds, and in a solar year if tolerably nursed increaseth to 28 pounds.

I grant this food will be somewhat dear, and therefore very

proper for landlords, who, as they have already devoured most of the parents, seem to have the best title to the children.

Infants' flesh will be in season throughout the year, but more plentiful in March, and a little before and after, for we are told by a grave author, an eminent French physician, that fish being a prolific diet, there are more children born in Roman Catholic countries about nine months after Lent than at any other season; therefore reckoning a year after Lent, the markets will be more glutted than usual, because the number of Popish infants is at least three to one in this kingdom, and therefore it will have one other collateral advantage by lessening the number of Papists among us.

I have already computed the charge of nursing a beggar's child (in which list I reckon all cottagers, labourers, and four-fifths of the farmers) to be about two shillings per annum, rags included, and I believe no gentleman would repine to give ten shillings for the carcass of a good fat child, which, as I have said, will make four dishes of excellent nutritive meat, when he hath only some particular friend or his own family to dine with him. Thus the Squire will learn to be a good landlord, and grow popular among his tenants, the mother will have eight shillings net profit, and be fit for work till she produces another child.

Those who are more thrifty (as I must confess the times require) may flay the carcass; the skin of which, artificially dressed, will make admirable gloves for ladies, and summer boots for fine gentlemen.

As to our City of Dublin, shambles may be appointed for this purpose, in the most convenient parts of it, and butchers we may be assured will not be wanting, although I rather recommend buying the children alive, and dressing them hot from the knife, as we do roasting pigs.

A very worthy person, a true lover of this country, and whose virtues I highly esteem, was lately pleased, in discoursing on this matter, to offer a refinement upon my scheme. He said that many gentlemen of this kingdom, having of late destroyed their deer, he conceived that the want of venison might be well supplied by the bodies of young lads and maidens, not exceeding fourteen years of age, nor under twelve, so great a number of

both sexes in every country being now ready to starve, for want
of work and service: and these to be disposed of by their parents if alive, or otherwise by their nearest relations. But with
due deference to so excellent a friend, and so deserving a pa-
triot, I cannot be altogether in his sentiments; for as to the
males, my American acquaintance assured me from frequent
experience that their flesh was generally tough and lean, like
that of our schoolboys, by continual exercise, and their taste
disagreeable, and to fatten them would not answer the charge.
Then as to the females, it would, I think with humble submis-
sion, be a loss to the public, because they soon would become
breeders themselves: And besides, it is not improbable that
some scrupulous people might be apt to censure such a practice (although indeed very unjustly) as a little bordering upon
cruelty, which, I confess, hath always been with me the strongest objection against any project, however so well intended.

But in order to justify my friend, he confessed that this expe-
dient was put into his head by the famous Psalmanazer, a native of the island Formosa, who came from thence to London,
above twenty years ago, and in conversation told my friend
that in his country when any young person happened to be put
to death, the executioner sold the carcass to persons of quality,
as a prime dainty, and that, in his time, the body of a plump girl
of fifteen, who was crucified for an attempt to poison the em-
peror, was sold to his Imperial Majesty's Prime Minister of
State, and other great Mandarins of the Court, in joints from
the gibbet, at four hundred crowns. Neither indeed can I deny
that if the same use were made of several plump young girls in
this town, who, without one single groat to their fortunes, cannot stir abroad without a chair, and appear at the playhouse,
and assemblies in foreign fineries, which they never will pay
for, the kingdom would not be the worse.

Some persons of a desponding spirit are in great concern
about that vast number of poor people, who are aged, diseased,
or maimed, and I have been desired to employ my thoughts
what course may be taken to ease the nation of so grievous an
encumbrance. But I am not in the least pain upon that matter,
because it is very well known that they are every day dying,

and rotting, by cold, and famine, and filth, and vermin, as fast as can be reasonably expected. And as to the younger labourers they are now in almost as hopeful a condition. They cannot get work, and consequently pine away for want of nourishment, to a degree, that if any time they are accidentally hired to common labour, they have not strength to perform it; and thus the country and themselves are happily delivered from the evils to come.

I have too long digressed, and therefore shall return to my subject. I think the advantages by the proposal which I have made are obvious and many, as well as of the highest importance.

For first, as I have already observed, it would greatly lessen the number of Papists, with whom we are yearly over-run, being the principal breeders of the nation, as well as our most dangerous enemies, and who stay at home on purpose with a design to deliver the kingdom to the Pretender, hoping to take their advantage by the absence of so many good Protestants, who have chosen rather to leave their country than stay at home, and pay tithes against their conscience to an Episcopal curate.

Secondly, the poorer tenants will have something valuable of their own, which, by law be made liable to distress, and help to pay their landlord's rent, their corn and cattle being already seized, and money a thing unknown.

Thirdly, whereas the maintenance of an hundred thousand children, from two years old, and upwards, cannot be computed at less than ten shillings a piece per annum, the nation's stock will be thereby increased fifty thousand pounds per annum, besides the profit of a new dish, introduced to the tables of all gentlemen of fortune in the kingdom, who have any refinement in taste, and the money will circulate among ourselves, the goods being entirely of our own growth and manufacture.

Fourthly, the constant breeders, besides the gain of eight shillings sterling per annum, by the sale of their children, will be rid of the charge of maintaining them after the first year.

Fifthly, this food would likewise bring great custom to taverns, where the vintners will certaintly be so prudent as to procure the best receipts for dressing it up to perfection, and consequently have their houses frequented by all the fine gentlemen, who justly value themselves upon their knowledge in good eating; and a skillful cook, who understands how to oblige his guests, will contrive to make it as expensive as they please.

Sixthly, this would be a great inducement to marriage, which all wise nations have either encouraged by rewards, or enforced by laws and penalties. It would increase the care and tenderness of mothers toward their children, when they were sure of a settlement for life, to the poor babes, provided in some sort by the public to their annual profit instead of expense. We should see an honest emulation among the married women, which of them could bring the fattest child to the market, men would become as fond of their wives during the time of their pregnancy, as they are now of their mares in foal, their cows in calf, or sows when they are ready to farrow, nor offer to beat or kick them (as it is too frequent a practice) for fear of a miscarriage.

Many other advantages might be enumerated: For instance, the addition of some thousand carcasses in our exportation of barrelled beef; the propagation of swine's flesh, and improvement in the art of making good bacon, so much wanted among us by the great destruction of pigs, too frequent at our tables, which are no way comparable in taste or magnificence to a well-grown, fat yearling child, which roasted whole will make a considerable figure at a Lord Mayor's feast, or any other public entertainment. But this and many others I omit, being studious of brevity.

Supposing that one thousand families in this city would be constant customers for infants' flesh, besides others who might have it at merry-meetings, particularly weddings and christenings, I compute that Dublin would take off annually about twenty thousand carcasses, and the rest of the kingdom (where probably they will be sold somewhat cheaper) the remaining eight thousand.

I can think of no one objection that will possibly be raised

against this proposal, unless it should be urged that the number
of people will be thereby much lessened in the kingdom. This I
freely own, and it was indeed one principal design in offering it
to the world. I desire the reader will observe, that I calculate
my remedy for this one individual Kingdom of Ireland, and for
no other that ever was, is, or, I think, ever can be upon earth.
Therefore let no man talk to me of other expedients: Of taxing
our absentees at five shillings a pound: Of using neither
clothes, nor household furniture, except what is of our own
growth and manufacture: Of utterly rejecting the materials and
instruments that promote foreign luxury: Of curing the expen-
siveness of pride, vanity, idleness, and gaming in our women:
Of introducing a vein of parsimony, prudence, and temper-
ance: Of learning to love our Country, wherein we differ even
from LAPLANDERS, and the inhabitants of TOPINAMBOO:
Of quitting our animosities and factions, nor act any longer like
the Jews, who were murdering one another at the very moment
their city was taken: Of being a little cautious not to sell our
country and consciences for nothing: Of teaching landlords to
have at least one degree of mercy toward their tenants. Lastly,
of putting a spirit of honesty, industry, and skill into our shopkeepers, who if a resolution could now be taken to buy only our
native goods, would immediately unite to cheat and exact upon
us in the price, the measure, and the goodness, nor could ever
yet be brought to make one fair proposal of just dealing, though
often and earnestly invited to it.

Therefore I repeat, let no man talk to me of these and the like
expedients, till he hath at least some glimpse of hope that there
will ever be some hearty and sincere attempt to put them in
practice.

But as to myself, having been wearied out for many years
with offering vain, idle, visionary thoughts, and at length utterly despairing of success, I fortunately fell upon this proposal,
which as it is wholly new, so it hath something solid and real, of
no expense and little trouble, full in our own power, and
whereby we can incur no danger in disobliging ENGLAND.
For this kind of commodity will not bear exportation, the flesh

being too tender a consistence to admit a long continuance in salt, although perhaps I could name a country which would be glad to eat up our whole nation without it.

After all I am not so violently bent upon my own opinion as to reject any offer, proposed by wise men, which shall be found equally innocent, cheap, easy, and effectual. But before something of that kind shall be advanced in contradiction to my scheme, and offering a better, I desire the author, or authors, will be pleased maturely to consider two points. First, as things now stand, how they will be able to find food and raiment for an hundred thousand useless mouths and backs. And secondly, there being a round million of creatures in human figure, throughout this kingdom, whose whole subsistence put into a common stock would leave them in debt two millions of pounds sterling; adding those, who are beggars by profession, to the bulk of farmers, cottagers, and labourers with their wives and children, who are beggars in effect. I desire those politicians, who dislike my overture, and may perhaps be so bold to attempt an answer, that they will first ask the parents of these mortals whether they would not at this day think it a great happiness to have been sold for food at a year old, in the manner I prescribe, and thereby have avoided such a perpetual scene of misfortunes as they have since gone through, by the oppression of landlords, the impossibility of paying rent without money or trade, the want of common sustenance, with neither house nor clothes to cover them from the inclemencies of the weather, and the most inevitable prospect of entailing the like, or greater miseries upon their breed for ever.

I profess in the sincerity of my heart that I have not the least personal interest in endeavoring to promote this necessary work, having no other motive than the public good of my country, by advancing our trade, providing for infants, relieving the poor, and giving some pleasure to the rich. I have no children by which I can propose to get a single penny; the youngest being nine years old, and my wife past child-bearing.

The easiest form of satire is to call a person names. This does little more than demonstrate your own anger. The satirist who is obviously controlled by the emotion of anger is like a prize fighter who forgets his training, his fight plan, and the rules of the ring. Though he may knock his opponent down and out, he hardly wins the fight. Good satire means above all else intellectual control.

Swift's "Modest Proposal" is calmly, almost lightly written, yet it is a savagely bitter piece of writing. This is achieved through the skillful use of irony. The reader realizes the impossibility of the solution presented, yet he also sees that the principles of the proposal are the principles which actually govern the relationship between landlord and peasant, rich and poor. The uneducated or economically handicapped person is considered inhuman, a beast of sorts. The way to reduce an animal population is to kill the young; if they can be eaten, so much the better. By carrying such principles to their logical extremes, Swift exposes their basic evil and the hypocrisy of their proponents. His own unfailing composure and self-confidence emphasize the blindness and inhumanity of people who would espouse such a way of life in any degree.

Irony may be said to be being serious about something we do not actually believe. The trick is to appear really serious.

QUESTIONS

1. How would you characterize the language in this essay? Does it resemble the language of any profession or scholarly pursuit?
2. Make a loose outline of the essay. How does its structure contribute to its satire?
3. How might the essay have become too obvious?

In his novel *1919* John Dos Passos uses another kind of satire in writing about the selection of the body of the Unknown Soldier.[3] The writer seems to jump from subject to subject. The form mirrors this, but in the end there is a strong unity. What is in this

[3] John Dos Passos, *1919* (New York: Harcourt, Brace & World, 1932), pp. 407–412.

piece besides scepticism? What makes the anger wider than the immediate source?

Whereasthe Congressoftheunitedstates byaconcurrentreso-lutionadoptedon the4thdayofmarch lastauthorizedthe Secre-taryofwar to cause to be brought to theunitedstatesthe body of an American whowasamemberoftheamericanexpeditionary-forcesineurope wholosthislifeduringtheworldwarandwhose-identityhasnotbeenestablished for burial inthememorialam-phitheatreofthe nationalcemeteryatarlingtonvirginia

In the tarpaper morgue at Chalons-sur-Marne in the reek of chloride of lime and the dead, they picked out the pine box that held all that was left of

enie menie minie moe plenty other pine boxes stacked up there containing what they'd scraped up of Richard Roe

and otherperson or persons unknown. Only one can go. How did they pick John Doe?

Make sure he aint a dinge, boys,

make sure he aint a guinea or a kike,

how can you tell a guy's a hundredpercent when all you've got's a gunnysack full of bones, bronze buttons stamped with the screaming eagle and a pair of roll puttees?

. . . and the gagging chloride and the puky dirt-stench of the yearold dead . . .

The day withal was too meaningful and tragic for applause. Silence, tears songs and prayer, muffled drums and soft music were the instrumentalities today of national approbation.

John Doe was born (thudding din of blood in love into the shuddering soar of a man and a woman alone indeed together lurching into

and ninemonths sick drowse waking into scared agony and the pain and blood and messof birth). John Doe was born

and raised in Brooklyn, in Memphis, near the lakefront in Cleveland, Ohio, in the stench of the stockyards in Ehi, on Bea-con Hill, in an old brick house in Alexandria Virginia, on Telegraph Hill, in a halftimbered Tudor cottage in Portland the city of roses,

in the Lying-In Hospital old Morgan endowed on Stuyvesant Square,

across the railroad tracks, out near the country club, in a shack cabin tenement apartmenthouse exclusive residential suburb;

scion of one of the best families in the social register, won first prize in the baby parade at Coronado Beach, was marbles champion of the Little Rock grammarschools, crack basketballplayer at the Booneville High, quarterback at the State Reformatory, having saved the sheriff's kid from drowning in the Little Missouri River was invited to Washington to be photographed shaking hands with the President on the White House steps;—

though this was a time of mourning, such an assemblage necessarily has about it a touch of color. In the boxes are seen the court uniforms of foreign diplomats, the gold braid of our own and foreign fleets and armies, the black of the conventional morning dress of American statesmen, the varicolored furs and outdoor wrapping garments of mothers and sisters come to mourn, the drab and blue of soldiers and sailors, the glitter of musical instruments and the white and black of a vested choir

—busboy harveststiff hogcaller boyscout champeen cornshucker of Western Kansas bellhop at the United States Hotel at Saratoga Springs office boy callboy fruiter telephone lineman longshoreman lumberjack plumber's helper,

worked for an exterminating company in Union City, filled pipes in an opium joint in Trenton, N.J.

Y.M.C.A. secretary, express agent, truckdriver, fordmechanic, sold books in Denver Colorado: Madam would you be willing to help a young man work his way through college?

President Harding, with a reverence seemingly more significant because of his high temporal station, concluded his speech:

We are met today to pay the impersonal tribute;

the name of him whose body lies before us took flight with his imperishable soul . . .

as a typical soldier of this representative democracy he fought and died believing in the indisputable justice of his country's cause . . .

by raising his right hand and asking the thousands within the sound of his voice to join in the prayer:

Our Father which art in heaven hallowed be thy name . . .

Naked he went into the army;

they weighed you, measured you, looked for flat feet, squeezed your penis to see if you had clap, looked up your anus to see if you had piles, counted your teeth, made you cough, listened to your heart and lungs, made you read the letters on the card, charted your urine and your intelligence.

gave you a service record for a future (imperishable soul)

and an identification tag stamped with your serial number to hang around your neck, issued O D regulation equipment, a condiment can and a copy of the articles of war.

Atten'SHUN suck in your gut you c——r wipe that smile off your face eyes right wattja tink dis is a choirch-social? For-war-D'ARCH.

John Doe

and Richard Roe and other person or person unknown

drilled hiked, manual of arms, ate slum, learned to salute, to soldier, to loaf in the latrines, forbidden to smoke on deck, overseas guard duty, forty men and eight horses, shortarm inspection and the ping of shrapnel and the shrill bullets combing the air and the sorehead woodpeckers the machineguns mud cooties gasmasks and the itch.

Say feller tell me how I can get back to my outfit.

John Doe had a head

for twentyodd years intensely the nerves of the eyes the ears the palate the tongue the fingers the toes the armpits, the nerves warmfelling under the skin charged the coiled brain with hurt sweet warm cold mine must dont sayings print headlines:

Thou shalt not the multiplication table long division, Now is the time for all good men knocks but once at a young man's door, It's a great life if Ish gebibbel, The first five years'll be the Safety First, Suppose a hun tried to rape your my country right or wrong, Catch 'em young, What he dont know wont treat 'em rough, Tell'em nothin, He got what was coming to him he got his, This is a white man's country, Kick the bucket, Gone west, If you dont like it you can croaked him

Say buddy cant you tell me how I can get back to my outfit?

Cant help jumpin when them things go off, give me the trots them things do. I lost my identification tag swimmin in the Marne, roughhousin with a guy while we was waitin to be deloused, in bed with a girl named Jeanne (Love moving picture wet French postcard dream began with saltpeter in the coffee and ended at the propho station);—

Say soldier for chrissake cant you tell me how I can get back to my outfit?

John Doe's

heart pumped blood:

alive thudding silence of blood in your ears

down in the clearing in the Oregon forest where the punkins were punkincolor pouring into the blood through the eyes and the fallcolored trees and the bronze hoopers were hopping through the dry grass, where tiny striped snails hung on the underside of the blades and the flies hummed, wasps droned, bumblebees buzzed, and the woods smelt of wine and mushrooms and apples, homey smell of fall pouring into the blood

and I dropped the tin hat and the seaty pack and lay flat with the dogday sun licking my throat and adamsapple and the tight skin over the breastbone.

The shell had his number on it.

The blood ran into the ground.

The service record dropped out of the filing cabinet where the quartermaster sergeant got blotto that time they had to pack up and leave the billets in a hurry.

The identification tag was in the bottom of the Marne.

The blood ran into the ground, the brains oozed out of the cracked skull and were licked up by the trenchrats, the belly swelled and raised a generation of bluebottle flies,

and the incorruptible skeleton,
and the scraps of dried viscera and skin bundled in khaki
they took to Chalons-sur-Marne
and laid it out neat in a pine coffin
and took it home to God'sCountry on a battleship
and buried it in a sarcophagus in the Memorial Amphithe-
atre in the Arlington National Cemetery
and draped the Old Glory over it
and the bugler played taps
and Mr. Harding prayed to God and the diplomats and the
generals and the admirals and the brasshats and the politicians
and the handsomely dressed ladies out of the society column of
the *Washington Post* stood up solemn
and thought how beautiful sad Old Glory God's Country it
was to have the bugler play taps and the three volleys made
their ears ring.
Where his chest ought to have been they pinned the Con-
gressional Medal,
the D.S.C., the Medaille Militaire, the Belgian Croix de
Guerre, the Italian gold medal, the Vitutea Militara sent by
Queen Marie of Rumania, the Czechoslovak war cross, the Vir-
tuti Militari of the Poles, a wreath sent by Hamilton Fish, Jr., of
New York, and a little wampum presented by a deputation of
Arizona redskins in warpaint and feathers. All the Washing-
tonians brought flowers.

Woodrow Wilson brought a bouquet of poppies.

The central device of Dos Passos' "Body of an American" is that
of contrast. On one hand we see the machinery of government at
work, bringing dignity to death, attempting to make it seem sweet
and fitting to die for one's country. But the wreaths, the pomp, the
ceremony, the top hats of the officials are in vicious contrast to the
scraps in the pine box, the scraps of Richard Roe.
The language of the biography is now grave, now harsh, now
repellently down-to-earth; and then suddenly so poetic that again
we see the contrast, not only see it but are hit hard by the horror of
the brains oozing out of the cracked skull while only a moment

before we were lost in the wood-smell of wine and mushrooms and apples, the homey odors of an American autumn.

The anger at what is lost in the waste of war surges through the essay under the skill of the writer. The unknown soldier becomes someone we know. Finally he becomes someone we are, gaining in identity through the complicated structure of the piece, the counterpoint of language and viewpoint the writer has created out of his anger. Read through the sketch again, listing the contrasts between the boy who sold books in Denver and the scraps of flesh in the box that is brought home.

QUESTIONS

1. How are clichés used effectively?
2. What is the purpose of repeatedly mentioning the soldier who can't find his outfit and the imperishable soul? How do these subjects develop through the writing?
3. Why does Dos Passos mention the specific gifts at the end?

Protest movements are almost inseparable from slogans and clichés. These undoubtedly have a certain kind of value in their given situation. But stronger than these are words which give a real sense of why the protest exists. Below, in an essay titled "12 Million Black Voices," Richard Wright attempts to convey a sense of slum life through the careful use of repetition.[4]

They say our presence in their neighborhoods lowers the value of their property. We do not understand why this should be so. We are poor; but they were once poor, too. They make up their minds, because others tell them to, that they must move at once if we rent an apartment near them. Having been warned against us by the Bosses of the Buildings, having heard tall

---

[4] Richard Wright, *Twelve Million Black Voices* (New York: Viking Press, 1941), pp. 103–111.

tales about us, about how "bad" we are, they react emotionally as though we had the plague when we move into their neighborhoods. Is it any wonder, then, that their homes are suddenly and drastically reduced in value? They hastily abandon them, sacrificing them to the Bosses of the Buildings, the men who instigate all this for whatever profit they can get in real-estate sales. And in the end we are the "fall guys." When the white folks move, the Bosses of the Buildings let the property to us at rentals higher than those the whites paid.

And the Bosses of the Buildings take these old houses and convert them into "kitchenettes," and then rent them to us at rates so high that they make fabulous fortunes before the houses are too old for habitation. What they do is this: they take, say, a seven-room apartment, which rents for $50 a month to whites, and cut it up into seven small apartments, of one room each; they install one small gas stove and one small sink in each room. The Bosses of the Buildings rent these kitchenettes to us at the rate of, say, $6 a week. Hence, the same apartment for which white people—who can get jobs anywhere and who receive higher wages than we—pay $50 a month is rented to us for $42 a week! And because there are not enough houses for us to live, because we have been used to sleeping several in a room on the plantations in the South, we rent these kitchenettes and are glad to get them. These kitchenettes are our havens from the plantations in the South. We have fled the wrath of Queen Cotton and we are tired.

Sometimes five or six of us live in a one-room kitchenette, a place where simple folk such as we should never be held captive. A war sets up in our emotions: one part of our feelings tells us that it is good to be in the city, that we have a chance at life here, that we need but turn a corner to become a stranger, that we no longer need bow and dodge at the sight of the Lords of the Land. Another part of our feelings tells us that, in terms of worry and strain, the cost of living in the kitchenettes is too high, that the city heaps too much responsibility upon us and gives too little security in return.

The kitchenette is the author of the glad tidings that new

suckers are in town, ready to be cheated, plundered, and put in their places.

The kitchenette is our prison, our death sentence without a trial, the new form of mob violence that assaults not only the lone individual, but all of us, in its ceaseless attacks.

The kitchenette, with its filth and foul air, with its one toilet for thirty or more tenants, kills our black babies so fast that in many cities twice as many of them die as white babies.

The kitchenette is the seed bed for scarlet fever, dysentery, typhoid, tuberculosis, gonorrhea, syphilis, pneumonia, and malnutrition.

The kitchenette scatters death so widely among us that our death rate exceeds our birth rate, and if it were not for the trains and autos bringing us daily into the city from the plantations, we black folks who dwell in northern cities would die out entirely over the course of a few years.

The kitchenette, with its crowded rooms and incessant bedlam, provides an enticing place for crimes of all sort—crimes against women and children or any stranger who happens to stray into its dark hallways. The noise of our living, boxed in stone and steel, is so loud that even a pistol shot is smothered.

The kitchenette throws desperate and unhappy people into an unbearable closeness of association, thereby increasing latent friction, giving birth to never-ending quarrels of recrimination, accusation, and vindictiveness, producing warped personalities.

The kitchenette injects pressure and tension into our individual personalities, making many of us give up the struggle, walk off and leave wives, husbands, and even children behind to shift as best they can.

The kitchenette creates thousands of one-room homes where our black mothers sit, deserted, with their children about their knees.

The kitchenette blights the personalities of our growing children, disorganizes them, blinds them to hope, creates problems whose effects can be traced in the characters of its child victims for years afterward.

The kitchenette jams our farm girls, while still in their teens, into rooms with men who are restless and stimulated by the noise and lights of the city; and more of our girls have bastard babies than the girls in any other sections of the city.

The kitchenette fills our black boys with longing and restlessness, urging them to run off from home, to join together with other restless black boys in gangs, that brutal form of city courage.

The kitchenette piles up mountains of profits for the Bosses of the Buildings and makes them ever more determined to keep things as they are.

The kitchenette reaches out with fingers full of golden bribes to the officials of the city, persuading them to allow old firetraps to remain standing and occupied long after they should have been torn down.

The kitchenette is the funnel through which our pulverized lives flow to ruin and death on the city pavements, at a profit.
. . .

Richard Wright's protest against slum conditions is written in the first person, but not the first-person singular. Wright's choice of the editorial *we* identifies the protest as belonging to a group rather than one irate individual. However, in doing this he has to be extremely careful to keep himself as an individual out of the writing; otherwise the illusion that this protest is the voice of many people, a chorus, would be destroyed.

The problem here is how to be concrete and general at the same time.

Lengthy expositions of cause and effect would lose the reader. The author wastes no time in focusing his essay on conditions that can be seen and heard and smelled. His history of the slum is as brief as possible; then we come to the kitchenette, which in this essay is as ever present and oppressive as it is in reality. By a measured and rhythmical repetition of the image of the kitchenette, he maintains a constant and concrete frame of reference. The tightness, the squalor, the noise, the crowding of the kitchenette are qualities which pervade the whole of slum life, inside or out.

The voice in which this is written has a lot to do with the effectiveness of the repetition. It is like a chant, a chorus of angry people. They are not literary people and the language is not literary. The repetition, the enumeration comes to us like a string of hot curses. Yet this could not have been written by just anyone. There is more to this essay than simple protest. There are no abstract condemnations, no wild name-calling. First there is the careful focus on the kitchenette. Then the economy of detail—quick, sensual, typical. Finally there is the underlying idea that the kitchenette exists not as an unalterable misery, not as fate, but as part of a corrupt society. We are introduced to this idea in the first paragraph where the bosses take over the neighborhood. It reappears throughout the essay in many forms and finds its strongest statement in the last sentence where it is placed beside the human tragedy of the kitchenette—the ruin and death of human beings for a profit.

QUESTIONS

1. How does Wright vary his repetition and actually use it to develop his themes of injustice and suffering?
2. How would you characterize the language, the choice of diction? Why did the author make this choice?
3. How does the mention of money help develop the main themes?

Clarence Darrow was one of America's most famous lawyers. He knew the law and he knew the human beings who made it and broke it. Because of the people and principles involved, he took on some of the most difficult cases of his day. When Leopold and Loeb, two brilliant University of Chicago students, killed a young boy, apparently for "thrills," Darrow defended them. What follows is part of his final plea for mercy.[5]

[5] Clarence Darrow, *Darrow for the Defense* (New York: Simon and Schuster, 1957), pp. 82–87.

Now, Your Honor, I have spoken about the war. I believed in
it. I don't know whether I was crazy or not. Sometimes I think
perhaps I was. I approved of it; I joined in the general cry of
madness and despair. I urged men to fight. I was safe because I
was too old to go. I was like the rest. What did they do? Right
or wrong, justifiable or unjustifiable—which I need not discuss
today—it changed the world. For four long years the civilized
world was engaged in killing men. Christian against Christian;
barbarians uniting with Christians to kill Christians; anything
to kill. It was taught in every school, aye in the Sunday schools.
The little children played at war. The toddling children on the
street. Do you suppose this world has ever been the same since
then? How long, Your Honor, will it take for the world to get
back to the humane emotions that were slowly growing before
the war? How long will it take the calloused hearts of men before the scars of hatred and cruelty shall be removed?

We read of killing one hundred thousand men in a day. We
read about it and we rejoiced in it—if it was the other fellows
who were killed. We were fed on flesh and drank blood. Even
down to the prattling babe. I need not tell Your Honor this, because you know; I need not tell you how many upright, honorable young boys have come into this court charged with murder, some saved and some sent to their death, boys who fought
in this war and learned to place a cheap value on human life.
You know it and I know it. These boys were brought up in it.
The tales of death were in their homes, their playgrounds, their
schools; they were in the newspapers that they read; it was a
part of the common frenzy. What was a life? It was nothing. It
was the least sacred thing in existence and these boys were
trained to this cruelty.

It will take fifty years to wipe it out of the human heart, if
ever. I know this, that after the Civil War in 1865, crimes of this
sort increased marvelously. No one needs to tell me that crime
has no cause. It has as definite a cause as any other disease, and
I know that out of the hatred and bitterness of the Civil War
crime increased as America had never known it before. I know
that growing out of the Napoleonic wars there was an era of

crime such as Europe had never seen before. I know that Europe is going through the same experience today; I know it has followed every war; and I know it has influenced these boys so that life was not the same to them as it would have been if the world had not been made red with blood. I protest against the crimes and mistakes of society being visited upon them. All of us have our share of it. I have mine. I cannot tell and I shall never know how many words of mine might have given birth to cruelty in place of love and kindness and charity.

Your Honor knows that in this very court crimes of violence have increased, growing out of the war. Not necessarily by those who fought but by those that learned that blood was cheap, and human life was cheap, and if the State could take it lightly why not the boy? There are causes for this terrible crime. There are causes, as I have said, for everything that happens in the world. War is a part of it; education is a part of it; birth is a part of it; money is a part of it—all these conspired to compass the destruction of these two poor boys.

Has the court any right to consider anything but these two boys? The State says that Your Honor has a right to consider the welfare of the community, as you have. If the welfare of the community would be benefited by taking these lives, well and good. I think it would work evil that no-one could measure. Has Your Honor a right to consider the families of these two defendants? I have been sorry, and I am sorry for the bereavement of Mr. and Mrs. Franks, for those broken ties that cannot be healed. All I can hope and wish is that some good may come from it all. But as compared with the families of Leopold and Loeb, the Franks are to be envied—and everyone knows it.

I do not know how much salvage there is in these two boys. I hate to say it in their presence, but what is there to look forward to? I do not know but that Your Honor would be merciful if you tied a rope around their necks and let them die; merciful to them, but not merciful to civilization, and not merciful to those who would be left behind. To spend the balance of their lives in prison is mighty little to look forward to, if anything. Is it anything? They may have the hope that as the years roll around they might be released. I do not know. I do not know. I will be honest with this court as I have tried to be from the beginning. I know that these boys are not fit to be at large. I believe they will not be until they pass through the next stage of life, at forty-five or fifty. Whether they will be then, I cannot tell. I am sure of this; that I will not be here to help them. So far as I am concerned, it is over.

I would not tell this court that I do not hope that some time, when life and age have changed their bodies, as it does, and has changed their emotions, as it does—that they may once more return to life. I would be the last person on earth to close the door to any human being that lives, and least of all to my clients. But what have they to look forward to? Nothing. And I think here of the stanza of Housman:

> Now hollow fires burn out to black,
> And lights are fluttering low:
> Square your shoulders, lift your pack
> And leave your friends and go.

> O never fear, lads, naught's to dread,
> Look not left nor right:
> In all the endless road you tread
> There's nothing but the night.

I care not, Your Honor, whether the march begins at the gallows or when the gates of Joliet close upon them, there is nothing but the night, and that is little for any human being to expect.

But there are others to consider. Here are these two families, who have led honest lives, who will bear the name that they bear, and future generations must carry it on.

Here is Leopold's father—and this boy was the pride of his life. He watched him, he cared for him, he worked for him; the boy was brilliant and accomplished, he educated him, and he thought that fame and position awaited him, as it should have awaited. It is a hard thing for a father to see his life's hopes crumble into dust.

Should he be considered? Should his brothers be considered? Will it do society any good or make your life safer, or any human being's life safer, if it should be handed down from generation to generation, that this boy, their kin, died upon the scaffold?

And Loeb's, the same. Here are the faithful uncle and brother, who have watched here day by day, while Dickie's father and his mother are too ill to stand this terrific strain, and shall be waiting for a message which means more to them than it can mean to you or me. Shall these be taken into account in this general bereavement?

Have they any rights? Is there any reason, Your Honor, why their proud names and all the future generations that bear them shall have this bar sinister written across them? How many boys and girls, how many unborn children, will feel it? It is bad enough, however it is. But it's not yet death on the scaffold. It's not that. And I ask Your Honor, in addition to all that I have said, to save two honorable families from a disgrace that never ends, and which could be of no avail to help any human being that lives.

Your Honor stands between the past and the future. You may hang these boys; you may hang them by the neck until they are dead. But in doing it you will turn your face toward the past. In doing it you are making it harder for every other boy who, in ignorance and darkness, must grope his way through the mazes which only childhood knows. In doing it you will make it harder for unborn children. You may save them and make it easier for every child that sometime may stand where these boys stand. You will make it easier for every human being with an aspiration and a vision and a hope and a fate.

I am pleading for the future; I am pleading for a time when hatred and cruelty will not control the hearts of men, when we can learn by reason and judgment and understanding and faith that all life is worth saving, and that mercy is the highest attribute of man.

I was reading last night of the aspiration of the old Persian poet, Omar Khayyam. It appealed to me as the highest that I can vision. I wish it was in my heart, and I wish it was in the hearts of all.

> So I be written in the Book of Love,
> I do not care about that Book above;
> Erase my name or write it as you will,
> So I be written in the Book of Love.

Put yourself in Darrow's place. You have two very bright boys guilty of a horrible crime, but you know that crimes like theirs do not simply "happen" out of nothing. Snuffing out their lives is not a remedy for any crime, past or future. The boys themselves will be in jail for life if they do not die. So Darrow, a keen observer of society and personality, began to build a picture of how these two boys related to their society. Perhaps he began by thinking of their crime as an act of violence. He may have worked from there to manifestations of violence in "normal" society. The pattern or picture he arrived at may not be acceptable to everyone; however, it convincingly conveyed to the court the fact that Leopold and Loeb were human beings and members of the same society as the court itself.

QUESTIONS

1. How does Darrow establish a theme and develop it?
2. This speech was made shortly after World War I. Do you think the language or content would have to be changed today? How?
3. Think of someone you know who has committed a crime of any sort—even a traffic violation. Suppose you were trying to explain the origin of the crime. How would you organize your material?

Does the student theme that follows show what anger is, and does it carry to the reader a sense of the writer's own hopeless rage over not being able to cash the check? In reading this paper, ask yourself if you would have reacted in the manner of the writer. Ask, too, why he started where he did, and whether he has written each paragraph without digressing from his main themes.

The most important question is what sort of picture the theme gives of the narrator. To some readers the writer seemed to have succeeded only in making his image of himself immature, unattractive, and deserving of worse treatment than the supermarket manager gave him.

Super market managers are the worst people alive; believe me. Ever since I tried to get a job in a grocery store at the age of sixteen, I've loathed them. I'd walk into a store and find the manager bagging groceries, pushing a broom, marking groceries, or doing some other associated task. I'd ask him if he needed any help at the store, and he'd tell me that he had too much help already. That's why he was doing that type of work. Sure. About every super market manager that I've seen was rude, stupid, niggardly, and narrow-minded. I knew one, once, who didn't seem to fit into that groove, but on the other hand, he was a Sunday School teacher, a Baptist Sunday School teacher, so maybe he did. I was only twelve when I knew him. If you get a thrill out of seeing a forty year old man pushing a broom, you're in for a real treat. But if you want to have an intelligent conversation, you're better off talking to a television set.

Because I considered myself somewhat of an expert on the psychology of super market managers, I had mixed feelings as I entered the Colonial Store with the hopes of cashing a check. In half an hour, I was to go home with my girlfriend, and the banks were closed, as it was Saturday, so the Colonial Store was about my only hope. I equated my chances of getting the check cashed by taking into account the fact that the manager was a Sunday School teacher, that I was a student, that the check was relatively small, and that the check was made out to me by my father; I equated about a fifty-fifty chance for success.

A clerk in the store told me that the manager could be found in the fruits section (appropriately enough), so I hiked over there. Sure enough, Mr. Williams was arranging a display of lemons. I approached him. I told him all about my being a student and having to leave town for the weekend. I also pointed out the fact that the check was made out by my father. It didn't have any effect. That stupid fool just told me that he only cashed checks for the amount of the purchase. I tried to use logic and to impress upon him the fact that he was the only person who could help me—trying to bring out the good Samaritan in him (and he wouldn't have to give any wine). It worked; I received a very sincere, apologetic refusal. He suggested a bank downtown. I told him that I didn't have enough time to search for the one bank that might be open. He told me how sorry he was, and I told him that he didn't have any idea how sorry he was. I told old Williams that I really appreciated it and said it in a very sarcastic tone of voice. That stupid man thought I was sincere! As I left, I called him a son-of-a-bitch and hurried off because I knew that I said a "wirty durd." The old trail fox stalked right after me, "Just a minute, son," he said. "I didn't particularly appreciate that."

"Oh, really, I didn't intend for you to." I told him all about my being a student, how I really needed the check cashed, that the check was good, and that it wouldn't hurt him to cash the check for me. This last speech wasn't an effort to get the check cashed, but an effort to show up Williams. God, I despised him! He kept trying to tell me that he just couldn't cash it. I informed him that he could but wouldn't. He conceded my correctness on that point. I walked away, thoroughly disgusted. Old Williams went back to his task of arranging lemons.

What I consider to be one of my main faults is my wit. It's not fast enough. I can come up with some of the choicest comments you've ever seen, but too much of the time I think of these prize comments when it's too late to use them, and I surely can't go up to this guy and say, "You remember about five minutes ago when you said . . . ? Well, here's my answer. . . ." It's ridiculous. Well, that's what happened to me that day after I got into the car and drove away. I really turned mad. In fact, I was so mad that I had to take my shirt off before my collar caught on fire. I looked in the mirror of the car and cursed old Williams out. I told him what a menial job he had and what a menial person he was. I also said that I prayed each night that I wouldn't grow up and be a super market manager.

The writer in this theme conveys the anger and the concrete details well enough, but he has not examined his experience thoroughly before writing. Since the writing is personal, he should have looked more closely at his own motivation and at the manager's side of the story. Only in doing this would he have developed a clear sense of the issues involved. Then he would have been able to see whether he was writing about an injustice or about unjustified anger. As it is, this is never clear.

Perhaps you will say the writer could never have made that examination of motives because he was too immature. If so, then do you deny that self-awareness can be initiated within the individual? One of the values of writing, besides communication, is that it forces us to scrutinize and order and criticize sense impressions, emotions, dreams, and ideas that would otherwise flow in and out of our minds unused.

QUESTIONS

1. Recreate, step by step, the process by which the author decided to write this theme. Include his decision on choosing this particular form.
2. How could the theme be rewritten to defend the narrator against the charge of immaturity and unjustified anger?

ASSIGNMENTS

1. Choose an incident or situation that at one time made you so angry you were unable to react in a practical manner. Write a description of it, using the third-person point of view. Avoid taking sides, yet make your writing show where the blame lay.

2. Does a particular local institution or law make you angry? Criticize the object of your anger in satire or in factual rebuttal. Choose something about which you have more than the usual newspaper and magazine facts.

CHAPTER 8

LOVE AND DELIGHT

Controlling Sentimentality

What we like or love or desire we usually want others to want or understand. Even when in love with another person, where we want no competition, we still want others to see the object of our love with the same heightened emotions we ourselves feel. Herein lies the principal source of trouble for anyone writing about love or desire. We tend to express the emotion in the abstract. We talk about how we feel, not about what we are and see and do. Whether our love is for another person or a landscape, we leap beyond the object of love and force our emotion directly upon the reader.

Children, with their blunt way of seeing things, often think love is "mushy." They, of course, are noticing that people are easily overcome by this emotion and lose their sense of proportion and even of reality. You can remember this from your own childhood. You probably know a number of your friends who have been overcome by this emotion. And when you yourself sit down to write about some form of love that you know, your hardest job will be to maintain accuracy and a sense of what distinguishes your experience from others.

Also, in writing about love or desire, even though you feel what is happening to you has never happened before, you do live in the twentieth century and follow in time many other writers who have experienced love and desire. They have tried to give form to their experience in poetry, novels, and in letters that would convey the heightened emotions they felt. You, as a latecomer, work under a handicap. For as Gertrude Stein said, words like *moon, sea,* and *love* were once words very strongly connected to actual presences, things, actions; but today the poet can no longer just say the word and invoke a strong sense of the thing itself. He has to seek his own new means of making language intense.

Miss Stein cannot tell a writer what to do, only what not to do. She believes you must find your own way of avoiding clichés and broad, meaningless abstractions—*burning passion, true love, throbbing heart strings, one and only, beautiful, wonderful, astonishing.* The list is endless—words that through too frequent usage have become labels for an emotion, not words used for their own meanings.

When one says, "my heart strings throbbed," he simply means his heart was beating faster or that he was excited. He doesn't believe there are strings in the heart. And the words like *beautiful, wonderful* and *marvellous* are too subjective really to describe anything. When we use them we simply demand the reader feel a certain way, feel as we do. He does not know why he should feel that way or why we feel that way. He does not see what the beauty or the wonder is.

These flaws in writing about things we love or desire can usually be lumped under the term *sentimentality*. Sentimentality is a condition in which the writer's emotion enters his writing so strongly that it covers up the real subject or severely distorts it. He asks us to believe in and share his emotion without giving any real proof that we should. What becomes most important in the writing is the emotion itself, not the unique relationship between the writer and his subject. The reader feels as if something is being hidden from him. This is often true. Perhaps the writer is unable to see beneath his own emotion and reveal anything deeper. Perhaps he is afraid to. To be really truthful about things we love can often be a very painful process of discovery. But at its best the act of writing is a discovery for the writer as well as the reader.

The writer's job is not to command his reader to feel and think a certain way. Even if your writing is an argument with a firm conclusion, you cannot expect to bring the reader to your conclusion unless you present the case to him as it exists. If you have nothing to say, you should discover this while you are preparing to write, not after you have already committed yourself to paper and cannot turn back.

This does not mean that you must present the kind of detailed, balanced picture one gets in a scientific report. The process of selecting and editing still plays its important role. You can, if you want, present only the good side of your subject—as long as you are faithful to both your subject and your own feelings. Look at this poem by the English poet Stephen Spender:

TO MY DAUGHTER

Bright clasp of her whole hand around my finger,
My daughter, as we walk together now.
All my life I'll feel a ring invisibly
Circle this bone with shining: when she is grown
Far from today as her eyes are far already.[1]

The poet's feelings for his daughter are quite evident. And to say that he will feel her hand all his life is certainly a subjective statement. But there is nothing in the poem that distorts the relationship between the two people. The poet simply gives us a picture of himself and his daughter and tells us what the result of this moment of consciousness will be. He does not drift off into abstractions in telling us. The poem is grounded in the concrete image of the two hands. When he uses the symbol of the ring, it is a symbol

[1] Stephen Spender, "To My Daughter," *Collected Poems* (New York; Random House, 1955).

that works—the shape of the child's hand *is* a ring and it *is* around one finger as a ring might be. Finally, there is the tension between the feeling of closeness that occasions the poem and the poet's awareness that despite this closeness there remains an indestructible gulf between any two people, even those who share love.

Compare the way Spender treats his subject to this stanza by Edgar Guest, who used to be one of America's most popular poets.

> Sue's got a baby now, an' she
> Is like her mother used to be;
> Her face seems prettier, an' her ways
> More settled-like. In these few days
> She's changed completely, an' her smile
> Has taken on the mother-style.
> Her voice is sweeter, an' her words
> Are clear as is the song of birds.
> She still is Sue, but not the same—
> She's different since the baby came.[2]

Do you really see anything important about Sue? How is her face changed? What is the "mother-style?" Can her voice really be "clear as is the song of birds?"

In reading the following selections, try to decide if there is any sentimentality. How do the authors try to avoid it? Why do they succeed or fail? And most important, what distinguishes each expression of love or desire from others? These are the questions you, too, will have to keep in mind as you write.

SELECTIONS

You have probably heard people trying to explain what it is like to be in love. They talk about things that seem to happen inside them, about feelings they have. Usually you think, "I know it's

[2] Edgar Guest, "Sue's Got a Baby," *Just Folks* (Chicago: Reilly and Lee, 1917), p. 134.

real, but he isn't getting across." Perhaps love can be effectively communicated without going "inside" the person in love. Ernest Hemingway was known for his use of "exterior" detail to reveal his characters' emotions. Could a story like the following, "Up in Michigan," be written about any of the people you have known who were in love? [3]

Jim Gilmore came to Hortons Bay from Canada. He bought the blacksmith shop from old man Horton. Jim was short and dark with big mustaches and big hands. He was a good horse-shoer and did not look much like a blacksmith even with his leather apron on. He lived upstairs above the blacksmith shop and took his meals at D. J. Smith's.

Liz Coates worked for Smith's. Mrs. Smith, who was a very large clean woman, said Liz Coates was the neatest girl she'd ever seen. Liz had good legs and always wore clean gingham aprons and Jim noticed that her hair was always neat behind. He liked her face because it was so jolly but he never thought about her.

Liz liked Jim very much. She liked it the way he walked over from the shop and often went to the kitchen door to watch for him to start down the road. She liked it about his mustache. She liked it about how white his teeth were when he smiled. She liked it very much that he didn't look like a black-smith. She liked it how much D. J. Smith and Mrs. Smith liked Jim. One day she found that she liked it the way the hair was black on his arms and how white they were above the tanned line when he washed up in the washbasin outside the house. Liking that made her feel funny.

Hortons Bay, the town, was only five houses on the main road between Boyne City and Charlevoix. There was the general store and post office with a high false front and maybe a wagon hitched out in front, Smith's house, Stroud's house, Dillworth's house, Horton's house and Van Hoosen's house. The houses were in a big grove of elm trees and the road was very sandy.

[3] Ernest Hemingway, "Up in Michigan," *The Short Stories of Ernest Hemingway* (New York: Charles Scribner's Sons, 1938), pp. 81–86.

There was farming country and timber each way up the road. Up the road a ways was the Methodist church and down the road the other direction was the township school. The black-smith shop was painted red and faced the school.

A steep sandy road ran down the hill to the bay through the timber. From Smith's back door you could look out across the woods that ran down to the lake and across the bay. It was very beautiful in the spring and summer, the bay blue and bright and usually whitecaps on the lake out beyond the point from the breeze blowing from Charlevoix and Lake Michigan. From Smith's back door Liz could see ore barges way out in the lake going toward Boyne City. When she looked at them they didn't seem to be moving at all but if she went in and dried some more dishes and then came out again they would be out of sight beyond the point.

All the time now Liz was thinking about Jim Gilmore. He didn't seem to notice her much. He talked about the shop to D. J. Smith and about the Republican Party and about James G. Blaine. In the evenings he read *The Toledo Blade* and the Grand Rapids paper by the lamp in the front room or went out spearing fish in the bay with a jacklight with D. J. Smith. In the fall he and Smith and Charley Wyman took a wagon and tent, grub, axes, their rifles and two dogs and went on a trip to the pine plains beyond Vanderbilt deer hunting. Liz and Mrs. Smith were cooking for four days for them before they started. Liz wanted to make something special for Jim to take but she didn't finally because she was afraid to ask Mrs. Smith for the eggs and flour and afraid if she bought them Mrs. Smith would catch her cooking. It would have been all right with Mrs. Smith but Liz was afraid.

All the time Jim was gone on the deer hunting trip Liz thought about him. It was awful while he was gone. She couldn't sleep well from thinking about him but she discovered it was fun to think about him too. If she let herself go it was better. The night before they were to come back she didn't sleep at all, that is she didn't think she slept because it was all mixed up in a dream about not sleeping and really not sleeping. When she saw the wagon coming down the road she felt weak and sick sort of inside. She couldn't wait till she saw Jim and it seemed as though everything would be all right when he came. The wagon stopped outside under the big elm and Mrs. Smith and Liz went out. All the men had beards and there were three deer in the back of the wagon, their thin legs sticking stiff over the edge of the wagon box. Mrs. Smith kissed D. J. and he hugged her. Jim said "Hello, Liz," and grinned. Liz hadn't known just what would happen when Jim got back but she was sure it would be something. Nothing had happened. The men were just home, that was all. Jim pulled the burlap sacks off the deer and Liz looked at them. One was a big buck. It was stiff and hard to lift out of the wagon.

"Did you shoot it, Jim?" Liz asked.

"Yeah. Ain't it a beauty?" Jim got it onto his back to carry to the smokehouse.

That night Charley Wyman stayed to supper at Smith's. It was too late to get back to Charlevoix. The men washed up and waited in the front room for supper.

"Ain't there something left in that crock, Jimmy?" D. J. Smith asked, and Jim went out to the wagon in the barn and fetched in the jug of whiskey the men had taken hunting with them. It was a four-gallon jug and there was quite a little slopped back and forth in the bottom. Jim took a long pull on his way back to the house. It was hard to lift such a big jug up to drink out of it. Some of the whiskey ran down on his shirt front. The two men smiled when Jim came in with the jug. D. J. Smith sent for glasses and Liz brought them. D. J. poured out three big shots.

"Well, here's looking at you, D. J.," said Charley Wyman.

"That damn big buck, Jimmy," said D. J.

"Here's all the ones we missed, D. J.," said Jim, and downed his liquor.

"Tastes good to a man."

"Nothing like it this time of year for what ails you."

"How about another, boys?"

"Here's how, D. J."

"Down the creek, boys."

"Here's to next year."

Jim began to feel great. He loved the taste and the feel of whiskey. He was glad to be back to a comfortable bed and warm food and the shop. He had another drink. The men came in to supper feeling hilarious but acting very respectable. Liz sat at the table after she put on the food and ate with the family. It was a good dinner. The men ate seriously. After supper they went into the front room again and Liz cleaned off with Mrs. Smith. Then Mrs. Smith went upstairs and pretty soon Smith came out and went upstairs too. Jim and Charley were still in the front room. Liz was sitting in the kitchen next to the stove pretending to read a book and thinking about Jim. She didn't want to go to bed yet because she knew Jim would be coming out and she wanted to see him as he went out so she could take the way he looked up to bed with her.

She was thinking about him hard and then Jim came out. His eyes were shining and his hair was a little rumpled. Liz looked down at her book. Jim came over back of her chair and stood there and she could feel him breathing and then he put his arms around her. Her breasts felt plump and firm and the nipples were erect under his hands. Liz was terribly frightened, no one had ever touched her, but she thought, "He's come to me finally. He's really come."

She held herself stiff because she was so frightened and did not know anything else to do and then Jim held her tight against the chair and kissed her. It was such a sharp, aching, hurting feeling that she thought she couldn't stand it. She felt Jim right through the back of the chair and she couldn't stand it and then something clicked inside of her and the feeling was warmer and softer. Jim held her tight hard against the chair and she wanted it now and Jim whispered, "Come on for a walk."

Liz took her coat off the peg on the kitchen wall and went out the door. Jim had his arm around her and every little way they stopped and pressed against each other and Jim kissed her. There was no moon and they walked ankle-deep in the sandy road through the trees down to the dock and the warehouse on the bay. The water was lapping in the piles and the point was dark across the bay. It was cold but Liz was hot all over from being with Jim. They sat down in the shelter of the warehouse and Jim pulled Liz close to him. She was frightened. One of Jim's hands went inside her dress and stroked over her breast and the other hand was in her lap. She was very frightened and didn't know how he was going to go about things but she snuggled close to him. Then the hand that felt so big in her lap went away and was on her leg and started to move up it.

"Don't, Jim," Liz said. Jim slid the hand further up.

"You mustn't, Jim. You mustn't." Neither Jim nor Jim's big hand paid any attention to her.

The boards were hard. Jim had her dress up and was trying to do something to her. She was frightened but she wanted it. She had to have it but it frightened her.

"You mustn't do it, Jim. You mustn't."

"I got to. I'm going to. You know we got to."

"No we haven't, Jim. We ain't got to. Oh, it isn't right. Oh, it's so big and it hurts so. You can't. Oh, Jim. Jim. Oh."

The hemlock planks of the dock were hard and splintery and cold and Jim was heavy on her and he had hurt her. Liz pushed him, she was so uncomfortable and cramped. Jim was asleep. He wouldn't move. She worked out from under him and sat up and straightened her skirt and coat and tried to do something with her hair. Jim was sleeping with his mouth a little open. Liz leaned over and kissed him on the cheek. He was still asleep. She lifted his head a little and shook it. He rolled his head over and swallowed. Liz started to cry. She walked over to the edge of the dock and looked down to the water. There was a mist coming up from the bay. She was cold and miserable and everything felt gone. She walked back to where Jim was lying and shook him once more to make sure. She was crying.

"Jim," she said, "Jim. Please Jim."

Jim stirred and curled a little tighter. Liz took off her coat and leaned over and covered him with it. She tucked it around him neatly and carefully. Then she walked across the dock and up the steep sandy road to go to bed. A cold mist was coming up through the woods from the bay.

The writer chooses the point of view of a sentimental girl but he himself controls the tone of his story. He shows us the girl at the same time he appears to be allowing the girl to show herself to the reader. How does Hemingway get this double perspective?

Is it through the dialogue? The people do not talk like everyday people. Are they characters the girl hears? Or does Hemingway fit their dialogue to his purposes? In real life we hesitate, change the tone of our talk, shift aimlessly to a new subject, or even forget what we started out to say. We may even rely on snatches of conversation when we are in contact with someone we know well. But in a story, if a character digresses or forgets what he has just said, it is because the author wants to show some trait in that character.

In this story about a girl's need for a man who is certain to leave her once he has possessed her, the characters say only what is necessary to bring them into the inevitable contact with each other. Even the words they omit help guide us to the point of the story. No excess talk. No characters explaining their feelings. Just names of people, of places, and talk of a dead deer. The dialogue is a taut wire of reality stretched through the action Hemingway is portraying.

The description is another control. Do we see only what the girl sees? The lake, we are told, is very beautiful in the spring and summer, the bay blue and bright. From her door, Liz could see ore barges way out in the lake. These barges did not seem to her to be moving at all but if she went into the kitchen and dried some more dishes and then came out again the barges would be out of sight beyond the point. We know the world beyond exists and we know how limited Liz's horizons are. But it has not been spelled out. The best way to see what Hemingway has done to this story is to ask yourself what it would have been like if Liz had written it. Using the third person, Hemingway does tell the story from Liz's point of view but in the voice which belongs to him as the artist who creates the story. It is a matter-of-fact voice that never takes sides in what could easily become a debate on morality rather than a clear and powerful picture of love and desire.

We say the story is told from Liz's point of view because almost everything we see and hear comes to us in the way she might see and hear. Even the vocabulary and some of the phrasing are like

Liz's. But Liz is never allowed to run away with the story the way her love runs away with her. Here we see the author's skill in selecting and editing in such a way that we get inside the characters without being confused or bored by an excess of detail and emotion.

In the end neither the author nor Liz have to tell us what the story "means." There is the girl, cold and miserable and alone. Yet she takes off her coat and meticulously wraps her unconscious lover in it. In this small concrete act is the new Liz—tougher, sadder, still capable of feeling for the man who used to be her idol. The reader does not need a moral or an analysis of the psychological actions and reactions. These would be to revert back to the abstract, to take a step away from life when the story has brought life closer and clearer than we generally see it in reality.

QUESTIONS

1. Suppose Liz were a real person. How would she write or tell this story?
2. How would the story be different if told from Jim's point of view? From an impartial point of view?
3. Try to put yourself in Hemingway's place. What were some of the reasons why he began this story?

Leo Tolstoy's writing seems at first very unlike Hemingway's. He tells us how characters feel and there is an obvious sympathy for his own characters. However, if you read carefully, you will find an essential similarity. Here is an excerpt from his long novel *Anna Karenina*. It is unfair to Tolstoy to present such a short excerpt from such an intricately woven story, but it is the way he writes that interests us most, not the structure of the whole book.

At four o'clock that afternoon Levin, conscious that his heart was beating rapidly, got out of the hired sledge at the Zoological Gardens and went down the path leading to the ice-hills and skating lake, sure of finding Kitty there, for he had noticed the Shcherbatskys' carriage at the entrance.

It was a clear frosty day. Carriages, private sledges, sledges for hire, and mounted police stood at the entrance. Well-dressed people, their hats shining in the sunlight, crowded at the gates and thronged the clean-swept paths between little houses built with carved eaves in Russian style. The bushy birch trees in the Garden with all their branches weighed down by snow seemed attired in new festive garments. He walked along the path leading to the skating lake, and kept repeating to himself: "I must not be excited. I must be quiet. . . . What are you doing? What's the matter? Be quiet, stupid!" he said to his heart. But the more he tried to be calm, the more laboured grew his breath. He met an acquaintance who called to him, but Levin did not even notice who it was. He approached the ice-hills and heard the clanking of the chains by which the sledges were being pulled up, their clatter as they descended the hills, and the sound of merry voices. A few more steps brought him to the skating lake, and among all the skaters he at once recognized her. He knew she was there by the joy and terror that took possession of his heart. She stood talking to a lady at the other end of the lake. There seemed to be nothing striking in her dress or attitude, but it was as easy for Levin to recognize her in that crowd as to find a rose among nettles. Everything was lit up by her. She was the smile that brightened everything around.

"Can I really step down on to the ice, and go up to her?" he thought. The spot where she stood seemed to him an unapproachable sanctuary, and there was a moment when he nearly went away, he was so filled with awe. He had to make an effort and reason with himself that all sorts of people were passing near her and he himself might have come just to skate. He stepped down, avoiding any long look at her as one avoids long looks at the sun, but seeing her as one sees the sun, without looking.

On that day of the week and at that hour, people belonging to the same set and acquainted with one another, met on the ice. Among them were masters of the art of skating showing off their skill, and beginners with timid and awkward movements holding on to the backs of chairs fitted with runners; boys, and old men skating for hygienic reasons; and they all seemed to Levin to be fortune's favourites because they were here near her. Yet skaters appeared quite calmly to gain on her, to catch her up, and even speak to her, and quite independently of her to amuse themselves enjoying the excellent ice and the fine weather.

Nicholas Shcherbatsky, Kitty's cousin, in a short jacket, tight trousers, with skates on his feet, was sitting on a bench, and seeing Levin, called out to him.

"Hullo, you Russian champion skater! When did you come? The ice is splendid—put on your skates!"

"I haven't any skates," answered Levin, wondering at such boldness and freedom of manner in her presence, and not losing sight of her for a moment although not looking at her. He felt the sun approaching him. She was turning a corner, her little feet, shod in high boots, kept close together, and she was skating timidly toward him. A little boy dressed in a Russian costume, violently swinging his arms and stooping very low, was overtaking her.

She was not very firm on her feet. Having drawn her hands from the muff that hung by a cord from her neck, she held them out and looking at Levin, whom she had recognized, she smiled at him and at her fears. Having turned the corner, she pushed off with an elastic little hold of him with her hand, nodded smilingly to Levin. She was more beautiful than he had imagined her.

When he thought about her he could vividly picture to himself her entire person, and especially the charm of her small, fair-haired head, so lightly poised on the shapely girlish shoulders, and the childlike look, combined with the slim beauty of her figure, lay her special charm; and this he thoroughly appreciated, but what always struck him afresh as unexpected was the expression in her eyes—mild, calm, and truthful,—and above all her smile, which carried him into a fairyland where he felt softened and filled with tenderness—as he remembered feeling on rare occasions in his early childhood.

"Have you been here long?" she said, shaking hands with him. "Thank you," she added as he picked up the handkerchief she had dropped from her muff.

"I? No, not long—since yesterday . . . I mean to-day . . ." replied Levin, in his excitement not quite taking in her question. "I wanted to come and see you," he went on, and then, remembering the reason why he wanted to see her he became abashed, and blushed. "I did not know that you skated, and so well."

She looked attentively at him as if wishing to understand his confusion.

"Your praise is valuable. There is a tradition here that you are the best skater," she said, flicking off with a small black-gloved hand some hoarfrost crystals that had fallen on her muff.

"Yes, I used to be passionately fond of skating. I wanted to be perfect at it."

"You seem to do everything passionately," she remarked with a smile. "I should so like to see you skate. Put on a pair and let us skate together."

"Skate together! Can it be possible?" thought Levin looking at her.

"I'll go and put them on at once," he said, and went to hire some skates.

"You've not looked us up for a long time, sir," said one of the attendants as, holding up Levin's foot, he bored a hole in the heel of his boot. "Since you left we have had no gentleman who is such a master at it as you! Is that right?" he added, pulling the strap tight.

"Yes, that's right, that's right! Please be quick!" answered Levin, trying to restrain the happy smile which appeared on his face. "Yes," he thought, "this is life—this is joy! She said, 'To-gether: let us skate together'! Shall I tell her now? But that's just why I'm afraid of speaking. Now I am happy, if only in my hopes—but then? . . . But I must . . . I must . . . I must . . . ! Away with this weakness!"

He stood up, took off his overcoat, and having given himself a start on the rough ice near the shelter, glided down to the smooth surface of the lake, increasing and diminishing his speed and shaping his course as if by volition only. He approached Kitty timidly, but her smile again tranquillized him.

She gave him her hand and they went on together, increasing their speed, and the faster they went the closer she pressed his hands.

"I should learn quicker with you; for some reason I feel confidence in you," she said.

"And I am confident of myself when you lean on me," he answered, and was immediately frightened of what he had said, and blushed. And in fact, as soon as he had uttered these words her face lost its kind expression—as when the sun hides behind a cloud—and Levin noticed that familiar play of her features which indicated an effort of mind: a wrinkle appeared on her smooth forehead.

"Has anything unpleasant happened . . . ? But I have no right to ask," he said hurriedly.

"Why? . . . No, nothing unpleasant has happened," she answered coldly, adding immediately: "You have not seen Mlle Linon?"

"Not yet."

"Go to her then, she is so fond of you."

"What does she mean? I have hurt her. Help me O Lord!" thought Levin, hastening toward the old Frenchwoman with the grey curls, who sat on one of the benches. She welcomed Levin as an old friend, showing her set of false teeth in a smile.

"Yes, you see we grow up," she said, indicating Kitty with a glance, "and grow old. 'Tiny Bear' is grown up!" continued the Frenchwoman, laughing and reminding him of his old joke when he called the three young ladies the Three Bears of the English fairy tale. "Do you remember when you used to call her so?"

He had not the faintest recollection of it, but she was fond of the joke and had laughed at it for the last ten years.

"Well, go—go and skate! Our Kitty is beginning to skate nicely, isn't she?"

When Levin returned to Kitty her face was no longer stern and her eyes had their former truthful, kindly look; but he thought there was an intentionally quiet manner in her affability and he felt sad. Having spoken about her old governess and her peculiarities, she asked him about his way of life.

"Do you really manage not to feel dull in the country in winter?" she said.

"I don't feel at all dull, I am very busy," he answered, conscious that she was subduing him to her quiet tone, from which —as had happened at the beginning of the winter—he would not be able to free himself.

"Have you come for long?" asked Kitty.

"I don't know," he answered, without thinking of what he was saying. The idea that if he accepted her tone of calm friendliness he would again go away without having settled anything occurred to him, and he determined to rebel.

"You don't know?"

"I don't. It all depends on you," he said, and was at once terrified at his own words.

Whether she had not heard his words or did not wish to hear them, anyhow, after slightly stumbling and striking her foot twice against the ice, she skated hurriedly away from him toward Mlle Linon, said something to her, and went toward the little house where the ladies took off their skates.

"My God! What have I done? O Lord, help me and teach me!" prayed Levin, and feeling at the same time a need of violent exercise, he got up speed and described inner and outer circles.

Just then a young man, the best of the new skaters, with a cigarette in his mouth and skates on, came out of the coffee-room, and taking a run, descended the steps leading to the lake, clattering with his skates as he jumped from step to step. He then flew down the slope and glided along the ice without so much as changing the easy position of his arms.

"Oh, that's a new trick!" said Levin, and at once ran up to that new trick.

"Don't hurt yourself—it needs practice!" Nicholas Shcherbatsky called out.

Levin went up the path as far back as he could to get up speed, and then slid downwards, balancing himself with his arms in this unaccustomed movement. He caught his foot on the last step, but, scarcely touching the ice with his hand, made a violent effort, regained his balance, and skated away laughing.

"Good! Dear man!" thought Kitty who at that moment was just coming out of the little house with Mlle Linon, looking at him with a smile of gentle tenderness as at a dear brother. "Can I really be guilty—have I really done anything wrong? They say it's coquetting. . . . I know it's not him I love, but still I feel happy with him, he is so charming! Only why did he say that?" she thought.

When he saw Kitty who was going away, and her mother who had met her on the steps, Levin, flushed with the violent exercise, stood still and considered. He then took off his skates and overtook mother and daughter at the gates of the Gardens.

"Very pleased to see you," said the Princess. "We are at home on Thursdays, as usual."

"And to-day is Thursday!"

"We shall be glad to see you," said the Princess drily.

Kitty was sorry to hear that dry tone and could not resist the desire to counteract her mother's coldness. She turned her head and said smilingly:

"Au revoir!"

Just then Oblonsky, his hat tilted on one side, with radiant face and eyes, walked into the Gardens like a joyous conqueror. But on approaching his mother-in-law he answered her questions about Dolly's health with a sorrowful and guilty air. After a few words with her in a subdued and mournful tone, he expanded his chest and took Levin's arm.

"Well, shall we go?" he asked. "I kept thinking about you, and am very, very glad you've come," he went on, looking significantly into Levin's eyes.

"Yes, yes! Let's go," answered the happy Levin, still hearing the voice saying: "Au revoir!" and still seeing the smile with which it had been said.

"The Angleterre, or the Hermitage?"

"I don't care."

"Well then, the Angleterre," said Oblonsky, choosing the Angleterre because he was deeper in debt to that restaurant than to the Hermitage, and therefore considered it wrong to avoid it. "Have you a sledge? . . . That's a good thing, because I've sent my coachman home."

The two friends were silent all the way. Levin was considering what the change in Kitty's face meant; now persuading himself that there was hope, now in despair, seeing clearly that such hope was madness; but yet feeling an altogether different being from what he had been before her smile and the words "Au revoir!"

Oblonsky during the drive was composing the menu of their dinner.

"You like turbot, don't you?" he asked, as they drove up to the restaurant.

"What?" said Levin. "Turbot? Oh yes, I am awfully fond of turbot!"

In this chapter from *Anna Karenina*, Tolstoy shows us the world through the eyes and thoughts of a lovestruck young man. Most of us are aware that love or infatuation makes us behave and think peculiarly. You have probably heard a number of songs which say the heart goes "flip-flop" or "zing," or the lover hears bells or gets dizzy. But that's in songs, you say. Of course, but how would you describe the special effect that being in love has on a person?

The problem is to avoid the usual clichés about cloud nine and being misty-eyed. These draw attention to the emotion, not to the person or particular situation.

Tolstoy at times talks directly about Levin's emotions, but only in relation to a specific situation—looking for Kitty on the ice, talking to her, saying good-bye. In other words, Tolstoy is very careful to place his lovestruck young man in the very concrete, real world. Levin's exaggerated sensitivity is balanced by the author continually keeping us aware of the world through which Levin moves, and which must register, at least subconsciously, on Levin's own mind. It is a world of ice, beginner skaters with chairs, old men exercising, skate-fitting, dinner menus, and even false teeth.

It is this confusion of the world lit by love and the world as we usually know it that causes us to be confused or act unusual when we are in love. So, through his careful mixing of internal and external detail and by keeping his character in motion through a certain period of time, one event or scene leading to another, Tolstoy brings an emotion into the real world.

QUESTIONS

1. Are there words and phrases or images you feel are too trite?
2. This love is much like other loves, yet the two people have distinct personalities. How is this done?
3. Suppose Hemingway were writing this episode. Would the effect be very different?

Study the following student poem. The title, "The Lover," indicates the focus is meant to include only one person. Read through the poem once without stopping, then look more closely. Try to form an idea of this "lover." Compare him to Levin in Tolstoy's writing.

> It's a pond. And it's my favorite place, especially
> in the spring when the sky is a perfect blue and the
> wind blows just enough to nudge the water. Acres of
> tall green grass encircle the pond and seem to protect
> it from being disturbed.
>
> If we ever go there,
> We'll take off our shoes
> And run through the grass
> And sing
> And laugh
> And play.
> The grass will tickle our feet
> And
> We'll tumble in it
> And
> Roll down the bank to the water.

Together
We can follow the water's edge,
Pretending that we're ten years old
Playing leap-frog in the sand.

We can be the king and queen in the world
And ride in a tasselled carriage.
Or we can be Hansel and Gretel
And look for our gingerbread house.

I'll put you in a little red rowboat and we'll just
drift around all day. You will feel so very happy
that you'll want to bring the whole world into the
boat and kiss each child and give flowers to everyone.

The author has grounded his emotion in very concrete images
even though the poem is a kind of daydream. There is a real unity
in the tone of the daydreaming and in the kinds of images which
convey the emotion. Some readers will find the material too
quaint, and some will think it is too much like pathetic fallacy—
nature agreeing with the emotions of the writer. The real question
is whether the author has a distinct impression to convey and if so,
whether he succeeds.

Questions

1. Does the digression into the imaginary country of Hansel and
   Gretel add to the poem?
2. Does the poem gain strength when the author directs it away
   from his own emotion to embrace the whole world?
3. Could this be just as effective as straight prose?

Antoine de Saint-Exupéry wrote many books about pilots and flying. Aviation for him had become something which was more than
technology or thrills. In the piece that follows, from *Night Flight,*

can you see any reasons why his work had such a great audience of people who knew nothing about flying? [4]

Already, beneath him, through the golden evening, the shadowed hills had dug their furrows and the plains grew luminous with long-enduring light. For in these lands the ground gives off this golden glow persistently, just as, even when winter goes, the whiteness of the snow persists.

Fabien, the pilot bringing the Patagonia air-mail from the far south to Buenos Aires, could mark night coming on by certain signs that called to mind the waters of a harbor—a calm expanse beneath, faintly rippled by the lazy clouds—and he seemed to be entering a vast anchorage, an immensity of blessedness.

Or else he might have fancied he was taking a quiet walk in the calm of evening, almost like a shepherd. The Patagonian shepherds move, unhurried, from one flock to another; and he, too, moved from one town to another, the shepherd of those little towns. Every two hours he met another of them, drinking at its riverside or browsing on its plain.

Sometimes, after a hundred miles of steppes as desolate as the sea, he encountered a lonely farm-house that seemed to be sailing backwards from him in a great prairie sea, with its freight of human lives; and he saluted with his wings this passing ship.

"San Julian in sight. In ten minutes we shall land."

The wireless operator gave their position to all the stations on the line. From Magellan Strait to Buenos Aires the airports were strung out across fifteen hundred miles and more, but this one led toward the frontiers of night, just as in Africa the last conquered hamlet opens on to the unknown.

The wireless operator handed the pilot a slip of paper: "There are so many storms about that the discharges are fouling my ear-phones. Shall we stop the night at San Julian?"

[4] Antoine de Saint-Exupéry, *Night Flight* (New York: Harcourt, Brace & World, 1941), pp. 3–11.

Fabien smiled; the sky was calm as an aquarium and all the stations ahead were signaling, Clear sky: no wind.

"No, we'll go on."

But the wireless operator was thinking: these storms had lodged themselves somewhere or other, as worms do in a fruit; a fine night, but they would ruin it, and he loathed entering this shadow that was ripe to rottenness.

As he slowed down his engine for the San Julian landing, Fabien knew that he was tired. All that endeared his life to man was looming up to meet him; men's houses, friendly little cafés, trees under which they walk. He was like some conqueror who, in the aftermath of victory, bends down upon his territories and now perceives the humble happiness of men. A need came over Fabien to lay his weapons down and feel the aching burden of his limbs—for even our misfortunes are a part of our belongings—and to stay, a simple dweller here, watching from his window a scene that would never change. This tiny village, he could gladly have made friends with it; the choice once made, a man accepts the issue of his venture and can love the life. Like love, it hems him in. Fabien would have wished to live a long while here—here to possess his morsel of eternity. These little towns, where he lived an hour, their gardens girdled by old walls over which he passed, seemed something apart and everlasting. Now the village was rising to meet the plane, opening out toward him. And there, he mused, were friendliness and gentle girls, white napery spread in quiet homes; all that is slowly shaped toward eternity. The village streamed past beneath his wings, yielding the secrets of closed gardens that their walls no longer guarded. He landed; and now he knew that he had seen nothing at all, only a few men slowly moving amongst their stones. The village kept, by its mere immobility, the secret of its passions and withheld its kindly charm; for, to master that, he would have needed to give up an active life.

The ten minutes' halt was ended and Fabien resumed his flight. He glanced back toward San Julian; all he now could see was a cluster of lights, then stars, then twinkling star-dust that vanished, tempting him for the last time.

"I can't see the dials; I'll light up."

He touched the switches, but the red light falling from the cockpit lamps upon the dial-hands was so diluted with the blue evening glow that they did not catch its color. When he passed his fingers close before a bulb, they were hardly tinged at all. "Too soon."

But night was rising like a tawny smoke and already the valleys were brimming over with it. No longer were they distinguishable from the plains. The villages were lighting up, constellations that greeted each other across the dusk. And, at a touch of his finger, his flying-lights flashed back a greeting to them. The earth grew spangled with light-signals as each house lit its star, searching the vastness of the night as a lighthouse sweeps the sea. Now every place that sheltered human life was sparkling. And it rejoiced him to enter into this one night with a measured slowness, as into an anchorage.

He bent down into the cockpit; the luminous dial-hands were beginning to show up. The pilot read their figures one by one; all was going well. He felt at ease up here, snugly ensconced. He passed his fingers along a steel rib and felt the stream of life that flowed in it; the metal did not vibrate, yet it was alive. The engine's five-hundred horse-power bred in its texture a very gentle current, fraying its ice-cold rind into a velvety bloom. Once again the pilot in full flight experienced neither giddiness nor any thrill; only the mystery of metal turned to living flesh.

So he had found his world again. . . .

A few digs of his elbow, and he was quite at home. He tapped the dashboard, touched the contacts one by one, shifting his limbs a little, and, settling himself more solidly, felt for the best position whence to gauge the faintest lurch of his five tons of metal, jostled by the heaving darkness. Groping with his fingers, he plugged in his emergency-lamp, let go of it, felt for it again, made sure it held; then lightly touched each switch, to be certain of finding it later, training his hands to function in a blind man's world. Now that his hands had learnt their role by heart, he ventured to turn on a lamp, making the cockpit bright with polished fittings and then, as on a submarine about to dive, watched his passage into night upon the dials only. Nothing shook or rattled, neither gyroscope nor altimeter flickered in the least, the engine was running smoothly; so now he relaxed his limbs a little, let his neck sink back into the leather padding and fell into the deeply meditative mood of flight, mellow with inexplicable hopes.

Now a watchman from the heart of night, he learnt how night betrays man's presence, his voices, lights, and his unrest. That star down there in the shadows, alone; a lonely house. Yonder a fading star; that house is closing in upon its love. . . . Or on its lassitude. A house that has ceased to flash its signal to the world. Gathered round their lamp-lit table, those peasants do not know the measure of their hopes; they do not guess that their desire carries so far, out into the vastness of the night that hems them in. But Fabien has met it on his path, when, coming from a thousand miles away, he feels the heavy ground-swell raise his panting plane and let it sink, when he has crossed a dozen storms like lands at war, between them neutral tracts of moonlight, to reach at last those lights, one following the other —and knows himself a conqueror. They think, these peasants, that their lamp shines only for that little table; but, from fifty miles away, some one has felt the summons of their light, as though it were a desperate signal from some lonely island, flashed by shipwrecked men toward the sea.

In this piece, Saint-Exupéry deals with the pastoral, peaceful side of the night and with the desire of the pilot to find his world —as he has found it before—in a flight that takes him through the velvet dark to a halting place along the way.

The sketch has such an immediacy that it actually seems to take the reader on the flight. Even when the pilot minimizes his own presence, referring to himself and his wireless operator only to acquaint the reader with the shadow of the storm, we feel that we are with the pilot at this moment in what is called the continuous present. We are in the sky, brought there by the ability of the author to make the flight take place *now*, even though technically the piece is in the past tense.

In part, the writer achieves this immediacy through using the framework of a journey, keeping us in movement simply because the plane itself is in movement. "We'll go on," Fabien says. In the calendar of the flight we do go on, past tiny villages where we could stay and make friends but do not because of the prescribed movement. The sense of immediacy is heightened, too, by the use of contrast. On one hand is the quiet of the villages, so entrancing, so temporary for the pilot; and on the other, the vastness of the night to which we always return, forced forward with the plane as it enters each new phase of darkness.

QUESTIONS

1. How would you characterize the author's interest in flying?
2. What theme controls the choice of detail and the organization of this piece? For instance, why is there not more detail of San Julian?
3. Make a sketchy outline of the thematic development of this piece.

It is almost a truism in popular psychology to say, "We desire most what we do not have." Many people have experienced this kind of desire at the end of a long journey. Writing about it generally sounds like a long sigh of relief or a grand musical finale. The individual experience is lost. Below, in an excerpt from *Travels with Charley*, John Steinbeck describes the end of a journey he took in a pickup truck accompanied by his poodle Charley.[5]

In the beginning of this record I tried to explore the nature of journeys, how they are things in themselves, each one an individual and no two alike. I speculated with a kind of wonder on the strength of the individuality of journeys and stopped on the postulate that people don't take trips—trips take people. That discussion, however, did not go into the life span of journeys.

[5] John Steinbeck, *Travels with Charley* (New York: Viking Press, 1962), pp. 243–246.

This seems to be variable and unpredictable. Who has not known a journey to be over and dead before the traveler returns? The reverse is also true: many a trip continues long after movement in time and space have ceased. I remember a man in Salinas who in his middle years traveled to Honolulu and back, and that journey continued for the rest of his life. We could watch him in his rocking chair on his front porch, his eyes squinted, half-closed, endlessly traveling to Honolulu.

My own journey started long before I left, and was over before I returned. I know exactly where and when it was over. Near Abingdon, in the dog-leg of Virginia, at four o'clock of a windy afternoon, without warning or good-by or kiss my foot, my journey went away and left me stranded far from home. I tried to call it back, to catch it up—a foolish and hopeless matter, because it was definitely and permanently over and finished. The road became an endless stone ribbon, the hills obstructions, the trees green blurs, the people simply moving figures with heads but no faces. All the food along the way tasted like soup, even the soup. My bed was unmade. I slipped into it for naps at long uneven intervals. My stove was unlighted and a loaf of bread gathered mold in my cupboard. The miles rolled under me unacknowledged. I know it was cold, but I didn't feel it; I know the countryside must have been beautiful, but I didn't see it. I bulldozed blindly through West Virginia, plunged into Pennsylvania and grooved Rocinante to the great wide turnpike. There was no night, no day, no distance. I must have stopped to fill my gas tank, to walk and feed Charley, to eat, to telephone, but I don't remember any of it.

It is very strange. Up to Abingdon, Virginia, I can reel back the trip like film. I have almost total recall, every face is there, every hill and tree and color, and sound of speech and small scenes ready to reply themselves in my memory. After Abingdon—nothing. The way was a gray, timeless, eventless tunnel, but at the end of it was the one shining reality—my own wife, my own house in my own street, my own bed. It was all there, and I lumbered my way toward it. Rocinante could be fleet, but I had not driven her fast. Now she leaped under my heavy relentless foot, and the wind shrieked around the corners of the house. If you think I am indulging in fantasy about the trip, how can you explain that Charley knew it was over too? He at least is no dreamer, no coiner of moods. He went to sleep with his head in my lap, never looked out the window, never said "Ftt," never urged me to a turn-out. He carried out his functions like a sleepwalker, ignored whole rows of garbage cans. If that doesn't prove the truth of my statement, nothing can.

New Jersey was another turnpike. My body was in a nerveless, tireless vacuum. The increasing river of traffic for New York carried me along, and suddenly there was the welcoming maw of Holland Tunnel and at the other end home.

A policeman waved me out of the snake of traffic and flagged me to a stop. "You can't go through the tunnel with that butane," he said.

"But officer, it's turned off."

"Doesn't matter. It's the law. Can't take gas into the tunnel."

And suddenly I fell apart, collapsed into a jelly of weariness. "But I want to get home," I wailed. "How am I going to get home?"

He was very kind to me, and patient too. Maybe he had a home somewhere. "You can go up and take George Washington Bridge, or you can take a ferry."

It was rush hour, but the gentle-hearted policeman must have seen a potential maniac in me. He held back the savage traffic and got me through and directed me with great care. I think he was strongly tempted to drive me home.

Magically I was on the Hoboken ferry and then ashore, far downtown with the daily panic rush of commuters leaping and running and dodging in front, obeying no signals. Every evening is Pamplona in lower New York. I made a turn and then another, entered a one-way street the wrong way and had to back out, got boxed in the middle of a crossing by a swirling rapids of turning people.

Suddenly I pulled to the curb in a no-parking area, cut my motor, and leaned back in the seat and laughed, and I couldn't stop. My hands and arms and shoulders were shaking with road jitters.

An old-fashioned cop with a fine red face and a frosty blue

eye leaned in toward me. "What's the matter with you, Mac, drunk?" he asked.

I said, "Officer, I've driven this thing all over the country—mountains, plains, deserts. And now I'm back in my own town, where I live—and I'm lost."

He grinned happily. "Think nothing of it, Mac," he said. "I got lost in Brooklyn only Saturday. Now where is it you were wanting to go?"

And that's how the traveler came home again.

Steinbeck starts his description of returning home with a kind of theoretical discussion of the nature of journeys. He then goes on to demonstrate this theory in terms of his own journey. However, he is doing more than setting up a theory in the first paragraph. This is not simply a scientific experiment about journeys. It is about a man's suddenly mounting desire to return home.

Before Abingdon, the author's desire was to see people and places. He was possessed by the spirit of the journey. His desire was to seek out new experiences. Suddenly the journey, mysterious thing that it is, deserts him while he is still several hundred miles from home. The first paragraph has prepared us for both this sudden cessation of the journey and its impact upon the individual.

The desire to return home builds up rapidly. Steinbeck does not tell us his feelings—loneliness, boredom, restlessness, apathy. These abstract words are never mentioned. What he does is put us in his place. He shows us how he sees people and landscapes, how he drives, sleeps, eats. When he does go inside his own thoughts, it is with the image of the tunnel with the "shining reality" at the other end. He also tells us how Charley acted.

He does all this very quickly. Almost half of this sketch takes place within a few miles from home. His desire to reach home, though never expressed as a pure emotion, has been so strong that he gets lost in his hometown. The reader, like the author, is at the end of a journey. And in the same way the author is kept from his goal by his delirious confusion, the reader is also held back. The process of reading, the actual design of the sketch, mirrors the events being described.

QUESTIONS

1. How does the theory stated in paragraph one remain present in the concrete detail of the rest of the writing?
2. Pick out three or four figures of speech. Are they just clever, or do they in some way help develop Steinbeck's particular themes?
3. Steinbeck writes in a very informal voice. How does that affect his writing and the reader?

In reading the student theme below, try to create an image of John Larson, the boy in love. Is the image you create yours, or is it one the author's writing has shaped and conveyed to you? Did he communicate something out of his experience and observation, or did he just stimulate some of your old memories and associations?

It wasn't but a year ago when one of my best friends, John Larson, fell in love for the first time in his life. John had dated many girls before, but had never remained with the same one for more than two months. Yet for some reason he began dating one particular girl for a much longer period of time. At first I doubted whether he had really fallen in love, but one thing was evident: this girl soon brought about a turning point in his life, for gradually his character changed as their relationship progressed.

These changes were not abrupt, but to an outsider, the differences in John's character were obvious. Before he fell for this girl, John was a carefree and independent person, quite active in many areas of social life. But his new love brought a sudden end to this way of living. He gave up his carefree existence in exchange for an earnest approach towards everyday life. His varied activities dwindled to the few which were in some way related to his girl. Along with these changes came new thoughts and attitudes which were contrary to those he had

previously held. For example, John had always believed that
the only way to get along with girls was to date as many as possible and avoid being serious with any. But this opinion was ill-
fated. Gradually, as he fell more and more in love, other females became less important to him, and this special girl was
the only one he cared to date. Thus one can easily see how love
can change an individual. Yet these visible changes alone are
not enough to convince the reader that this boy had found true
love. Only after I had had several long talks with John did I
finally realize he had really fallen in love.

It was during one of these discussions that John explained to
me why he felt so strongly towards this girl. He told me that for
the first time in his life he really depended on someone,
through his total faith and trust in the girl. He sensed that their
relationship gave him greater self-confidence. This feeling, he
explained, was the result of the great pride he had in himself, in
her, and in their relationship. John continued and told me of
the deep inner satisfaction he received as a result of his love for
her and from the security he felt in sharing so many things with
another. What seemed to be the most important factor was the
bright future that he knew his love promised for him. For the
first time in his life, John couldn't laugh away the thought of
marriage. By then I had no doubt in the sincerity of the love he
had for the girl.

Superficially this sketch seems to have a unity in the author's
movement from doubt to certainty, concerning his friend's love.
The trouble is that the sketch is not really about the author. Yet it
never is really about the boy in love, either. The author's mistake
is in naming the changes in the boy rather than in showing them
in concrete language. The result is the kind of emotional note-
taking that is often used as the basis for a real portrait, but that
gives no one but the author a real sense of an individual's life.

The way the author talks, it seems he believed he was being
very vivid. He says the changes in John's behavior were obvious
and he proceeds to give what he believes are good examples. The
examples are not changes in behavior. They are simply abstractions about the changes. Behavior is a concrete pattern of thought

and action. It is the "stuff" of a person's active life. To believe that abstraction is the same thing as behavior is to believe that saying is doing. When you believe that, you are risking your life.

Questions

1. Sketch a concrete beginning paragraph that would also establish the author's interest in the theme of change.
2. Why do you think the author did not ground his description in concrete detail?
3. If the author wanted to keep himself in the sketch, how could he have made his presence a real unifying device?

Assignments

1. Describe someone you knew who was in love. Avoid the usual clichés about "walking on air" and being a "new man." Try to capture what it meant to that person at that time. Use concrete detail to ground the emotion in the facts of human behavior. (Desire or delight may be substituted for love.)
2. Attempt to define love in psychological terms. Avoid such abstractions and subjective terms as *beauty, harmony, peacefulness,* and *eternal.* Use concrete examples or images to support your definition. Be sure the organization of your paper is planned and relevant to your approach. You are not writing for the dictionary.

CHAPTER 9

SORROW AND

LAUGHTER

Controlling Pathos and Absurdity

Sorrow and laughter often have a common source. This is never more evident than when someone else's misfortune is the occasion of our laughter. Most of us have at one time or another laughed at someone hitting his thumb with a hammer or stubbing his toe unexpectedly. Granted this is a long way from laughing at another's genuine illness or grief. However, we have done even this, though we have disguised the fact to ourselves.

As a child you probably laughed at the misfortunes of a clown. Later you began to laugh at jokes in which the main character really suffers. If you have laughed at what we call "sick jokes," then you have probably laughed at sorrows that in real life would be too grim to talk about. In listening to news of war you may have laughed at some ingenious rout of the enemy, but to the enemy it was far from funny.

The jokes point up an important fact about writing from laughter and sorrow. The joke could have been real life, couldn't it? Suppose it was? Whether words make us laugh or feel sorrow is very much a matter of how they are chosen, arranged, and fitted to the subject (of course, the reader's personality is also involved). The writer must be constantly aware that what may be funny or serious to him may be just the opposite to the reader, even if the writer's intent is obvious. Probably you have, at one time or another, told a joke or a funny story and had someone say, "I don't see what's so funny about that." What caused the misunderstanding? Your audience did not receive the joke or story in the personal point of view from which you gave it. Your words failed to convey that point of view.

It is not how you feel, but how you write, that is going to influence the reader's feelings.

When Christoper Isherwood and Terry Southern wrote the script for the film *The Loved One*, a spoof of the American funeral and cemetery system, they had as their starting point an acute awareness of how absurd our "way of death" has become. In their film version of Evelyn Waugh's novel *The Loved One*, the feelings and words and motions connected with death became comic. In both film and novel this was the intended effect. The outsider can see the comedy. He can laugh at what the characters and their real-life counterparts feel is very serious and joyless. As have many people, Isherwood and Southern looked at American funeral practices and found them often so extreme as to be absurd. Their task was to show the audience that a custom which had become too serious for its content, was now absurd. Seriousness, overdone, had become comedy.

What is it about a clown or a comedian or a character in comic writing that allows us to laugh at misfortune? Usually there are very definite signs that tell us we are in a special situation. The most obvious signal is for the character or narrator to laugh, like the friend who writes, "If I don't pass this quiz I'm going to take a bottle of sleeping pills. Ha, ha, ha." But a good comedian does not have to laugh at his own jokes. The signals are in the manner of presentation.

Here again we have some obvious examples: the clown's cos-

tume and makeup, a special tone of voice, glib phrases, clever and
playful twists of thought, and all kinds of deliberate exaggeration.
A writer of comedy has signals too, but he tries to make them a
part of his whole effort. As Max Eastman said, humor is "being in
fun," not just saying you are. The idea of "play" is clarified by the
following passage from Eastman's *Enjoyment of Laughter:*

> Perhaps the best way to convince yourself of this is to ob-
> serve the play of animals—or better still, play with them.
> When you go into a rough-and-tumble with a young and un-
> trained fighting dog, you rely absolutely upon his sensing and
> responding to the mood of play. You stake your life upon it. You
> seize him by the ears or throat, you thrust your hand between
> his teeth, you fling him this way and that, and backward clear
> across the sidewalk, and he barks and snarls, intense and seem-
> ingly ferocious, crouching for a leap—and yet you have no
> fear. You do not cry out, "When you bark that way, smile!" or,
> "Remember now, it is all in fun, we're only fooling!" You know
> without the smile that he is fooling. You know it by the move-
> ment of his tail. It is a fact of nature, not an acquired idea, that
> he is fooling.
>
> Psychologists, although they have been trying to of late, will
> never get away from that fact of nature. Play is not merely, as
> some now think it sophisticated to say, "a name for the activi-
> ties of children." Didn't you ever hear a child say, "All right,
> then I won't play!"? And didn't he know what he was saying?
> Play is a socio-physiological state or posture of instinctive life.
> It is not only something that we do, but something that we are
> while we do it.[1]

However, look at this passage from a serious and famous work of
fiction:

> "Uncle, you are not looking well to-night."
> "I am not well, Florence. I sometimes doubt if I shall ever be
> any better."

[1] Max Eastman, *Enjoyment of Laughter* (New York: Simon and Schuster, 1936), p. 16.

"Surely, uncle, you cannot mean—"

"Yes, my child, I have reason to believe that I am nearing the end."

"I cannot bear to hear you speak so, uncle," said Florence Linden, in irrepressible agitation. "You are not an old man. You are but fifty-four."

"True, Florence, but it is not years only that make a man old. Two great sorrows have embittered my life. First, the death of my dearly loved wife, and next the loss of my boy, Harvey."

"It is long since I have heard you refer to my cousin's loss. I thought you had become reconciled—no, I do not mean that, I thought your regret might be less poignant."

"I have not permitted myself to speak of it, but I have never ceased to think of it day and night."

John Linden paused sadly, then resumed:

"If he had died, I might, as you say, have become reconciled; but he was abducted at the age of four by a revengeful servant whom I had discharged from my employment. Heaven knows whether he is living or dead, but it is impressed upon my mind that he still lives, it may be in misery, it may be as a criminal, while I, his unhappy father, live on in a luxury which I cannot enjoy, with no one to care for me—"

Florence Linden sank impulsively on her knees beside her uncle's chair.

"Don't say that, uncle," she pleaded. "You know that I love you, Uncle John."

"And I, too, uncle."

There was a shade of jealousy in the voice of Curtis Waring as he entered the library through the open door, and, approaching his uncle, pressed his hand.

He was a tall, dark-complexioned man, of perhaps thirty-five, with shifty black eyes and thin lips, shaded by a dark moustache. It was not a face to trust.[2]

If you laughed, you probably recognized that the characters were not very realistic. The writing seems almost a parody of sorrow.

[2] Horatio Alger, *Adrift in New York* (New York: The Odyssey Press, 1966), p. 3–4.

The writer might have profited from the advice Chekhov once gave. He advised the writer of a highly emotional story to be very reserved or "cold" when describing sad or unfortunate characters. He felt that in this way the author's coldness provided a background and relief for the character's emotions.

Think of the occasions on which you have heard people express sorrow. Aren't the numerous expressions very similar? But you didn't laugh because you knew the situation firsthand or because you were face to face with a sad person. When you write about sorrow your reader will not have these advantages. You will have to get behind the clichés and make the situation and emotion real for him.

In writing out of sorrow and laughter more than in any other kind of writing the final judge will be the reader. If he laughs at your sorrow or is repelled by your laughter, you have not only wasted your effort and lost your reader, but you have also turned him in exactly the opposite direction from the one you wished.

Again this demonstrates the fact that sorrow and laughter may have a common source. Your job is to take that source and work it into a pattern of seeing that is your own, yet a pattern into which the reader can also fit.

You can begin to do this by examining your own experience of the emotion. Did you react honestly, or only as you were expected to? For instance, when Grandma died did you cry because your parents cried or because you knew Grandma was dead? If you received a "Dear John," were you sorry for losing the partner or for your own loneliness?

This kind of questioning is only a beginning. First you must see the emotion honestly. Then you must see it in a perspective the reader will understand, and you must see it concretely. Try to see its pattern in events and things, as well as in internal impressions. Concreteness is where you and your reader meet most safely. If you forget to be concrete and wail when no one else understands why, you are apt to be called a crybaby or a "little old lady." If you find yourself laughing before anyone else, watch out. Laughter is not as contagious as some people say. In fact, if you go on laughing like that, somebody is apt to take you seriously and lock you up.

S ELECTIONS

Many people say, "Kids grow up so much faster today." This is probably true, but many of the problems remain similar. The fifteen-year-old boy we see in this excerpt from Sherwood Anderson's story "I Want To Know Why" is probably a younger fifteen than you were.[3] Nevertheless, his disappointment with the adult world may be like one of your own. This is the end of a story about a boy who has been working at the racetrack.

The track in Saratoga is near the edge of town. It is all polished up and trees around, the evergreen kind, and grass and everything painted and nice. If you go past the track you get to a hard road made of asphalt for automobiles, and if you go along this for a few miles there is a road turns off to a little rummy-looking farm house set in a yard.

That night after the race I went along that road because I had seen Jerry and some other men go that way in an automobile. I didn't expect to find them. I walked for a ways and then sat down by a fence to think. It was the direction they went in. I wanted to be as near Jerry as I could. I felt close to him. Pretty soon I went up the side road—I don't know why—and came to the rummy farm house. I was just lonesome to see Jerry, like wanting to see your father at night when you are a young kid. Just then an automobile came along and turned in. Jerry was in it and Henry Rieback's father, and Arthur Bedford from home, and Dave Williams and two other men I didn't know. They got out of the car and went into the house, all but Henry Rieback's father who quarreled with them and said he wouldn't go. It was only about nine o'clock, but they were all drunk and the rummy looking farm house was a place for bad women to stay in. That's what it was. I crept up along a fence and looked through a window and saw.

[3] Sherwood Anderson, *The Triumph of the Egg* (London: B. W. Huebsch, Inc., 1921), pp. 16–20.

It's what give me the fantods. I can't make it out. The women in the house were all ugly mean-looking women, not nice to look at or be near. They were homely too, except one who was tall and looked a little like the gelding Middlestride, but not clean like him, but with a hard ugly mouth. She had red hair. I got up by an old rose bush by an open window and looked. The women had on loose dresses and sat around in chairs. The men came in and some sat on the women's laps. The place smelled rotten and there was rotten talk, the kind a kid hears around a livery stable in a town like Beckersville in the winter but don't ever expect to hear talked when there are women around. It was rotten. A nigger wouldn't go into such a place. I looked at Jerry Tillford. I've told you how I had been feeling about him on account of his knowing what was going on inside of Sunstreak in the minute before he went to the post for the race in which he made a world's record.

Jerry bragged in that bad woman house as I know Sunstreak wouldn't never have bragged. He said that he made that horse, that it was him that won the race and made the record. He lied and bragged like a fool. I never heard such silly talk.

And then, what do you suppose he did! He looked at the woman in there, the one that was lean and hard-mouthed and looked a little like the gelding Middlestride, but not clean like him, and his eyes began to shine just as they did when he looked at me and at Sunstreak in the paddocks at the track in the afternoon. I stood there by the window—gee!—but I wished I hadn't gone away from the tracks, but had stayed with the boys and the niggers and the horses. The tall rotten looking woman was between us just as Sunstreak was in the paddocks in the afternoon.

Then, all of a sudden, I began to hate that man. I wanted to scream and rush in the room and kill him. I never had such a feeling before. I was so mad clean through that I cried and my fists were doubled up so my finger nails cut my hands.

And Jerry's eyes kept shining and he waved back and forth, and then he went and kissed that woman and I crept away and went back to the tracks and to bed and didn't sleep hardly any, and then next day I got the other kids to start home with me and never told them anything I seen.

I been thinking about it ever since. I can't make it out. Spring has come again and I'm nearly sixteen and go to the tracks mornings same as always, and I see Sunstreak and Middlestride and a new colt named Strident I'll bet will lay them all out, but no one thinks so but me and two or three niggers.

But things are different. At the tracks the air don't taste as good or smell as good. It's because a man like Jerry Tillford, who knows what he does, could see a horse like Sunstreak run, and kiss a woman like that the same day. I can't make it out. Darn him, what did he want to do like that for? I keep thinking about it and it spoils looking at horses and smelling things and hearing niggers laugh and everything. Sometimes I'm so mad about it I want to fight someone. It gives me the fantods. What did he do it for? I want to know why.

Sherwood Anderson was noted for his sensitivity to the many small events and people that were the life of American towns and villages in the first decades of this century. Here we see a segment of that life, which Anderson has made into a story. To reveal a certain meaning and unity in his subject, Anderson works through the sensibility of a fifteen-year-old boy. The boy may be Anderson as a youth or he may be an acquaintance or he may be simply invented. The point is that he holds together as a character, as a sensitivity, and as an observer. Because he seems real, he is allowed to see for the reader.

The things seen are governed by the boy's interests, and the language mirrors his thought. The seer and the seen embody innocence and worldliness. The author brings them to the agonizing point of first contact. Perhaps the boy is facing a vision of his own future.

QUESTIONS

1. How does the language mirror the boy's thought? Why does an author do this? (Be specific.)
2. Why aren't the women described more fully (excepting the one that looks like Middlestride)?
3. The questions at the end seem unnecessary to some readers. Do

they fit the narrator's (not the author's style)? Why does the author include them?

4. What might have been the steps by which the author moved from his personal observations and experience to making this story? Try to put yourself in his place by working on material from your own hometown.

Christopher Isherwood's novel *A Single Man* follows an aging college professor named George through a single day. George leads a quiet and perhaps an empty life. His one lasting relationship was with his friend Jim, who has been dead several years. In the last pages of the book the author describes the simple act of George going to bed.[4]

> Within this body on the bed, the great pump works on and on, needing no rest. All over this quietly pulsating vehicle the skeleton crew make their tiny adjustments. As for what goes on topside, they know nothing of this but danger signals, false alarms mostly: red lights flashed from the panicky brain stem, curtly contradicted by green all clears from the level-headed cortex. But now the controls are on automatic. The cortex is drowsing; the brain stem registers only an occasional nightmare. Everything seems set for a routine run from here to morning. The odds are enormously against any kind of accident. The safety record of this vehicle is outstanding.
>
> Just let us suppose, however . . . .
>
> Let us take the particular instant, years ago, when George walked into The Starboard Side and set eyes for the first time on Jim, not yet demobilized and looking far stunning beyond words in his Navy uniform. Let us then suppose that, at that same instant, deep down in one of the major branches of George's coronary artery, an unimaginably gradual process be-

[4] Christopher Isherwood, *A Single Man* (New York: Simon and Schuster, 1964), pp. 184–186.

gan. Somehow—no doctor can tell us exactly why—the inner lining begins to become roughened. And, one by one, on the roughened surface of the smooth endothelium, ions of calcium, carried by the bloodstream, begin to be deposited. . . . Thus, slowly, invisibly, with the utmost discretion and without the slightest hint to those old fussers in the brain, an almost independently melodramatic situation is contrived: the formation of the atheromatous plaque.

Let us suppose this, merely. (The body on the bed is still snoring.) This thing is wildly improbable. You could bet thousands of dollars against its happening, tonight or any night. And yet it *could*, quite possibly, be about to happen—within the next five minutes.

Very well—let us suppose that this is the night, and the hour, and the appointed minute.

Now—

The body on the bed stirs slightly, perhaps; but it does not cry out, does not wake. It shows no outward sign of the instant, annihilating shock. Cortex and brain stem are murdered in the blackout with the speed of an Indian strangler. Throttled out of its oxygen, the heart clenches and stops. The lungs go dead, their power line cut. All over the body, the arterials contract. Had this blockage not been absolute, had the occlusion occurred in one of the smaller branches of the artery, the skeleton crew could have dealt with it; they are capable of engineering miracles. Given time, they could have rigged up bypasses, channeled out new collateral communications, sealed off the damaged area with a scar. But there is no time at all. They die without warning at their posts.

For a few minutes, maybe, life lingers in the tissues of some outlying regions of the body. Then, one by one, the lights go out and there is total blackness. And if some part of the nonentity we called George has indeed been absent at this moment of terminal shock, away out there on the deep waters, then it will return to find itself homeless. For it can associate no longer with what lies here, unsnoring, on the bed. This is now cousin to the garbage in the container on the back porch. Both will have to be carted away and disposed of, before too long.

Within the detail of the simple act of sleeping, Isherwood explores a problem that has been written about for over two thousand years—the human soul or spirit imprisoned in vulnerable and limited flesh. Unlike "philosophical" writers, he does not take off from the facts of George's life and produce an abstract meditation on body and soul. If the problem is to be relevant to his story, he must work through his material, not outside it.

Although George has been made a very real personality, Isherwood now pictures him as a kind of machine, a vehicle. This metaphor enables the reader to consider George more objectively. It also sums up the irony of George's fate as a human being. Metaphor is a means of recreating ideas and emotions as concrete experience. If the metaphor works well, there is no need to tack an explanation on the end of it. If you are hit over the head with a pipe, it would be anticlimactic for someone to explain why the pipe hurt.

QUESTIONS

1. There is a time for explaining and a time for presenting. Why does Isherwood choose presentation?
2. The author seems to be writing a scientifically objective description of death from coronary occlusion. In what words and phrases is the author present?
3. Why does Isherwood extend the metaphor so far rather than doing the job in one short paragraph?
4. Why does the author speak so matter-of-factly? (The last sentence is an example.)

Some things are so absurd they could never be written about seriously. Below in his short story "The Night the Bed Fell," James Thurber describes a family crisis in which the combination of characters and events could never be treated seriously.[5] However,

[5] James Thurber, "The Night the Bed Fell," *My Life and Hard Times* (New York: Harper & Row, 1933), pp. 1–15.

this does not mean the comedy comes easily. In considering this piece, work beyond the obvious comic devices and try to see why there is more than cleverness in this writing.

I suppose that the high-water mark of my youth in Columbus, Ohio, was the night the bed fell on my father. It makes a better recitation (unless, as some friends of mine have said, one has heard it five or six times) than it does a piece of writing, for it is almost necessary to throw furniture around, shake doors, and bark like a dog, to lend the proper atmosphere and verisimilitude to what is admittedly a somewhat incredible tale. Still, it did take place.

It happened, then, that my father had decided to sleep in the attic one night, to be away where he could think. My mother opposed the notion strongly because, she said, the old wooden bed up there was unsafe: it was wobbly and the heavy headboard would crash down on father's head in case the bed fell, and kill him. There was no dissuading him, however, and at a quarter past ten he closed the attic door behind him and went up the narrow twisting stairs. We later heard ominous creakings as he crawled into bed. Grandfather, who usually slept in the attic bed when he was with us, had disappeared some days before. (On these occasions he was usually gone six or eight days and returned growling and out of temper, with the news that the federal Union was run by a passel of blockheads and that the Army of the Potomac didn't have any more chance than a fiddler's bitch.)

We had visiting us at this time a nervous first cousin of mine named Briggs Beall, who believed that he was likely to cease breathing when he was asleep. It was his feeling that if he were not awakened every hour during the night, he might die of suffocation. He had been accustomed to setting an alarm clock to ring at intervals until morning, but I persuaded him to abandon this. He slept in my room and I told him that I was such a light sleeper that if anybody quit breathing in the same room with me, I would wake instantly. He tested me the first night—which I had suspected he would—by holding his breath after my regular breathing had convinced him I was asleep. I was not asleep, however, and called to him. This seemed to allay his fears a little, but he took the precaution of putting a glass of spirits of camphor on a little table at the head of his bed. In case I didn't arouse him until he was almost gone, he said, he would sniff the camphor, a powerful reviver. Briggs was not the only member of his family who had his crotchets. Old Aunt Melissa Beall (who could whistle like a man, with two fingers in her mouth) suffered under the premonition that she was destined to die on South High Street, because she had been born on South High Street and married on South High Street. Then there was Aunt Sarah Shoaf, who never went to bed at night without the fear that a burglar was going to get in and blow chloroform under her door through a tube. To avert this calamity—for she was in greater dread of anesthetics than of losing her household goods—she always piled her money, silverware, and other valuables in a neat stack just outside her bedroom, with a note reading: "This is all I have. Please take it and do not use your chloroform, as this is all I have." Aunt Gracie Shoaf also had a burglar phobia, but she met it with more fortitude. She was confident that burglars had been getting into her house every night for forty years. The fact that she never missed anything was to her no proof to the contrary. She always claimed that she scared them off before they could take anything, by throwing shoes down the hallway. When she went to bed she piled, where she could get at them handily, all the shoes there were about her house. Five minutes after she had turned off the light, she would sit up in bed and say "Hark!" Her husband, who had learned to ignore the whole situation as long ago as 1903, would either be sound asleep or pretend to be sound asleep. In either case he would not respond to her tugging and pulling, so that presently she would arise, tiptoe to the door, open it slightly and heave a shoe down the hall in one direction and its mate down the hall in the other direction. Some nights she threw them all, some nights only a couple of pair.

But I am straying from the remarkable incidents that took place during the night that the bed fell on father. By midnight

we were all in bed. The layout of the rooms and the disposition
of their occupants is important to an understanding of what
later occurred. In the front room upstairs (just under father's
attic bedroom) were my mother and my brother Herman, who
sometimes sang in his sleep, usually "Marching Through Geor-
gia" or "Onward, Christian Soldiers." Briggs Beall and myself
were in a room adjoining this one. My brother Roy was in a
room across the hall from ours. Our bull terrier, Rex, slept in
the hall.

My bed was an army cot, one of those affairs which are made
wide enough to sleep on comfortably only by putting up, flat
with the middle section, the two sides which ordinarily hang
down like the sideboards of a drop-leaf table. When these sides
are up, it is perilous to roll too far toward the edge, for then the
cot is likely to tip completely over, bringing the whole bed
down on top of one with a tremendous banging crash. This, in
fact, is precisely what happened, about two o'clock in the morning. (It was my mother who, in recalling the scene later, first
referred to it as "the night the bed fell on your father.")

Always a deep sleeper, slow to arouse (I had lied to Briggs), I
was at first unconscious of what had happened when the iron
cot rolled me onto the floor and toppled over on me. It left me
still warmly bundled up and unhurt, for the bed rested above
me like a canopy. Hence I did not wake up, only reached the
edge of consciousness and went back. The racket, however, instantly awakened my mother, in the next room, who came to
the immediate conclusion that her worst dread was realized:
the big wooden bed upstairs had fallen on father. She therefore
screamed, "Let's go to your poor father!" It was this shout,
rather than the noise of my cot falling, that awakened my
brother Herman, in the same room with her. He thought that
mother had become, for no apparent reason, hysterical. "You're
all right, mamma!" he shouted, trying to calm her. They ex-
changed shout for shout for perhaps ten seconds: "Let's go to
your poor father!" and "You're all right!" That woke up Briggs.
By this time I was conscious of what was going on, in a vague
way, but did not yet realize that I was under my bed instead of
on it. Briggs, awakening in the midst of loud shouts of fear and

apprehension, came to the quick conclusion that he was suffo-
cating and that we were all trying to "bring him out." With a
low moan, he grasped the glass of camphor at the head of his
bed and instead of sniffing it poured it over himself. The room
reeked of camphor. "Ugf, ahfg!" choked Briggs, like a drowning man, for he had almost succeeded in stopping his breath
under the deluge of pungent spirits. He leaped out of bed and
groped toward the open window, but he came up against one
that was closed. With his hand, he beat out the glass, and I
could hear it crash and tinkle in the alley-way below. It was at
this juncture that I, in trying to get up, had the uncanny sensation of feeling my bed above me! Foggy with sleep, I now suspected, in my turn, that the whole uproar was being made in a
frantic endeavor to extricate me from what must be an unheard-
of and perilous situation. "Get me out of this!" I bawled. "Get
me out!" I think I had the nightmarish belief that I was en-
tombed in a mine. "Gugh!" gasped Briggs, floundering in his
camphor.

By this time my mother, still shouting, pursued by Herman,
still shouting, was trying to open the door to the attic, in order
to go up and get my father's body out of the wreckage. The
door was stuck, however, and wouldn't yield. Her frantic pulls
on it only added to the general banging and confusion. Roy and
the dog were now up, the one shouting questions, the other
barking.

Father, farthest away and soundest sleeper of all, had by this
time been awakened by the battering on the attic door. He decided that the house was on fire. "I'm coming, I'm coming!" he
wailed in a slow, sleepy voice—it took him many minutes to
regain full consciousness. My mother, still believing he was
caught under the bed, detected in his "I'm coming!" the
mournful, resigned note of one who is preparing to meet his
Maker. "He's dying!" she shouted.

"I'm all right!" Briggs yelled, to reassure her. "I'm all right!"
He still believed that it was his own closeness to death that was
worrying mother. I found at last the light switch in my room,
unlocked the door, and Briggs and I joined the others at the
attic door. The dog, who never did like Briggs, jumped for him

—assuming that he was the culprit in whatever was going on —and Roy had to throw Rex and hold him. We could hear father crawling out of bed upstairs. Roy pulled the attic door open, with a mighty jerk, and father came down the stairs, sleepy and irritable but safe and sound. My mother began to weep when she saw him. Rex began to howl. "What in the name of God is going on here?" asked father.

The situation was finally put together like a gigantic jigsaw puzzle. Father caught a cold from prowling around in his bare feet but there were no other bad results. "I'm glad," said mother, who always looked on the bright side of things, "that your grandfather wasn't here."

Thurber tells his story like an anecdote, but whether you call it anecdote or story, there is more in it than in most funny stories people tell. As Eastman said, the writer of comedy must achieve a state of "being in fun." Thurber does this by creating a playful world for his story. He chooses playful names, uses playful language, and exaggerates the characters peculiar habits and mannerisms. This seems easy enough (especially in the abstract). A much more difficult achievement sustains the quality of this story. The narrator (as opposed to the author) is matter-of-fact, almost serious. He is the author, acting as if Aunt Sarah Shoaf and Briggs Beall were real relatives of his. The narrator provides the bridge between the reader's world and the world of humor where neurotic people and dangerous accidents can be funny.

In using a narrator like this, the writer walks a difficult tightrope. He must be like people in the story, but he must never get carried away by it. If he is laughing at the typewriter as he writes, he is probably not laughing at the story so much as at the poor narrator who is forced to take it all seriously.

QUESTIONS

1. What is the purpose of talking about the story in paragraph one?
2. How are the exaggerated characters kept from being dull stereo-

types? In E. M. Forster's terms (see Chapter 5, p. 93) how are the
flat characters made interesting?
3. Think of someone you know whose life could provide the kind
of humor Thurber has written. How would you write about this
person?

Parkinson's Law is a book which its author, C. Northcote Parkinson, calls "studies in administration." [6] Modern business has been the object of both much serious study and much laughter. Most of the laughter originates with the stereotypes held by the nonbusiness mind. Professor Parkinson creates his humor out of the admixture of scholarly knowledge of fact and practical experience. Here is the beginning of a chapter on an administrative disease —injelititis, or palsied paralysis.

> We find everywhere a type of organization (administrative, commercial, or academic) in which the higher officials are plodding and dull, those less senior are active only in intrigue against each other, and the junior men are frustrated or frivolous. Little is being attempted. Nothing is being achieved. And in contemplating this sorry picture, we conclude that those in control have done their best, struggled against adversity, and have finally admitted defeat. It now appears from the results of recent investigation, that no such failure need be assumed. In a high percentage of the moribund institutions so far examined the final state of coma is something gained of set purpose and after prolonged effort. It is the result, admittedly, of a disease, but of a disease that is largely self-induced. From the first signs of the condition, the progress of the disease has been encouraged, the causes aggravated, and the symptoms welcomed. It is the disease of induced inferiority, called Injelititis. It is a commoner ailment than is often supposed, and the diagnosis is far easier than the cure.

[6] C. Northcote Parkinson, *Parkinson's Law* (Boston: Houghton Mifflin, 1957), pp. 78–82.

Our study of this organizational paralysis begins, logically, with a description of the course of the disease from the first signs to the final coma. The second stage of our inquiry concerns symptoms and diagnosis. The third stage should properly include some reference to treatment, but little is known about this. Nor is much likely to be discovered in the immediate future, for the tradition of British medical research is entirely opposed to any emphasis on this part of the subject. British medical specialists are usually quite content to trace the symptoms and define the cause. It is the French, by contrast, who begin by describing the treatment and discuss the diagnosis later, if at all. We feel bound to adhere in this to the British method, which may not help the patient but which is unquestionably more scientific. To travel hopefully is better than to arrive.

The first sign of danger is represented by the appearance in the organization's hierarchy of an individual who combines in himself a high concentration of incompetence and jealousy. Neither quality is significant in itself and most people have a certain proportion of each. But when these two qualities reach a certain concentration—represented at present by the formula I^3J^5—there is a chemical reaction. The two elements fuse, producing a new substance that we have termed "injelitance." The presence of this substance can be safely inferred from the actions of any individual who, having failed to make anything of his own department, tries constantly to interfere with other departments and gain control of the central administration. The specialist who observes this particular mixture of failure and ambition will at once shake his head and murmur, "Primary or idiopathic injelitance." The symptoms, as we shall see, are quite unmistakable.

The next or secondary stage in the progress of the disease is reached when the infected individual gains complete or partial control of the central organization. In many instances this stage is reached without any period of primary infection, the individual having actually entered the organization at that level. The injelitant individual is easily recognizable at this stage from the persistence with which he struggles to eject all those abler than himself, as also from his resistance to the appointment or promotion of anyone who might prove abler in course of time. He dare not say, "Mr. Asterisk is too able," so he says, "Asterisk? Clever perhaps—but is he *sound?* I incline to prefer Mr. Cypher." He dare not say, "Mr. Asterisk makes me feel small," so he says, "Mr. Cypher appears to me to have the better judgment." Judgment is an interesting word that signifies in this context the opposite of intelligence; it means, in fact, doing what was done last time. So Mr. Cypher is promoted and Mr. Asterisk goes elsewhere. The central administration gradually fills up with people stupider than the chairman, director, or manager. If the head of the organization is second-rate, he will see to it that his immediate staff are all third-rate; and they will, in turn, see to it that their subordinates are fourth-rate. There will soon be an actual competition in stupidity, people pretending to be even more brainless than they are.

The next or tertiary stage in the onset of this disease is reached when there is no spark of intelligence left in the whole organization from top to bottom. This is the state of coma we described in our first paragraph. When that stage has been reached the institution is, for all practical purposes, dead. It may remain in a coma for twenty years. It may quietly disintegrate. It may even, finally, recover. Cases of recovery are rare. It may be thought odd that recovery without treatment should be possible. The process is quite natural, nevertheless, and closely resembles the process by which various living organisms develop a resistance to poisons that are at first encounter fatal. It is as if the whole institution had been sprayed with a DDT solution guaranteed to eliminate all ability found in its way. For a period of years this practice achieves the desired result. Eventually, however, individuals develop an immunity. They conceal their ability under a mask of imbecile good humor. The result is that the operatives assigned to the task of ability-elimination fail (through stupidity) to recognize ability when they see it. An individual of merit penetrates the outer defenses and begins to make his way toward the top. He wanders on, babbling about golf and giggling feebly, losing documents and forgetting names, and looking just like everyone else. Only when he has reached high rank does he suddenly throw off the mask and appear like the demon king among a crowd of pantomime fairies. With shrill screams of dismay the high executives find ability right there in the midst of them. It is too late by then to do anything about it. The damage has been done, the disease is in retreat, and full recovery is possible over the next ten years. But these instances of natural cure are extremely rare. In the more usual course of events, the disease passes through the recognized stages and becomes, as it would seem, incurable.

Sooner or later, most of us will find ourselves working among people who form a miniature society of their own. This is true of schools, corporations, the arts, and professions like law or medicine. These miniature societies also have patterns of behavior and unwritten codes of law that are peculiar to them. Those who are not aware of the special situation they work in often become so captive to it that it becomes their entire world. To others, these people are often both sad and funny. Northcote Parkinson has studied one pattern in the world of business administration and saw how it corresponded with another pattern—a medical pattern.

Parkinson begins with a concise picture of a typical administrative problem. His summary is presented in words common to many business studies. He does not linger with the commonplace, but uses his quick "businesslike" manner to launch the reader into his own thesis.

To explain this thesis, Parkinson develops the metaphor of a disease. The structure for his sketch is medical. He follows stages of the disease to its unusual cure or its incurable stabilization. All the while he is careful not to become so involved in the language of the metaphor that he forgets his original subject.

QUESTIONS

1. How could the medical metaphor ruin this piece?
2. Recreate what you think could have been the steps in conceiving and writing this piece.

3. While the author does not enter the writing, his voice is distinct. How would you characterize the voice that describes injelititis? How does this affect the writing?

4. Read a description of business or of a businessman from David Riesman's *The Lonely Crowd,* or C. Wright Mills' *White Collar.* How would you explain the differences between this writing and Parkinson's?

Russell Baker's regular *New York Times* columns are terse, pointed, and matter of fact, like this sample, "The Disposable Man," from a collection called *All Things Considered.*[7] You can usually call his columns "funny," but as with many good "funny" writers, the fun is serious. The writer's ability to play meaningfully with serious material is an indication of inward calm and control. Despite people around him, and even his own inclinations, he can assume an attitude he feels will be more effective in communicating his knowledge to a reader.

How far is American know-how from producing a disposable man?

Closer perhaps than it seems. Sears, Roebuck and Company is already marketing a stingless bee, for people who want to keep bees without really being bothered. The stingless bee, of course, was inevitable, just as the disposable man is. It is merely the latest in a long line of technological breakthroughs that have brought us into the Nothing Generation or, as social psychologists might call it, the Non Age.

The purpose of the Non Age is to make it possible for the Nothing Generation to get through a complete non-life without any of the untidy bothers of living, like bee stings. Hence, the non-bee.

Other adjuncts of the good non-life include the fuzzless peach, the seedless grape, and odorless booze (vodka). All

[7] Russell Baker, "The Disposable Man," *All Things Considered* (Philadelphia: J. B. Lippincott Co., 1962).

serve the same basic function as the stingless bee. They relieve man of the need to come to grips with nature by devising schemes to keep peach fuzz off his chin, seeds out of his appendix and neighbors from knowing that he is snockered.

The child of the Nothing Generation is naturally swaddled in a disposable diaper. As he grows he goes to the painless dentist. His father lives in a no-down-payment house and wears a wrinkle-free, drip-dry wardrobe. On formal occasions, he wears a clip-on tie.

The essence of non-life is non-involvement, more positively known as playing it safe. And so literature has created the anti-hero for the anti-theater and the anti-novel. The anti-hero sits around in garbage cans doing nothing for hours, except saying "no" to life and waiting to be disposed of. He is a great favorite of the Nothing Generation, which can listen to him for hours, even on caffeine-free coffee.

When the anti-hero wants to carbonate his stomach he takes a non-caloric soft drink. It comes in a disposable, no-deposit no-return bottle, or a throwaway can. For amusement he sits in dehumidified air watching non-actors perform non-dramas about non-people and absorbing advertisements that tell how to take the misery out of washday, the odors out of living and the challenge out of opening a milk can.

The beauty of the Non Age is that it makes non-life so easy, and creates so much leisure time to enjoy non-living. The disposable diaper, for example, not only takes half the agony out of parenthood, but also gives the parents time to drink more odorless booze, without offending baby's delicate nose.

The throwaway bottle saves them from the unpleasantness of seeing junior sulk when ordered to take the bottles back to the store. It also gives them a chance to worry each other about why junior has nothing to do with his time but wolf fuzzless peaches and seedless grapes.

The Non Age, fortunately, provides for junior, should the non-life hang heavily on his hands and make him edgy. The doctor will prescribe some tranquillizers to keep him in a non-emotional state. The prescription will be written with a throwaway pen.

In this state junior may be induced to turn down the anti-music on the phonograph and turn his hand to something perfectly unchallenging, like keeping stingless bees.

The stingless bee, incidentally, reached the market at the same time as the topless bathing suit and the topless evening gown, which had just appeared in London. Both will soon take the last disturbing shred of curiosity out of anti-hero.

What next in the march toward a better non-life for all Americans? The workless job is already well developed. The disposable conscience is old hat. There is room perhaps, as recent events in the old South suggest, for the painless truncheon, though a case can be made that when safe, uninvolved non-living becomes absolute, everything will be painless.

No. What the Nothing Generation needs for self-completion is the disposable man. He will be able to pass from disposable diaper to the trash can, leaving no trace but an irrevocable trust for his disposable children.

Often, when an absurd idea seems to enter our thoughts from no conceivable source, we dismiss it quickly. Russell Baker could have done this with the idea of a disposable man. However, some absurd ideas stick with us, and if examined closely enough they are seen to be not so absurd after all. When examining the relation of these ideas to things that already exist, we find either that the ideas are not so absurd or that some things in the world around us are more absurd than we ever thought.

In his essay on disposable man, Baker's point is obvious, but not *too* obvious. He doesn't beat us over the head with it or wave it around saying, "Aren't I clever?" He uses it economically and concretely. He begins with the ultimate product of what he calls the Non Age—the disposable man. It seems complete fantasy until he talks about similar products already widely accepted by the readers—you and me.

Among descriptions of these familiar things, he carefully repeats his idea word, *non.* This repetition could be boring if it were not attached to the concrete subjects. This attachment, as well as Baker's varying the negative *non* to *anti, nothing, no, un-,* and *less,* make the repetition interesting and a demonstration of the reality of the Non Age.

QUESTIONS

1. Can you imagine a wordier version of this essay?
2. Can you see any organization in the presentation of details?
3. What makes this piece funny and Isherwood's serious?

When someone begins to ruin something you care about deeply, sorrow, anger, or both are often the result. Biologist Rachel Carson wrote a best-selling book on pesticides, *The Silent Spring.*[8] It was a best seller not because readers were deeply interested in pesticides, but because as a writer, Rachel Carson conveyed a strong sense of sorrow and loss. In this story of Long Island, New York, how does she use documentation to help convey her emotion?

From small beginnings over farmlands and forests the scope of aerial spraying has widened and its volume has increased so that it has become what a British ecologist recently called "an amazing rain of death" upon the surface of the earth. Our attitude toward poisons has undergone a subtle change. Once they were kept in containers marked with skull and crossbones; the infrequent occasions of their use were marked with utmost care that they should come in contact with the target and with nothing else. With the development of the new organic insecticides and the abundance of surplus planes after the Second World War, all this was forgotten. Although today's poisons are more dangerous than any known before, they have amazingly become something to be showered down indiscriminately from

[8] Rachel Carson, *The Silent Spring* (Boston: Houghton Mifflin, 1962), pp. 155–161.

the skies. Not only the target insect or plant, but anything—human or nonhuman—within range of the chemical fallout may know the sinister touch of the poison. Not only forests and cultivated fields are sprayed, but towns and cities as well.

A good many people now have misgivings about the aerial distribution of lethal chemicals over millions of acres, and two mass-spraying campaigns undertaken in the late 1950's have done much to increase these doubts. These were the campaigns against the gypsy moth in the northeastern states and the fire ant in the South. Neither is a native insect but both have been in this country for many years without creating a situation calling for desperate measures. Yet drastic action was suddenly taken against them, under the end-justifies-the-means philosophy that has too long directed the control divisions of our Department of Agriculture.

The gypsy moth program shows what a vast amount of damage can be done when reckless large-scale treatment is substituted for local and moderate control. The campaign against the fire ant is a prime example of a campaign based on gross exaggeration of the need for control, blunderingly launched without scientific knowledge of the dosage of poison required to destroy the target or of its effects on other life. Neither program has achieved its goal.

The gypsy moth, a native of Europe, has been in the United States for nearly a hundred years. In 1869 a French scientist, Leopold Trouvelot, accidentally allowed a few of these moths to escape from his laboratory in Medford, Massachusetts, where he was attempting to cross them with silkworms. Little by little the gypsy moth has spread throughout New England. The primary agent of its progressive spread is the wind; the larval, or caterpillar, stage is extremely light and can be carried to considerable heights and over great distances. Another means is the shipment of plants carrying the egg masses, the form in which the species exists over winter. The gypsy moth, which in its larval stage attacks the foliage of oak trees and a few other hardwoods for a few weeks each spring, now occurs in all the New England states. It also occurs sporadically in New Jersey, where it was introduced in 1911 on a shipment of spruce trees from Holland, and in Michigan, where its method of entry is not known. The New England hurricane of 1938 carried it into Pennsylvania and New York, but the Adirondacks have generally served as a barrier to its westward advance, being forested with species not attractive to it.

The task of confining the gypsy moth to the northeastern corner of the country has been accomplished by a variety of methods, and in the nearly one hundred years since its arrival on this continent the fear that it would invade the great hardwood forests of the southern Appalachians has not been justified. Thirteen parasites and predators were imported from abroad and successfully established in New England. The Agriculture Department itself has credited these importations with appreciably reducing the frequency and destructiveness of gypsy moth outbreaks. This natural control, plus quarantine measures and local spraying, achieved what the Department in 1955 described as "outstanding restriction of distribution and damage."

Yet only a year after expressing satisfaction with the state of affairs, its Plant Pest Control Division embarked on a program calling for the blanket spraying of several million acres a year with the announced intention of eventually "eradicating" the gypsy moth. ("Eradication" means the complete and final extinction or extermination of a species throughout its range. Yet as successive programs have failed, the Department has found it necessary to speak of second or third "eradications" of the same species in the same area.)

The Department's all-out chemical war on the gypsy moth began on an ambitious scale. In 1956 nearly a million acres were sprayed in the states of Pennsylvania, New Jersey, Michigan, and New York. Many complaints of damage were made by people in the sprayed areas. Conservationists became increasingly disturbed as the pattern of spraying huge areas began to establish itself. When plans were announced for spraying 3 million acres in 1957 opposition became even stronger. State and federal agriculture officials characteristically shrugged off individual complaints as unimportant.

The Long Island area included within the gypsy moth spraying in 1957 consisted chiefly of heavily populated towns and suburbs and of some coastal areas with bordering salt marsh. Nassau County, Long Island, is the most densely settled county in New York apart from New York City itself. In what seems the height of absurdity, the "threat of infestation of the New York City metropolitan area" has been cited as an important justification of the program. The gypsy moth is a forest insect, certainly not an inhabitant of cities. Nor does it live in meadows, cultivated fields, gardens, or marshes. Nevertheless, the planes hired by the United States Department of Agriculture and the New York Department of Agriculture and Markets in 1957 showered down the prescribed DDT-in-fuel-oil with impartiality. They sprayed truck gardens and dairy farms, fish ponds and salt marshes. They sprayed the quarter-acre lots of suburbia, drenching a housewife making a desperate effort to cover her garden before the roaring plane reached her, and showering insecticide over children at play and commuters at railway stations. At Setauket a fine quarter horse drank from a trough in a field which the planes had sprayed; ten hours later it was dead. Automobiles were spotted with the oily mixture; flowers and shrubs were ruined. Birds, fish, crabs, and useful insects were killed.

A group of Long Island citizens led by the world-famous ornithologist Robert Cushman Murphy had sought a court injunction to prevent the 1957 spraying. Denied a preliminary injunction, the protesting citizens had to suffer the prescribed drenching with DDT, but thereafter persisted in efforts to obtain a permanent injunction. But because the act had already been performed the courts held that the petition for an injunction was "moot." The case was carried all the way to the Supreme Court, which declined to hear it. Justice William O. Douglas, strongly dissenting from the decision not to review the case, held that "the alarms that many experts and responsible officials have raised about the perils of DDT underline the public importance of this case."

The suit brought by the Long Island citizens at least served to focus public attention on the growing trend to mass application of insecticides, and on the power and inclination of the control agencies to disregard supposedly inviolate property rights of private citizens.

The contamination of milk and of farm produce in the course of the gypsy moth spraying came as an unpleasant surprise to many people. What happened on the 200-acre Waller farm in northern Westchester County, New York, was revealing. Mrs. Waller had specifically requested Agriculture officials not to spray her property, because it would be impossible to avoid the pastures in spraying the woodlands. She offered to have the land checked for gypsy moths and to have any infestation destroyed by spot spraying. Although she was assured that no farms would be sprayed, her property received two direct sprayings and, in addition, was twice subjected to drifting spray. Milk samples taken from the Wallers' purebred Guernsey cows 48 hours later contained DDT in the amount of 14 parts per million. Forage samples from fields where the cows had grazed were of course contaminated also. Although the county Health Department was notified, no instructions were given that the milk should not be marketed. This situation is unfortunately typical of the lack of consumer protection that is all too common. Although the Food and Drug Administration permits no residues of pesticides in milk, its restrictions are not only inadequately policed but they apply solely to interstate shipments. State and county officials are under no compulsion to follow the federal pesticides tolerances unless local laws happen to conform—and they seldom do.

Truck gardeners also suffered. Some leaf crops were so burned and spotted as to be unmarketable. Others carried heavy residues; a sample of peas analyzed at Cornell University's Agricultural Experiment Station contained 14 to 20 parts per million of DDT. The legal maximum is 7 parts per million. Growers therefore had to sustain heavy losses or find themselves in the position of selling produce carrying illegal residues. Some of them sought and collected damages.

As the aerial spraying of DDT increased, so did the number of suits filed in the courts. Among them were suits brought by beekeepers in several areas of New York State. Even before the 1957 spraying, the beekeepers had suffered heavily from use of

DDT in orchards. "Up to 1953 I had regarded as gospel everything that emanated from the U.S. Department of Agriculture and the agricultural colleges," one of them remarked bitterly. But in May of that year this man lost 800 colonies after the state had sprayed a large area. So widespread and heavy was the loss that 14 other beekeepers joined him in suing the state for a quarter of a million dollars in damages. Another beekeeper, whose 400 colonies were incidental targets of the 1957 spray, reported that 100 per cent of the field force of bees (the workers out gathering nectar and pollen for the hives) had been killed in forested areas and up to 50 per cent in farming areas sprayed less intensively. "It is a very distressful thing," he wrote, "to walk into a yard in May and not hear a bee buzz."

The gypsy moth programs were marked by many acts of irresponsibility. Because the spray planes were paid by the gallon rather than by the acre there was no effort to be conservative, and many properties were sprayed not once but several times. Contracts for aerial spraying were in at least one case awarded to an out-of-state firm with no local address, which had not complied with the legal requirement of registering with state officials for the purpose of establishing legal responsibility. In this exceedingly slippery situation, citizens who suffered direct financial loss from damage to apple orchards or bees discovered that there was no one to sue.

After the disastrous 1957 spraying the program was abruptly and drastically curtailed, with vague statements about "evaluating" previous work and testing alternative insecticides. Instead of the 3½ million acres sprayed in 1957, the treated areas fell to ½ million in 1958 and to about 100,000 acres in 1959, 1960, and 1961. During this interval, the control agencies must have found news from Long Island disquieting. The gypsy moth had reappeared there in numbers. The expensive spraying operation that had cost the Department dearly in public confidence and good will—the operation that was intended to wipe out the gypsy moth for ever—had in reality accomplished nothing at all.

This section from *The Silent Spring* is preceded by chapters on how pesticides affect plants, soil, water, and animals. Later the author writes about the human consequences. Throughout the book she keeps man's responsibility as her central theme.

In the section on the gypsy moth she tries to develop an image of man foolishly using insecticide—not against insects but against himself. From her masses of documentation she chose one case —not an exceptional case, but one that would provide both proof and thematic continuity. The theme is in the first paragraph—our attitude toward poisons. The gypsy moth case embodies this attitude as well as proves irresponsibility.

The author's sense of loss is strong and probably accompanied by anger, but if she did not choose her documentation carefully, readers would accuse her of propaganda. They would not believe in the cause of her sorrow or anger. The same result would occur if she were not careful with her language. The use of highly emotional language here could cover up the real situation, which includes both reader and writer.

QUESTIONS

1. Examine Miss Carson's use of adjectives and adverbs. Do you think they are well used or too abundant and obvious?
2. Imagine this essay as a lecture on responsibility. Rewrite one or two paragraphs so they are completely theoretical or abstract.
3. Juxtaposition (placing side by side) of detail is important in creating the emotion. Identify several juxtapositions you feel are deliberate and forceful. How do you think they work on the reader's mind?

As you read the following student theme, "Christmas Morning," concentrate on the tone of the writing. When are you sure if it is comic or serious?

Christmas for me has always been a time of getting. As a kid you are overpowered by the givers, so you become used to receiving. That is just how Christmas works nowadays. So when I was five years old Christmas came along with its usual promises. I gave the department store Santa Claus a long list of toys, including a bone and a bed for my retriever Colonel.

Colonel was an extension of my own personality, the only extension outside myself. Just as kids aren't really allowed to give, they're not really allowed to extend their personalities either. Anyway, Colonel got on the Christmas list not because I was a good guy, but for selfish reasons.

Christmas Eve when I came home from church I took Colonel up to my room and told him what he and I were going to get in the morning. I asked my mother if I could keep him up in my room so he would be surprised, but she said no. (I never was allowed to have him in my room at night.)

The next morning when I woke up I listened to see if my parents were up already. I wanted to be first. I couldn't hear any dishes or voices. I went downstairs in my pajamas, and without even going to the Christmas tree I opened the cellar door to call up Colonel. The door was open.

"Colonel," I yelled into the cellar.

No answer. Maybe he is up, I thought and went to the tree in the dining room. Colonel was lying under the tree in his bed, a big wicker thing with a cushion. I kneeled down to rumple him up, but when I touched him his whole body shook like a piece of wood. Oddly enough, my first thought was that this was a fake model of Colonel, but of course Colonel was dead, right under the tree.

The author of this theme set out not only to describe an incident, but to do something with the themes of giving and receiving. The presence of these themes unifies his writing. However, in intending to convey sorrow along with his images of giving and receiving, the writer has misplaced his emphasis.

The sorrow comes entirely in the last sentences of the last paragraph. The author knows all along where he is going, but the reader does not. As he writes the author bears the sorry end in mind; the reader is simply puzzled or curious. The result is that what seems like a neat flowering of grief to the author is simply shock to the reader. And in this case, the shock is so ironic as to be almost absurd. The result is more like a cruelty joke than a sad story. In fact, it is told like a joke—the punch line held off until the very last. Some readers will begin to wonder if this was not the intended effect.

You may argue that the author seeks this ambiguity, perhaps to mirror certain ambiguities in life. If this is the case, why all the detail about the boy? Why not just say a boy's pet was found dead under a Christmas tree? However, once there is a personality created, we want to see the relationships. We want communication, not riddles. There is usually enough mystery in the concrete facts of life, as it is.

QUESTIONS

1. How could this have been made an effective comic sketch? What tone of voice and point of view would have been used?
2. What would be the effect of reorganizing the sketch so the dog's death was first or at least near the beginning?
3. Could the self-analysis (about the dog as an extension of personality) be used more effectively, or replaced?
4. What further thinking could the author have done before he actually started writing?

ASSIGNMENTS

1. Describe the loss of someone or something you valued or failure to reach an expected goal. Be sure you know whether you are describing merely your feelings, or the actual loss. Can you make your feelings concrete? Will the reader see why the loss caused sorrow, or will he think the effect too grandiose for the cause?
2. Are you usually able to laugh at adversity and trouble, or do you find the world too serious and dark to laugh at? Limiting yourself to a particular incident, place, or group, write a description which will make the reader share your light or dark vision. Do not tell the reader how to see; let your organization, choice of detail, and language do the work.

PART FOUR

THE WRITER'S
RESPONSIBILITY

CHAPTER *10*

YOUR WRITING

AND YOU

There are two reasons why most people do not become good writers. First, writing is work. Not only do you have to be able to sit still in one place with your seat glued to a chair, but you have to think hard before you write; and after you write you must be willing to re-evaluate all of what you have done. By now you probably know this and will be able to sympathize with Mark Harris' southpaw.

It is now 3 A.M. in the morning, and I am disgusted. It is a very cold winter night out, and I have got a fire in the fireplace.

I begun this book last October, and it is now January, and I doubt that I am halfway through. I will give 1 word of advice to any sap with the itch to write a book—do not begin it in the first place.

I got 12 chapters wrote on this blasted thing and it was not easy. My hand does not grip a pencil so good, for it is rather large, and I went and bought a couple big fat pencils called an

Eagle number 4 from Fred Levine that does not make my hand so tired. Fred is still rather cool to me.

After I got through the 12 chapters I bumped into Aaron yesterday morning, and he said, "Well, Henry, I do not see much of you any more. Ain't you afraid of putting on weight staying indoors like that?"

"I have wrote 12 chapters," I said, "and lost 12 pounds at the least."

"I admire your get up and go," he said.

"Get up and go hell," said I. "It is the sit down and stay that gets books wrote," and he got a great laugh out of that.[1]

The second reason most beginning writers fail is because writing requires honesty—the honesty to look long and hard at your own self and the honesty to put what you find on paper where total strangers might see it. To be vague, to use meaningless clichés or glittering generalities, to propagandize, to use sentimentality— all are forms of dishonesty. You can be dishonest as much in what you do not do as in what you do. Honest writing is a little like walking down the street naked: It takes a good deal of confidence and trust and courage.

There is only one level on which to fight dishonesty in writing —within the individual. You must fight before you write. Fighting with yourself is difficult and hurts the ego, but since all good writing must originate with your personal involvement, the fight is yours. It does no good to try to bully others into liking your writing.

Though there are many forms of symbolic communication for man, language is one of the most personal. Silently or aloud, most men talk to themselves a good part of their waking hours. In our minds we try to "discuss" our problems, feelings, and ideas, or we analyze our experience. But even with all this "talking," how often are we ever sure about our conclusions? And rather than admit uncertainty and seek to learn, we adopt someone else's idea because it sounds good. Often enough thinking harder and longer about our feelings and ideas would make us more certain. Yet

[1] Mark Harris, *The Southpaw* (Indianapolis: The Bobbs-Merrill Co., 1953), p. 105.

through fear or laziness or blindness when we are talking about those things that mean most to us we usually resort to saying, "I can't really describe it."

If you say that in writing, you are really saying you cannot write about what you want to. Then why write about that subject at all? (Unless you expect to dazzle your readers with abstractions and evasions. These will fool some readers and will be appreciated by others who want to be fooled.) As a reader how far would you go in the student essay "An Amazing Man," ·the first paragraph of which follows?

> Somehow Mr. Frank Dixon is the most amazing man in town. He is the mayor of Norwich and everybody knows him by sight. Though he is of average height, there is something about his walk and his face that distinguishes him. He dresses well too. But these are only surface characteristics. It's an indescribable inner uniqueness that is the essence of the man.

Upon examination by other students, this writer admitted (or perhaps discovered) that his basis for describing Mr. Dixon as amazing was mainly that everyone in town described him that way. The writer himself did not know why. He simply believed it and set out to show it. The entire theme was as vague as that first paragraph. The writer *felt* his belief, but because there was no foundation in concrete detail, he spent all his words labeling how he felt about Dixon. The reader never got to know the "amazing man."

This writer failed his first responsibility—to himself. He assumed he had something worth writing about, but he did not examine his knowledge of the subject. In fulfilling the assignments of this book you have probably felt the weight of this responsibility. Perhaps you felt it only after the class or your instructor commented.

When under pressure, as one is in any good writing, to say what you really mean, you are tempted by many escapes. As in "An Amazing Man," the escape may be as obvious as vagueness, generality, and abstraction. But there are also much more subtle and dangerous escapes, and you may convince yourself that your escape is the real thing. Have you ever bought something which was not very good, then convinced yourself it really was good? Have you ever started to "fall in love" just because you were lonely? Have you believed your own mistakes were caused by someone else? Have you ever seriously used a stereotype to describe someone you do or don't like? In all these cases you used some device of language to convince yourself of something false.

Your writing *is* your personality. Just as you may not see some faults in yourself, you may not see them in your writing. A critic will say, "That's not logical," and you might reply sincerely, "That's the way I see it." But in saying so you have only changed the critic's remark to "*You* see things illogically."

You are not entirely at fault for the lack of honesty that often threatens your writing. For one thing, you are constantly being bombarded by words that are not yours. Often these words are made so much a part of daily life that you begin thinking they are yours. For the sake of convenience, you use them. You can probably find in your speech words, phrases, and patterns of thought from radio, movies, records, and television. There is nothing wrong with using words which others have used. Language belongs to everyone. But you must be aware of which words are yours and which are not. You must know when your thinking is being slave to the words and when you are using the words to serve your thought.

No one can force you to adopt the conventions and clichés of language that you do not want. In this respect, you are freer as a writer than you are as a businessman, a scientist, a family man, a carpenter, or a driver. This freedom is certainly essential, but it can also be detrimental, as it was for novelist Joyce Cary. At school Cary was encouraged to write by his teacher Sydney Irwin,

> who opened his library to me. Irwin was a precise and careful scholar who did, I believe, a good deal of reviewing for *The Times* of that date. And he encouraged me to write. Unluckily, he was anxious not to impress his own judgments, he tried as far as possible to leave me to express my own ideas in my own way. The result was that I did not learn to use language with precision, and years later had to struggle with problems that I should have had solved for me at school. I found these prize

essays some years ago, and they had the faults no schoolboy should be allowed to commit, and what's more, their ideas were extremely conventional.[2]

As a writer you must not only be responsive to outside criticism, but you must seek it as a way of keeping yourself honest. To avoid criticism of this kind is a sign of fear and lack of confidence. It is like trying to play tennis by batting a lot of balls over the net and having no opponent to return them.

While you must seek outside criticism, you must also be selective where you look for it. Polite readers usually say nothing, flatter, or remain noncommital. Your best critics will be blunt and honest, and they will probably understand what you are trying to do. Public praise (or condemnation) is usually worth little in evaluating your work.

Here is how Henry Miller felt about the belated public acclaim he won in the United States.

INTERVIEWER: How does it feel to be a best-seller after enduring the plight of the creative artist all these years?

MILLER: I really have no feelings about it. It's unreal to me, the whole thing. I don't find myself involved. In fact I rather dislike it. It gives me no pleasure. All I see is more disruption in my life, more intrusions, more nonsense. People are concerned about something which no longer concerns me. That book doesn't mean anything to me any more. People think because they're all worked up about it that I am too. They think it's a great thing for me that I'm accepted at last. Well, I feel that I'd been accepted long before, at least by those I cared to be accepted by. To be accepted by the mob doesn't mean a thing to me. In fact it's rather painful. Because I'm being accepted for the wrong reasons. It's a sensational affair, it doesn't mean that I am appreciated for my true worth.

INTERVIEWER: But this is part of the recognition that you've always known would come to you.

[2] Joyce Cary, *Art and Reality* (New York: Harper & Row, 1958), pp. 63–64.

MILLER: Yes, of course. But then, don't you see, the only real recognition comes from those who are on the same level with you, from your peers. That's the only kind that matters, and I've had that. I've had it for years now.[3]

SELECTIONS

The selections which follow are by professional writers, but what they say applies to all good writing. As we have said often throughout this book, good writing is within anyone's reach. There are not two ways of writing, one for pros and one for students. The basis of *War and Peace* or Franklin's *Autobiography* or Huxley's essays is the basis for your writing too—a personal involvement and vision. You may never tackle subjects as difficult or profound as these writers' subjects, but you have plenty to write about. If you don't have plenty to write about, you are ready for a psychiatrist or you are a new kind of machine.

Leo Tolstoy's essay "What Is Art" considers many theories and finds that they are all forgetting one simple condition that must be met before art can exist.[4] Does this condition apply to your work?

All these theories forget one chief thing—that neither importance, nor beauty, nor sincerity, provides the requisite for works of art, but that the basic condition of the production of such works is that the artist should be conscious of something new and important; and that therefore, just as it always has been, so it always will be, necessary for a true artist to be able to perceive something quite new and important. For the artist to see what is new, it is necessary that he should observe and think, and not occupy his life with trifles which hinder his attentive penetration into, and meditation on, life's phenomena. In order that the new things he sees may be important ones, the

[3] Henry Miller interview, *Writers at Work: The Paris Review Interviews,* Second Edition (New York: The Viking Press, 1963).

[4] Leo Tolstoy, "What Is Art," *What Is Art,* trans. Louise and Aylmer Maude (London: Oxford University Press, 1930).

artist must be a morally enlightened man, and he must not live a selfish life but must share the common life of humanity.

If only he sees what is new and important he will be sure to find a form which will express it, and the sincerity which is an essential content of artistic production will be present. He must be able to express the new subject so that all may understand it. For this he must have such mastery of his craft that when working he will think as little about the rules of that craft as a man when walking thinks of the laws of motion. And in order to attain this, the artist must not look round on his work and admire it, must not make technique his aim—as one who is walking should not contemplate and admire his gait—but should be concerned only to express his subject, and in such a way as to be intelligible to all.

Finally, to work at his subject not for external ends but to satisfy his inner need, the artist must rise superior to motives of avarice and vanity. He must love with his own heart and not with another's, and not pretend that he loves what others love or consider worthy of love.

And to attain all this the artist must do as Balaam did when the messengers came to him and he went apart awaiting God so as to say only what God commanded; and he must not do as that same Balaam afterwards did when, tempted by gifts he went to the king against God's command, as was evident even to the ass on which he rode, though not perceived by him while blinded by avarice and vanity.

QUESTIONS

1. What does Tolstoy mean by "morally enlightened," and why does he place such stress on the nonwriting part of a man's life?
2. Why is a writer "sure to find a form" if he has "found what is new and important"?
3. Explain the Biblical example at the end.

For centuries people have tried to formulate rules for writing. Here, in a passage from *The Summing Up*, Somerset Maugham tells how someone applied rules to his writing.[5]

I have never had more than two English lessons in my life, for though I wrote essays at school, I do not remember that I ever received any instruction on how to put sentences together. The two lessons I have had were given me so late in life that I am afraid I cannot hope greatly to profit by them. The first was only a few years ago. I was spending some weeks in London and had engaged as temporary secretary a young woman. She was shy, rather pretty, and absorbed in a love affair with a married man. I had written a book called *Cakes and Ale* and, the typescript arriving one Saturday morning, I asked her if she would be good enough to take it home and correct it over the week-end. I meant her only to make a note of mistakes in spelling that the typist might have made and point out errors occasioned by a handwriting that is not always easy to decipher. But she was a conscientious young person and she took me more literally than I intended. When she brought back the typescript on Monday morning it was accompanied by four foolscap sheets of corrections. I must confess that at the first glance I was a trifle vexed; but then I thought that it would be silly of me not to profit, if I could, by the trouble she had taken and so sat me down to examine them. I suppose the young woman had taken a course at a secretarial college and she had gone through my novel in the same methodical way as her masters had gone through her essays. The remarks that filled the four neat pages of foolscap were incisive and severe. I could not but surmise that the professor of English at the secretarial college did not mince matters. He took a marked line, there could be no doubt about that; and he did not allow that there might be two opinions about anything. His apt pupil would have nothing to do with a preposition at the end of a sentence. A mark of exclamation betokened her disapproval of a colloquial

[5] Somerset Maugham, *The Summing Up*, First Edition (New York: Doubleday, 1938), pp. 25–30.

phrase. She had a feeling that you must not use the same word twice on a page and she was ready every time with a synonym to put in its place. If I had indulged myself in the luxury of a sentence of ten lines, she wrote: "Clarify this. Better break it up into two or more periods." When I had availed myself of the pleasant pause that is indicated by a semicolon, she noted: "A full stop"; and if I had ventured upon a colon she remarked stingingly: "Obsolete." But the harshest stroke of all was her comment on what I thought was rather a good joke: "Are you sure of your facts?" Taking it all in all I am bound to conclude that the professor at her college would not have given me very high marks.

Questions

1. Does Maugham advocate having no rules at all?
2. What principles govern Maugham's grammar besides tradition or usage?
3. Why does Maugham's use of grammar involve responsibility?

We have emphasized that your own personality should be in your writing. One of the greatest fears any writer has is that if he puts his own self into his writing, readers may say, "Who's interested in you?" Stephen Spender, a British poet, has written an autobiography entitled *The Making of a Poem*.[6] Below he talks about the problems and values of autobiography, particularly why one might feel justified in writing about himself. Could his reasoning apply to other forms of personal writing?

The dictionary definition of the word *Autobiography* is: 'the story of one's life written by himself.' This starts a train of thought in my mind. 'One's life written by himself'—just as if

[6] Stephen Spender, "Confession and Autobiography," *The Making of a Poem* (New York: W. W. Norton, 1955), pp. 63–67.

himself were A, B, or C, or some other writing his biography. Of course, the dictionary is right, but there is a world of difference in that 'himself'. Brown's Life written by Brown is—to my mind—a different proposition from Brown's Life written by Jones or Smith. At all events, it is a different proposition in the mind of Brown when he takes up his pen, remembering himself: though, in fact, he may well decide to pretend that he is Smith, writing his life as though he were another person. He may say: 'What is significant about me in the minds of others is that which Jones or Smith would write as my biography. So let me pretend that I am Jones or Smith, and enter into a neighbour's-eye-view of myself.' Yet in saying this, isn't Brown taking a tremendous step? In deciding to write his own biography, as though he were Jones or Smith, isn't he excluding a whole world, which is himself as he appears, not to Jones or Smith, but to himself?

Perhaps I over-dramatize the affair: generals, statesmen, and big-game hunters—to take some random examples—may really appear to themselves exactly as they appear to other people. To themselves they are historic forces giving orders on battlefields, making speeches in Parliament, or moving through forests armed with guns like sticks, which they point at lions, tigers, and elephants. If there is anything left over from all this which is themselves, it is either unpublishable or else a charming proof to others of their humanity. For in the case of public personalities humanity seems to begin where eccentricity appears, when they think or act in a way which is inconsistent with being general, statesman, or big-game hunter.

Yet unless one is to oneself entirely public, it seems that the problem of an autobiographer, when he considers the material of his own past, is that he is confronted not by one life—which he sees from the outside—but by two. One of these lives is himself as others see him—his social or historic personality—the sum of his achievements, his appearances, his personal relationships. All these are real to him as, say, his own image in a mirror. But there is also himself known only to himself, himself seen from the inside of his own existence. This inside self has a history which may have no significance in any objective 'history of his time'. It is the history of himself observing the observer, and not as the observed of others.

· · · ·

We are seen from the outside by our neighbours; but we remain always at the back of our eyes and our senses, situated in our bodies, like a driver in the front seat of a car seeing the other cars come towards him. A single person, instead of being a tiny little automatism in a vast concourse of traffic which is the whole of humanity, is one consciousness within one machine confronting all the other traffic. From this point of view, being born into the world is like being a rocket shot on to the moon. And who knows whether being projected on to the moon would actually be so very different from being born into the world? At first one would perhaps feel very strange. But soon, one would—in the manner of all men—take one's own presence on the moon for granted, just as one takes the world, and accepts oneself as one of the others.

To feel strange, to retain throughout life the sense of being a voyager on the earth come from another sphere, to whom everything remains wonderful, horrifying, and new, is, I suppose, to be an artist. Artists—whether they are writers or painters—are people who continue throughout life to realize that every experience is a unique event in time and space, occurring for the first and last time.

It might seem then, that autobiography was the most stimulating of forms for a writer. For here he is dealing with his life in the raw at the point where it is also his art in the raw. He can describe, through the history of his meeting with the people and things outside him, those opposite beings whom from the back of himself he sees coming towards him, the very sensation of being alive, and being alone.

Yet, just because a writer is so rawly and newly in contact with his material, even because in his writing he draws so much on this new experience of ever first-seen life, autobiography may be especially difficult for him. For in this work, the expression of such naked solitude may be just what he wishes to avoid. He uses his observation in order to relate one thing to another, not to state experiences which are unrelated. Until his subjective experiences have become objectified—have become of a kind that he can identify and project into life outside himself—they are no use to him for his art.

The essence of art is that opposite is related to its opposite. The subject has to be made object, the chaotic the formal, the unique the generally shared experience. Thus, although for a writer his autobiography is the vast mine from which he smelts ore to put into his works, it is also his aim to convert this ore into forms which are outside the writer's own personal ones.

In literature the autobiographical is transformed. It is no longer the writer's own experience: it becomes everyone's. He is no longer writing about himself: he is writing about life. He creates it, not as an object which is already familiar and observed, as he is observed by others, but as a new and revealing object, growing out of and beyond observation. Thus characters in a novel are based on the novelist's observation of real people, and of himself. Yet they would not be 'living' if they were just reported. They are also invented, that is new characters, living in the scene of life which is his novel, and independent of the material of real observation from which they came.

Thus autobiography does set him a very special problem. The theme of his book is himself. Yet if he treats this theme as though he were another person writing about himself, then he evades the basic truth of autobiography which is: 'I am alone in the universe'.

There may of course be many good reasons for refusing this truth. It may not be the writer's purpose to deal with it at all. He may be writing about himself because he is a part of history and his own best historian. Perhaps he thinks that the contribution he has made to politics or thought in his time should be recorded and that, being closest to it, he is the best person to record it. Thus we have in our time, by Albert Schweitzer, Freud, and Croce, excellent examples of objective, depersonalized autobiography. Then also there are reminiscences, like Sir Osbert Sitwell's volumes which are revealing of his family, but tell us little about what it feels like to be in Sir Osbert's skin.

●　●　●　●

All this is perfectly justified. One does not have to defend it. Indeed, what one has to defend is the autobiographers who write about the intimate experience of being themselves. They are indiscreet, they are too interested in themselves, they write about things which are not important to others, they are ego-maniacs. The nature of the inner human personality is such, that if they tell what it is like to be themselves, they are immoralists, exhibitionists, pornographers. The inner voice of self-awareness is no respecter of human institutions, betrays other people, and reveals oneself as base. Maine de Biran—about whose *Intimate Journal* Mr. Aldous Huxley has written—expressed a doubt which the portrayer of the intimate self feels himself. After discussing all his weaknesses, he reflects that perhaps the worst crime is all this interest in oneself.

Self-revelation of the inner life is perhaps a dirty business. Nevertheless—even in its ugliest forms—we cannot afford altogether to despise anyone who—for whatever reasons—is the humblest and ugliest servant of truth. Human beings are instruments crawling about the surface of the earth, registering their reactions to one another and to things. Some of them are very crude instruments, others exact and sensitive. A human instrument is most exact about objective things when it is most detached from them. The effort to create form and objectivity in literature is detachment: and whoever writes of that which is most close to him—himself—is unlikely to achieve detachment.

Nevertheless in a day of pseudo-science when sociologists and psychologists are for ever measuring the behaviour of their neighbours, there is a justification for the autobiography which reminds us how little objective human beings, who set themselves up as observing instruments, really are. The self-revelation of the experience of the self is a measuring of the human instrument by itself. The observer is self-observed.

QUESTIONS

1. What does autobiography do for the writer?
2. Why do we read autobiography?

3. What distinguishes autobiography from biography?
4. Could you support the argument that almost all writing is in some way autobiographical?

Educators used to feel that the more you wrote, the better you wrote. A course at Yale called Daily Themes operated on that premise, and is described by Calvin Trillin in his *New Yorker* article "No Telling, No Summing Up." [7] While the method has been abandoned, the course illustrated many problems faced by student writers trying to be original writers.

Benjamin Nangle, a Yale English professor who has been one of the instructors of a fiction-writing course called Daily Themes since 1923, has read about so many young couples parting forever that he long ago lost count. Boys and girls have said goodbye at railroad stations, in dormitory rooms, in cars parked in the suburbs of Midwestern cities, in the booths of dingy restaurants—almost anyplace where the girl can walk slowly out of sight, or the boy can hang his head and listen to the retreating footsteps, or the girl can slam the door. "Boy-girl themes generally fall into two equally bad types," James Folsom, another Daily Themes instructor, once said in a speech. "The first of these deals with a boy—or occasionally a girl— innocent beyond belief, high-minded, studious, morally beyond reproach, who, for some reason which remains unfathomable, is treated with inhuman cruelty by someone of the opposite sex—someone cunningly disguised as a normal human being but in actuality heartless, vicious, sadistic, and corrupt. The second type details the fortunes of two young people who, through the malevolence of fate—or occasionally the malevolence of someone acting through incomprehensible motives of the purest evil—are separated from each other forever."

[7] Calvin Trillin, "No Telling, No Summing Up," *The New Yorker* (June 11, 1966). Reprinted by permission; © 1966 by The New Yorker Magazine, Inc.

Undergraduates might be expected to consider experiences with girls important enough to write down; undergraduates taking Daily Themes, under pressure to produce a three-hundred-word piece of fiction every day for eight or nine weeks, eventually consider experiences with almost anyone important enough to write down. They begin to observe their roommates. Folsom considers the themes produced by roommate observation better, by and large, than those that result from recalling romances, though he admitted, in the same speech, "It is true that the general picture one gets of roommates when surveying the sizable field of roommate literature as a whole is that they are universally the most nasty, unwholesome, stupid, and despicable young men ever gathered together in one spot."

Yale English instructors have been reading daily themes for about sixty years—to the background music of countless writers saying that it is futile to try to teach something so obviously a matter of divine gift as writing, and of countless professors hinting that it is vaguely disreputable to try to teach something so obviously unscholarly as writing. From the start, a theme has been defined as "a part of a short story," a page or two long. "Daily" has always meant daily, or almost daily. "The title of the course is somewhat misleading," the lecturer often says at the first meeting of the class. "There are no themes due on either Saturday or Sunday, or on Thanksgiving. In other respects, however, the course title is not misleading. We mean that one theme is due every day. The first theme is due tomorrow." Undergraduates who are inclined to endure this regimen do not expect their burden to be lightened very often by praise from above. Daily Themes has always been one of the few courses in Yale College to use letter grades (later translated into the numerical grades used in Yale records), and the grade after D has always been W. Nobody is certain what W stands for, but most people believe it means "Worthless." An undergraduate on the way to his weekly conference with his instructor, where he receives marks and criticism on his last five themes, walks in the presence of W's. From the outset, it has been a tenet of Daily Themes that a student should not be per-

mitted to leave a conference without a ray of hope—that somewhere in his five themes there must be at least one adjective
that can be commended, or one phrase that is not as bad as all
the others—but it is common for an instructor to leave the impression that a ray of hope was not easy to find.

   To demonstrate what is *not* a daily theme, a lecturer sometimes reads to one of the early classes something called the
Jawbone Theme—in which a man wanders through a ghost
ship that has washed ashore, idly comes across a human jawbone, and suddenly realizes, to his distress, that he is holding
the jawbone of his beloved. Trick endings are anathema to
Daily Themes instructors, and telling an anecdote is a foolproof
method of receiving a W. In fact, *telling* anything in Daily
Themes is dangerous. Like most courses in writing, Daily
Themes demands that its students "show, not tell"—show
through dialogue and description, rather than tell by pronouncement or plot summary. "Telling" written in the margin
of a daily theme is severe criticism, and so is "Summing up"—
trying to explain what should have been revealed in the action
by tacking on what is meant to be a pregnant last sentence. The
most vivid event in the memory of one Daily Themes veteran is
a lecture by Nangle that ended with the evils of "summing up."
Nangle appealed to the class, almost poignantly, not to submit
to him any more themes that ended with the sentence "He
walked away in disgust." Wearily leaning over the lectern, he
tried to make clear how many themes he had read over the
years that ended that way, and how many he was likely to read
in the future, no matter how many appeals he made. At that
thought, he walked away in disgust.

   Daily Themes instructors stress that what they consider a
good theme is a scene—however mundane—that reveals
something about the people in it. "We outlast them," Folsom
says. "They run out of the experiences they had always thought
they would write up someday, and they have to look around."
Looking around, undergraduates are never quite convinced
that their daily lives are the stuff that action is made of. After
the first week or so, most of them begin to find their supply of
memorable adventures running thin, and then even mundane

scenes seem to disappear from their lives. The world becomes a blank in the twenty-four hours between themes. The normal mood of Daily Themes students on a week night is desperation. They cull anecdotes (and W's) from their friends. They try to goad their roommates into behaving in nasty, unwholesome, stupid, or despicable ways. They probe their memories for goodbyes in high school or during summer vacations. They think of people they have disliked in the past. They strain their ears for overheard dialogue while waiting for green lights. When something out of the ordinary happens on the campus, they feel delivered. For many years, Yale undergraduates were required to attend morning chapel, and they would all go from there to the post office to pick up their mail. An old vender with a horse and wagon was stationed between the two spots to catch the passing trade. One day, just after chapel was dismissed, the vender's aged horse fell to the pavement and, after a twenty-minute delay, died. Daily Themes instructors say that no horse's death has ever been more widely celebrated in fiction.

Normally, girls surpass horses as a subject of daily themes, but that triumph is fairly recent. For forty years—from 1909 to 1949—a collection of daily themes was produced in book form every year, each student contributing his favorite theme and his share of the printing bill. (The books were discontinued when printing costs got too high, and were resumed last year with the money from a recent bequest.) Richard Sewall, who taught Daily Themes for several years in the forties, once read through the hundred or so themes preserved from 1911, and he found only three girls—all of them pleasant and none of them saying goodbye. (One of them, a laundry-bill collector described as "one of those many old-faced little daughters of the poor," belonged to the small band of little old ladies, decrepit panhandlers, quaint Italians, and pathetic young girls who used to creep through the early themes as representatives of the lower classes.) Parents and their ilk appeared as rarely and as pleasantly. The one theme in the 1909 book that deals with generational relations is narrated by a young man who was reluctant to spend an evening with some friends of his parents but later concludes, "No small talk here of the belle of the ball, whose sheltered life furnished naught else; nor the crude accounts of the young men's coatroom, bred of an unbalanced outlook on life. That evening with experience-silvered heads— I would not give ten Proms for it."

A hero in last year's Daily Themes book found himself in a similar position:

"Mother, will you please just leave me alone for a while?"

"Can't you at least come down and say hello to them?"

"No—they're your friends, not mine. I don't give a damn whether they ever come over. I don't care about them."

"Well, they care about you. They want to see you."

"Well, good for them. I don't want to see them—I don't want to see anyone right now."

"I don't see how anyone can be so perverse. Is something bothering you?"

"Yes, the whole damn world bothers me right now so I want to be up here by myself and I especially don't feel like going down there and being hypocritically pleasant and civil to the Bayleys."

The early writers of daily themes had no precise substitutes for girls and parents, but they seemed to derive a lot of enjoyment from the look of the campus and the wonders of nature. A good number of burning logs crackled in cheerful campfires in those days, and a lot of snow was driven against the glistening windowpanes of rustic cabins. A typical nature lover of 1910 wrote, "Around the bend in the piney mountain trail where first the sapphire lake flashes into view I swing, just as the flaming sun sinks below the last azure hill of the intervale, flecking with pink and gold every fleecy August cloud." Going through most of the old Daily Themes books, Sewall found that the subject matter had not been greatly affected by the upheavals of the First World War and the Depression—both of which were pretty much ignored as subjects themselves. In the twenties and thirties, the language of the themes gradually lost some of its nineteenth-century flavor, but if the writers were having any serious confrontations with girls or parents or roommates, they were unwilling to write them down. The subject matter of the themes began to broaden at the time of the Second World War, but even today half the themes are still about college life. Some subjects are so common that instructors talk of the Mixer Theme, the Shoot Down (it is usually the boy who is shot down by the girl, occasionally at a mixer), the Lonely Theme (people are often lonely at mixers and after being shot down), and—a voice from the past—the Panhandler Theme. "There is also the Summer Job Theme and the Growing Up Theme," Folsom says. "And the theme about adventures in New York. There's a strong sub-genre of the New York Theme about being approached by a homosexual." Daily Themes writers are not known for their upbeat endings. Michael Cowan, who is one of the instructors of the course this year, says, "Although you can find happiness experiences, fulfillment experiences—sexual fulfillment or a guy getting elected to a club—the average story turns the other way. People laugh if someone reads a theme that implies any sort of easy happiness." There is some evidence, however, that today's undergraduates are not as far from musing on the beauties of azure hills as they seem. "Now we get the guy sitting on the beach musing about the girl he's slept with the night before," Folsom says. "Sometimes I think they've just replaced Swinburne romanticism with Hemingway romanticism."

Before the Daily Themes course was five years old, John Berdan, who taught it from 1907 until his retirement, in 1941, had established the criteria governing the themes in the form of eight slogans, most of which lasted, without alteration, for more than fifty years. (But by the fifties the same slogans that had once brought forth flowery descriptions of nature and football were producing spare dialogues between surly boy and unwilling girl, or careful accounts of the most disgusting event of the weekend.) For the past several years, the slogans have not been used word for word as lecture topics, and teaching methods have become more varied now that the regular course has been supplemented by sophomore seminars at some of Yale's residential colleges. But Berdan's influence remains, even if modern students miss the opportunity of seeing him chalk a slogan in huge letters on the blackboard, turn to the class, and announce, "Individualize by Specific Detail!" Speaking before secondary-school English teachers at a conference sponsored by the Yale Master of Arts in Teaching Program, Sewall called Individualize by Specific Detail the eyeopener in Daily Themes' attempt to revive the sensitivity to detail that is often buried in secondary schools under the weight of parsed sentences and dull source themes—a "return to the vivid, honest, and direct observation of children." At a later conference, Nangle cited "A young, rather attractive girl stood on the street corner" as an example of the type of sentence that young, rather unsuspecting Daily Themes writers offer up for annihilation during the first week of the course. "Young?" Nangle asked. "How young? Two? Five? Twelve? Eighteen? Twenty-six? Attractive? What constitutes attraction? Color of hair, beauty of face or figure, mode of attire? Attractive to what instinct—the maternal, the sexual, the aesthetic, or some other? Can you see her?" After a conference or two, Daily Themes students who have been observing their roommates begin to observe them a bit more closely.

"Vivify by Range of Appeal!" Berdan would exhort after he had despaired of making any progress in persuading students to Individualize by Specific Detail. "Characterize by Speech and Gesture! Clarify by Point of View! Unify by a Single Impression! Combine Details for Coherence! Charge Words with Connotation! Choose Words for their Sounds!" In an effort to remind students that they had sound and odor as well as sight at their disposal (Vivify by Range of Appeal), Berdan would write a word like "garbage" or "perfume" on the board and wordlessly pass out paper. At the following lecture, with the reeking results in his hand, he would preach moderation in all things.

Today, the slogans have been replaced by "a kind of brush-fire approach," Folsom says—concentrating on whatever evils seem most widespread in the week's themes. There is never any shortage of horrible examples. Inevitably, some of the themes turned in during the first week of lectures are sensational tales of horrifying violence, and they are often followed by what Folsom calls Lost in the Jungle Week. Discouraged from the sensational ("Gentlemen, it is not necessary to kill off your grandmother for our benefit"), undergraduates often turn toward the scatological. The use of obscenity and swearing for effect is a fairly recent phenomenon. Looking through the themes of the Roaring Twenties, Sewall found "only a few 'damns,' one timid 'goddamn,' and one mild four-letter word." This and the fact that most of the themes seemed more romantic than roaring led him to conclude that Yale was suffering from a slight cultural lag. (The Class Book poll of seniors in 1925 showed their favorite novel to be "A Tale of Two Cities.") By 1933, Daily Themes writers were catching up, with sentences like "When in hell would the damn music end?" For the past several years, Folsom has found it necessary to explain in an early lecture that realism cannot be obtained merely by sprinkling the page arbitrarily with obscenity. In a theme of only three hundred words or so, it is often not very difficult to see where the writer went wrong, and the clinker caused by an ill-chosen word can be deafening. (Nangle's favorite is a romantic description of a lovely girl that ends with the sun striking her "shiny blond pate.") The themes read in class remain anonymous, and some who have taken the course believe that the most important lesson it teaches an undergraduate is how to look as contemptuous as everyone else in the room while his own theme is being read.

When Daily Themes advocates are told that writing courses belong in trade schools, they often answer that Daily Themes is the best course in literary criticism at Yale—that, as Folsom once said in a speech, it teaches "by example, rather than by precept, that the proper question to ask in the interpretation of literature is not 'What does the story mean?' but, rather, 'How does the story work?' " To those who say that writing cannot be taught, the instructors answer that it can at least be criticized, and that, to judge from the results, it can be improved by taking Daily Themes—although they don't pretend to know just what it is in the process that causes the improvement. "At least, it purges some of the nonsense from their style," says Sewall. "Sure, it may be rule of thumb, and a refined mind can find all kinds of philosophical arguments against it, but, damn it, it works. At the end of the semester, they write better than they did at the beginning."

Harry Berger, who once taught Daily Themes and is now chairman of the English Department of the University of California at Santa Cruz, says that the Daily Themes method is "fine as an exercise—a way of getting guys to do certain aspects of craft that they otherwise wouldn't do," but he adds, "The danger is that guys really think they're getting some kind of magic formula for being successful writers." Some students do fall into a formula. Attempting to avoid some of the more obvious means of getting a W, they tend to write in the flat dialogues that are associated with Hemingway or John O'Hara, and the dictum that they must show rather than tell can force them to put a character through some strenuous exercises in order to avoid telling the reader outright what is going on. But Daily Themes instructors say that after Thanksgiving, when the themes give way to weekly short stories, the undergraduates feel no special allegiance to the rules that haunted their autumn evenings.

Before that emancipation, most Daily Themes students accept the combination of daily grind and faint encouragement stoically, like Marine recruits who know they are voluntarily enduring consistent mistreatment. Occasionally, though, it all becomes too much to bear, and the student reacts (as he reacts to many of his daily difficulties) by writing a theme about it—purging himself of his anger and solving the problem of what to hand in the next morning. The exasperation of taking the course is one of the few theme subjects that have remained constant through the years. One piece of particularly angry interior dialogue that Nangle has saved was written by an undergraduate named Johnson in the early fifties. It begins, "By God he better understand this one. That old Wilder bastard better get *this* one. Ten themes of mine he's read now—ten themes and I don't think he's caught one thing I've said. Jesus, that guy must still be in the eighteenth century. Well, um, kaff, Mr. Jacobi, it's perfectly obvious that the girl here is in perfect control of the situation, um, kaff. No, Mr. Wilder, you blind old bastard, the girl is *not* in control of the situation, the girl is making an *ass* of herself, and if you had one-half an eye in your head you'd see that. . . . *I* get it. My *roommates* get it. My *friends* get it. . . . How did an old quack like you ever get to teach this course anyway?"

Johnson got a B for that one.

QUESTIONS

1. Why were there so many similar themes?
2. Other than looking for novel subject matter, how might students have made their themes more original?
3. Analyze the themes from your course. Can you see any patterns in the content or attitudes?

One of our national vices is that the public assumes politicians cannot say exactly what they think. As a political columnist and author of many books, Walter Lippmann has tried for more than fifty years to explain not only what politicians say, but why they say it. Though written in 1922 this essay on stereotypes, from Lippmann's book *Public Opinion*, is relevant to your writing now.[8]

Each of us lives and works on a small part of the earth's surface, moves in a small circle, and of these acquaintances knows only a few intimately. Of any public event that has wide effects we see at best only a phase and an aspect. This is as true of the eminent insiders who draft treaties, make laws, and issue orders, as it is of those who have treaties framed for them, laws promulgated to them, orders given at them. Inevitably our opinions cover a bigger space, a longer reach of time, a greater number of things, than we can directly observe. They have, therefore, to be pieced together out of what others have reported and what we can imagine.

Yet even the eyewitness does not bring back a naïve picture

[8] Walter Lippmann, *Public Opinion* (New York: The Macmillan Company, 1922).

of the scene.° For experience seems to show that he himself brings something to the scene which later he takes away from it, that oftener than not what he imagines to be the account of an event is really a transfiguration of it. Few facts in consciousness seem to be merely given. Most facts in consciousness seem to be partly made. A report is the joint product of the knower and known, in which the rôle of the observer is always selective and usually creative. The facts we see depend on where we are placed, and the habits of our eyes.

An unfamiliar scene is like the baby's world, "one great, blooming, buzzing confusion." † This is the way, says Mr. John Dewey,‡ that any new thing strikes an adult, so far as the thing is really new and strange. "Foreign languages that we do not understand always seem jibberings, babblings, in which it is impossible to fix a definite, clearcut, individualized group of sounds. The countryman in the crowded street, the landlubber at sea, the ignoramus in sport at a contest between experts in a complicated game, are further instances. Put an inexperienced man in a factory, and at first the work seems to him a meaningless medley. All strangers of another race proverbially look alike to the visiting stranger. Only gross differences of size or

° *E.g. cf.* Edmond Locard, *L'Enquête Criminelle et les Méthodes Scientifiques.* A great deal of interesting material has been gathered in late years on the credibility of the witness, which shows, as an able reviewer of Dr. Locard's book says in *The Times* (London) Literary Supplement (August 18, 1921), that credibility varies as to classes of witnesses and classes of events, and also as to type of perception. Thus, perception of touch, odor, and taste have low evidential value. Our hearing is defective and arbitrary when it judges the sources and direction of sound, and in listening to the talk of other people "words which are not heard will be supplied by the witness in all good faith. He will have a theory of the purport of the conversation, and will arrange the sounds he heard to fit it." Even visual perceptions are liable to great error, as in identification, recognition, judgment of distance, estimates of numbers, for example, the size of a crowd. In the untrained observer the sense of time is highly variable. All these original weaknesses are complicated by tricks of memory, and the incessant creative quality of the imagination. *Cf.* also Sherrington, *The Integrative Action of the Nervous System*, pp. 318–327.

The late Professor Hugo Münsterberg wrote a popular book on this subject called *On the Witness Stand.*

† Wm. James, *Principles of Psychology*, Vol. I, p. 488.

‡ John Dewey, *How We Think*, p. 121.

color are perceived by an outsider in a flock of sheep, each of which is perfectly individualized to the shepherd. A diffusive blur and an indiscriminately shifting suction characterize what we do not understand. The problem of the acquisition of meaning by things, or (stated in another way) of forming habits of simple apprehension, is thus the problem of introducing (1) *definiteness* and *distinction* and (2) *consistency* or *stability* of meaning into what is otherwise vague and wavering."

But the kind of definiteness and consistency introduced depends upon who introduces them. In a later passage ° Dewey gives an example of how differently an experienced layman and a chemist might define the word metal. "Smoothness, hardness, glossiness, and brilliancy, heavy weight for its size . . . the serviceable properties of capacity for being hammered and pulled without breaking, of being softened by heat and hardened by cold, of retaining the shape and form given, of resistance to pressure and decay, would probably be included" in the layman's definition. But the chemist would likely as not ignore these esthetic and utilitarian qualities, and define a metal as "any chemical element that enters into combination with oxygen so as to form a base."

For the most part we do not first see, and then define, we define first and then see. In the great blooming, buzzing confusion of the outer world we pick out what our culture has already defined for us, and we tend to perceive that which we have picked out in the form stereotyped for us by our culture. Of the great men who assembled at Paris to settle the affairs of mankind, how many were there who were able to see much of the Europe about them, rather than their commitments about Europe? Could anyone have penetrated the mind of M. Clemenceau, would he have found there images of the Europe of 1919, or a great sediment of stereotyped ideas accumulated and hardened in a long and pugnacious existence? Did he see the Germans of 1919, or the German type as he had learned to see it since 1871? He saw the type, and among the reports that came to him from Germany, he took to heart those reports, and, it

° *Op. cit.*, p. 133.

seems, those only, which fitted the type that was in his mind. If a junker blustered, that was an authentic German; if a labor leader confessed the guilt of the empire, he was not an authentic German.

At a Congress of Psychology in Göttingen an interesting experiment was made with a crowd of presumably trained observers.°

"Not far from the hall in which the Congress was sitting there was a public fête with a masked ball. Suddenly the door of the hall was thrown open and a clown rushed in madly pursued by a negro, revolver in hand. They stopped in the middle of the room fighting; the clown fell, the negro leapt upon him, fired, and then both rushed out of the hall. The whole incident hardly lasted twenty seconds.

"The President asked those present to write immediately a report since there was sure to be a judicial inquiry. Forty reports were sent in. Only one had less than 20% of mistakes in regard to the principal facts; fourteen had 20% to 40% of mistakes; twelve from 40% to 50%; thirteen more than 50%. Moreover in twenty-four accounts 10% of the details were pure inventions and this proportion was exceeded in ten accounts and diminished in six. Briefly a quarter of the accounts were false.

"It goes without saying that the whole scene had been arranged and even photographed in advance. The ten false reports may then be relegated to the category of tales and legends; twenty-four accounts are half legendary, and six have a value approximating to exact evidence."

Thus out of forty trained observers writing a responsible account of a scene that had just happened before their eyes, more than a majority saw a scene that had not taken place. What then did they see? One would suppose it was easier to tell what had occurred, than to invent something which had not occurred. They saw their stereotype of such a brawl. All of them had in the course of their lives acquired a series of images of brawls, and these images flickered before their eyes. In one man these images displaced less than 20% of the actual scene, in thirteen men more than half. In thirty-four out of the forty ob-

° A von Gennep, *La formation des légendes*, pp. 158–159. Cited F. van Langenhove, *The Growth of a Legend*, pp. 120–122.

servers the stereotypes preëmpted at least one-tenth of the scene.

A distinguished art critic said ° that "what with the almost numberless shapes assumed by an object. . . . What with our insensitiveness and inattention, things scarcely would have for us features and outlines so determined and clear that we could recall them at will, but for the stereotyped shapes art has lent them." The truth is even broader than that, for the stereotyped shapes lent to the world come not merely from art, in the sense of painting and sculpture and literature, but from our moral codes and our social philosophies and our political agitations as well. Substitute in the following passage of Mr. Berenson's the words 'politics,' 'business,' and 'society,' for the word 'art' and the sentences will be no less true: ". . . unless years devoted to the study of all schools of art have taught us also to see with our own eyes, we soon fall into the habit of moulding whatever we look at into the forms borrowed from the one art with which we are acquainted. There is our standard of artistic reality. Let anyone give us shapes and colors which we cannot instantly match in our paltry stock of hackneyed forms and tints, and we shake our heads at his failure to reproduce things as we know they certainly are, or we accuse him of insincerity."

Mr. Berenson speaks of our displeasure when a painter "does not visualize objects exactly as we do," and of the difficulty of appreciating the art of the Middle Ages because since then "our manner of visualizing forms has changed in a thousand ways." † He goes on to show how in regard to the human figure we have been taught to see what we do see. "Created by Donatello and Masaccio, and sanctioned by the Humanists, the new

° Bernard Berenson, *The Central Italian Painters of the Renaissance*, pp. 60, *et seq.*

† *Cf.* also his comment on *Dante's Visual Images, and his Early Illustrators* in *The Study and Criticism of Italian Art* (First Series), p. 13. "We cannot help dressing Virgil as a Roman, and giving him a 'Classical profile' and 'statuesque carriage,' but Dante's visual image of Virgil was probably no less mediaeval, no more based on a critical reconstruction of antiquity, than his entire conception of the Roman poet. Fourteenth Century illustrators make Virgil look like a mediaeval scholar, dressed in cap and gown, and there is no reason why Dante's visual image of him should have been other than this."

canon of the human figure, the new cast of features . . . presented to the ruling classes of that time the type of human being most likely to win the day in the combat of human forces.
. . . Who had the power to break through this new standard
of vision and, out of the chaos of things, to select shapes more
definitely expressive of reality than those fixed by men of genius? No one had such power. People had perforce to see things
in that way and in no other, and to see only the shapes de-
picted, to love only the ideals presented. . . ." °

If we cannot fully understand the acts of other people, until
we know what they think they know, then in order to do justice
we have to appraise not only the information which has been at
their disposal, but the minds through which they have filtered
it. For the accepted types, the current patterns, the standard
versions, intercept information on its way to consciousness.
Americanization, for example, is superficially at least the sub-
stitution of American for European stereotypes. Thus the peasant who might see his landlord as if he were the lord of the
manor, his employer as he saw the local magnate, is taught by
Americanization to see the landlord and employer according to
American standards. This constitutes a change of mind, which
is, in effect, when the inoculation succeeds, a change of vision.
His eyes see differently. One kindly gentlewoman has confessed that the stereotypes are of such overwhelming importance, that when hers are not indulged, she at least is unable to
accept the brotherhood of man and the fatherhood of God: "we
are strangely affected by the clothes we wear. Garments create a
mental and social atmosphere. What can be hoped for the
Americanism of a man who insists on employing a London
tailor? One's very food affects his Americanism. What kind of
American consciousness can grow in the atmosphere of sauer-
kraut and Limburger cheese? Or what can you expect of the
Americanism of the man whose breath always reeks of gar-
lic?" †

This lady might well have been the patron of a pageant

° *The Central Italian Painters*, pp. 66–67.
† Cited by Mr. Edward Hale Bierstadt, *New Republic*, June 1, 1921, p. 21.

which a friend of mine once attended. It was called the Melting Pot, and it was given on the Fourth of July in an automobile town where many foreign-born workers are employed. In the center of the baseball park at second base stood a huge wooden and canvas pot. There were flights of steps up to the rim on two sides. After the audience had settled itself, and the band had played, a procession came through an opening at one side of the field. It was made up of men of all the foreign nationalities employed in the factories. They wore their native costumes, they were singing their national songs; they danced their folk dances, and carried the banners of all Europe. The master of ceremonies was the principal of the grade school dressed as Uncle Sam. He led them to the pot. He directed them up the steps to the rim, and inside. He called them out again on the other side. They came, dressed in derby hats, coats, pants, vest, stiff collar and polka-dot tie, undoubtedly, said my friend, each with an Eversharp pencil in his pocket, and all singing the Star-Spangled Banner.

To the promoters of this pageant, and probably to most of the actors, it seemed as if they had managed to express the most intimate difficulty to friendly association between the older peoples of America and the newer. The contradiction of their stereotypes interfered with the full recognition of their common humanity. The people who change their names know this. They mean to change themselves, and the attitude of strangers toward them.

There is, of course, some connection between the scene outside and the mind through which we watch it, just as there are some long-haired men and short-haired women in radical gatherings. But to the hurried observer a slight connection is enough. If there are two bobbed heads and four beards in the audience, it will be a bobbed and bearded audience to the reporter who knows beforehand that such gatherings are composed of people with these tastes in the management of their hair. There is a connection between our vision and the facts, but it is often a strange connection. A man has rarely looked at a landscape, let us say, except to examine its possibilities for division into building lots, but he has seen a number of landscapes hanging in the parlor. And from them he has learned to think of a landscape as a rosy sunset, or as a country road with a church steeple and a silver moon. One day he goes to the country, and for hours he does not see a single landscape. Then the sun goes down looking rosy. At once he recognizes a landscape and exclaims that it is beautiful. But two days later, when he tries to recall what he saw, the odds are that he will remember chiefly some landscape in a parlor.

Unless he has been drunk or dreaming or insane he did see a sunset, but he saw in it, and above all remembers from it, more of what the oil painting taught him to observe, than what an impressionist painter, for example, or a cultivated Japanese would have seen and taken away with him. And the Japanese and the painter in turn will have seen and remembered more of the form they had learned, unless they happen to be the very rare people who find fresh sight for mankind. In untrained observation we pick recognizable signs out of the environment. The signs stand for ideas, and these ideas we fill out with our stock of images. We do not so much see this man and that subject; rather we notice that the thing is man or sunset, and then see chiefly what our mind is already full of on those subjects.

There is economy in this. For the attempt to see all things freshly and in detail, rather than as types and generalities, is exhausting, and among busy affairs practically out of the question. In a circle of friends, and in relation to close associates or competitors, there is no shortcut through, and no substitute for, an individualized understanding. Those whom we love and admire most are the men and women whose consciousness is peopled thickly with persons rather than with types, who know us rather than the classification into which we might fit. For even without phrasing it to ourselves, we feel intuitively that all classification is in relation to some purpose not necessarily our own; that between two human beings no association has final dignity in which each does not take the other as an end in himself. There is a taint on any contact between two people which does not affirm as an axiom the personal inviolability of both.

But modern life is hurried and multifarious, above all physical distance separates men who are often in vital contact with each other, such as employer and employee, official and voter. There is neither time nor opportunity for intimate acquaintance. Instead we notice a trait which marks a well known type, and fill in the rest of the picture by means of the stereotypes we carry about in our heads. He is an agitator. That much we notice, or are told. Well, an agitator is this sort of person, and so *he* is this sort of person. He is an intellectual. He is a plutocrat. He is a foreigner. He is a "South European." He is from Back Bay. He is a Harvard Man. How different from the statement: he is a Yale Man. He is a regular fellow. He is a West Pointer. He is an old army sergeant. He is a Greenwich Villager: what don't we know about him then, and about her? He is an international banker. He is from Main Street.

The subtlest and most pervasive of all influences are those which create and maintain the repertory of stereotypes. We are told about the world before we see it. We imagine most things before we experience them. And those preconceptions, unless education has made us acutely aware, govern deeply the whole process of perception. They mark out certain objects as familiar or strange, emphasizing the difference, so that the slightly familiar is seen as very familiar, and the somewhat strange as sharply alien. They are aroused by small signs, which may vary from a true index to a vague analogy. Aroused, they flood fresh vision with older images, and project into the world what has been resurrected in memory. Were there no practical uniformities in the environment, there would be no economy and only error in the human habit of accepting foresight for sight. But there are uniformities sufficiently accurate, and the need of economizing attention is so inevitable, that the abandonment of all stereotypes for a whole innocent approach to experience would impoverish human life.

What matters is the character of the stereotypes, and the gullibility with which we employ them. And these in the end depend upon those inclusive patterns which constitute our philosophy of life. If in that philosophy we assume that the world is codified according to a code which we possess, we are likely to make our reports of what is going on describe a world run by our code. But if our philosophy tells us that each man is only a small part of the world, that his intelligence catches at best only phases and aspects in a coarse net of ideas, then, when we use our stereotypes, we tend to know that they are only stereotypes, to hold them lightly, to modify them gladly. We tend, also, to realize more and more clearly when our ideas started, where they started, how they came to us, why we accepted them. All useful history is antiseptic in this fashion. It enables us to know what fairy tale, what school book, what tradition, what novel, play, picture, phrase, planted one preconception in this mind, another in that mind.

Those who wish to censor art do not at least underestimate this influence. They generally misunderstand it, and almost always they are absurdly bent on preventing other people from discovering anything not sanctioned by them. But at any rate, like Plato in his argument about the poets, they feel vaguely that the types acquired through fiction tend to be imposed on reality. Thus there can be little doubt that the moving picture is steadily building up imagery which is then evoked by the words people read in their newspapers. In the whole experience of the race there has been no aid to visualization comparable to the cinema. If a Florentine wished to visualize the saints, he could go to the frescoes in his church, where he might see a vision of saints standardized for his time by Giotto. If an Athenian wished to visualize the gods he went to the temples. But the number of objects which were pictured was not great. And in the East, where the spirit of the second commandment was widely accepted, the portraiture of concrete things was even more meager, and for that reason perhaps the faculty of practical decision was by so much reduced. In the western world, however, during the last few centuries there has been an enormous increase in the volume and scope of secular description, the word picture, the narrative, the illustrated narrative, and finally the moving picture and, perhaps, the talking picture.

Photographs have the kind of authority over imagination today, which the printed word had yesterday, and the spoken word before that. They seem utterly real. They come, we imagine, directly to us without human meddling, and they are the most effortless food for the mind conceivable. Any description in words, or even any inert picture, requires an effort of memory before a picture exists in the mind. But on the screen the whole process of observing, describing, reporting, and then imagining, has been accomplished for you. Without more trouble than is needed to stay awake the result which your imagination is always aiming at is reeled off on the screen. The shadowy idea becomes vivid; your hazy notion, let us say, of the Ku Klux Klan, thanks to Mr. Griffiths, takes vivid shape when you see *The Birth of a Nation*. Historically it may be the wrong shape, morally it may be a pernicious shape, but it is a shape, and I doubt whether anyone who has seen the film and does not know more about the Ku Klux Klan than Mr. Griffiths, will ever hear the name again without seeing those white horsemen.

And so when we speak of the mind of a group of people, of the French mind, the militarist mind, the bolshevik mind, we are liable to serious confusion unless we agree to separate the instinctive equipment from the stereotypes, and the formulae which play so decisive a part in building up the mental world to which the native character is adapted and responds. Failure to make this distinction accounts for oceans of loose talk about collective minds, national souls, and race psychology. To be sure a stereotype may be so consistently and authoritatively transmitted in each generation from parent to child that it seems almost like a biological fact. In some respects, we may indeed have become, as Mr. Wallas says,° biologically parasitic upon our social heritage. But certainly there is not the least scientific evidence which would enable anyone to argue that men are born with the political habits of the country in which they are born. In so far as political habits are alike in a nation, the first places to look for an explanation are the nursery, the school, the church, not in that limbo inhabited by Group Minds

° Graham Wallas, *Our Social Heritage*, p. 17.

and National Souls. Until you have thoroughly failed to see tradition being handed on from parents, teachers, priests, and uncles, it is a solecism of the worst order to ascribe political differences to the germ plasm.

It is possible to generalize tentatively and with a decent humility about comparative differences within the same category of education and experience. Yet even this is a tricky enterprise. For almost no two experiences are exactly alike, not even of two children in the same household. The older son never does have the experience of being the younger. And therefore, until we are able to discount the difference in nurture, we must withhold judgment about differences of nature. As well judge the productivity of two soils by comparing their yield before you know which is in Labrador and which is in Iowa, whether they have been cultivated and enriched, exhausted, or allowed to run wild.

QUESTIONS

1. How would you define *innocence* and explain its value for a writer?
2. What stereotypes did you grow up with?
3. How have stereotypes played a part in the way schools are run?

If you have had trouble with writing, or if you consider yourself a poor writer, you may claim you are not to blame. Teacher Louis Zahner explains, in an excerpt from *Composition at the Barricades*, where some of the blame rests.[9] His descriptions are general, but you can easily see if they apply to your own experience.

In his struggle to save the written language, today's teacher of English stands almost alone. There was a time when the study of other subjects called naturally for written reports and

[9] Louis Zahner, "Composition at the Barricades," *Atlantic Monthly Magazine* (November 1959).

essays and, at the least, for written answers of some length on examinations.

The essay test—that is, the examination which demands original thinking and writing—is dead. It had a decent funeral, with orations, and its many mourners have now left the churchyard. But the fall of the essay examination as a college entrance test is perhaps the greatest single cause of the decline of the teaching of composition in the schools. The use of objective tests in schools and for college entrance has not only decreased practice in writing. It has given the schools the idea that the colleges do not put much value any more on a sound training in writing. If a student can enter college without ever having written a composition in his school, is composition worth teaching? Under these conditions, who can blame the teachers for wondering whether writing is any longer one of the essential three R's?

The colleges and their examining agencies are in no way culpable. To save the essay test they have tried every known means and experimented with countless new ones. They have met today's more and more complex and exacting demands of testing for college entrance brilliantly and fairly. In their determination not to direct the schools, however, they have underestimated an inevitable power that they never wished to have. The colleges once exerted considerable influence upon written composition through their entrance examinations; they could, if they would, bring to bear such influence quietly but effectively through other means. If, in doing so, they would unobtrusively consider their obligation to be the improvement of the teaching of composition not only to the college-bound but to every student everywhere who has it in him to think and write straightforward prose, an abandoned salient will have been re-established and widened.

In addition to removing the necessity and the incentive for writing, the objective test has had a less obvious but even more corrosive effect upon writing. Calling for facts and information rather than original thinking, it does not require the student to reach and support generalizations and conclusions of his own. Under its influence, teachers are putting more and more emphasis on memorization of facts and storage of information rather than on understanding. Expressed another way, students do not have much to write about. They can put facts together like glass beads on a string, and if they can do it without making any mistakes, they get the impression that they are writing. Teaching the mechanics and techniques of writing to empty students is an immoral business, a waste of everybody's time.

The only remedy is an increase in the number of enlightened teachers in all subjects, teachers who are bent on educating their pupils, tests or no tests. They will soon discover that the best preparation they can give their students for taking an objective test is to forget the test and to get to work on reading, thinking, and writing. Mere facts and information take care of themselves in the process.

The schools are beset by another difficulty that cripples the teaching of language. It is a commonplace that year by year, subject by subject, more and more ground has to be covered. Not enough of the old can be jettisoned to make room for the new. Hence, to save time, subject matter must be presented condensed and processed. More and more, teaching is by abstractions and prefabricated generalizations and conclusions, not by cases, particulars, or illustrations. There is no time for inductive teaching.

The result is a learning through mere words almost wholly removed from any firsthand experience, even from any suspicion that words have anything to do with experience. They are just words that, at a pinch, can be defined by other words, generalizations that can be supported by other generalizations, or even by a rewording of the same ones. Here are the seeds of what later flowers into pure jargon and rich gobbledygook.

Holding fast the connections between words and the realities of experience is the essence of all use and understanding of language, its use in thinking and in writing and speaking, its understanding in reading and listening. Fortunately, making these connections is a natural process. It is the way a child learns his native language. His first question is, "What is that?" He sees and touches the object before he asks for and is given the word that names it. Later, the question becomes, "What does that word mean?" That is the critical point in his whole education in language. If the answer is given by specific examples within his own experience, he is learning language. If it is given as a rewording in equally abstract and remote words, he is learning incantation.

When this natural process asserts itself in the English classroom it can fare badly. Asked to define "terror," a child naturally says something like "Terror is when you are almost hit by an automobile." The teacher corrects him: "It is wrong to say 'Terror is *when*.'" The learner keeps trying until he gets "Terror is a state of fear approaching panic." He wins an A and the damage is done. Similarly, much isolated vocabulary drill hopefully undertaken by the schools in preparation for aptitude tests is excellent training in the use of language as incantation and as an ornate cloak for vacuity.

The remedy for this lies in the lower grades. Teaching in the eleventh and twelfth grades must continue to be carried on in relatively high abstractions. But in the lower grades, little by little, a habit of mind can be established that will not let any generalization slip by without a quick mental checkup by illustration and example, or any abstraction without a down-to-earth operational definition. Taught and practiced in the grades, the process of relating language to actual experience can become the established way the mind works. There have been and are mature men incapable of thinking in any other way. Mr. Justice Holmes and Judge Learned Hand come readily to mind.

This matter of dealing with abstract words and generalizations is only one detail of a large issue—the teaching of language in the schools. It is an open question whether what is taught in the schools really is the English language.

The idea that English grammar and structure are identical with those of Latin is implicit in much of the teaching, and methods once used for teaching Latin live on under a disguise of very fancy modern dress. Contemporary studies of the language are beginning to take hold, but much remains to be done for, and to, the classroom teacher before he can use them effectively.

The study of the intricate ways of language in the interchange of ideas and feelings—what it can state, what it can suggest; how it can clarify, how mislead; the almost limitless variety of meanings and shades of meaning it can convey—this also is beginning to gain a foothold.

But the linguists and the operationalists (to coin a stand-in for "semanticists," which seems to have taken on an emotional tinge) still work apart and even at cross-purposes. What must come if the English language is to be effectively taught in the schools is a revival of the trivium, the union of grammar, logic, and rhetoric, done into modern English, and with the full enlistment of modern knowledge.

Teachers should also take a new look at usage. The old formalist view that nothing is right unless it conforms to classical grammar and the best literary standards mercifully has gone. In its place, however, is established an equally undiscriminating pronouncement, "Anything goes. If enough people use it, it is right." The obvious exception is made of illiterate expressions which, though clear in meaning, damage the user: "I seen him when he wasn't hardly trying."

In addition to making heroic and mildly manic efforts to banish such expressions, teachers and others keep alive the venerable argument about locutions that depart from traditional grammar but are not as yet fully accepted. It is more generally understood that such usage will in time be accepted and called idiom. The slang dictionary of fifty years ago reads today like a list of literary, even diplomatic phrases. But there is always a line where the advancing front encounters rear-guard action. "It's me" is no sooner in occupied territory than the battle rages at the *like—as* salient.

All this ado is harmless except that, in treating current usage as a matter of manners, not of meanings, it diverts attention from the important issue.

The distinction between inventive and preventive usage is

never considered. New usage can be inventive, bringing into the language useful and vitalizing expressions—"egghead," for example. Or it can be preventive, destroying the power of the language to make useful distinctions, or even to express what its users want to say. If, within the space of half an hour, someone hears, as (or, if you prefer, *like*) I recently did, that it is a "terrific" day (the sun was shining, the air balmy), that these new birthday cards are really "terrific," obviously "made up by some artist with a terrific sense of humor," and that a new policy is "a terrific deal insurancewise," what can he call a hurricane that scared him to death and blew his garage roof away? And will he be fully understood and considered to be moderately literate if he says "It doesn't cost me much to run my car" instead of "My car is terrific expensewise"? Or does an admissions officer reading on a candidate's report that "he does not take too much interest in athletics" know for sure whether the writer means that the candidate takes scarcely any interest at all or that he takes a great deal but does not let athletics interfere with his studies? One principal might mean the first, another the second. The admissions officer can only wait and see.

A detailed study of usage that does more than record and count and describe is overdue. The key question is not whether a new expression is considered by so many people to be at this or that level of usage but whether it is inventive or preventive.

The teacher of language, especially of writing, is working under another handicap. The gap between speech and proficient writing is widening. The student does not hear much good, let alone distinguished, English. Reading aloud in the home is an archaic pastime. Conversation is a lost art. Radio and television, their language aimed at catching and entertaining the customer, talk to him in his own easy jargon and patois. There are a few programs on which guests, commentators, and even announcers speak literate English. There are still some great preachers. But all these put together are far outnumbered. The language our pupils hear is not the language from which clear, coherent writing is easily developed.

Nor does the student's reading help his writing much. Radio

cut into his reading, though not dangerously; he learned to read against a background of music and voices. Television cuts deeper; it does not mix with reading.

More detrimental to the student's reading than the possible falling off in the amount he reads, however, is the emphasis now put by schools and colleges upon the speed of reading. If he is to get through the amount of reading required by his school and college, he must be trained to read faster. He is drilled to read by eye alone. Hearing in the mind the sound of the language being silently read is a fault that must be overcome.

The result is that writing too becomes the business of the eye alone. The mind's ear grows deaf. Unless the pupil's pen is the tongue of a ready speaker, we cannot hope for even moderately effective writing.

The teacher and poet in Robert Frost spoke together when he wrote: "A dramatic necessity goes deep into the nature of the sentence. Sentences are not different enough to hold the attention unless they are dramatic. No ingenuity of varying structure will do. All that can save them is the speaking tone of voice somehow entangled in the words and fastened to the page for the ear of the imagination. That is all that can save poetry from sing-song, all that can save prose from itself."

Methods for the use of the voice in teaching composition could quite easily be developed. They would include the use of the pupil's own voice in the writing and revision of his work. Supplemented by sound films and recordings made especially for the purpose and by facilities for pupils to read aloud to themselves, they might well help to solve the problem of teaching composition to large classes and reduce the teacher's overwhelming load of students' papers to correct.

Whatever is done to improve the writing of English must be done in the elementary and secondary schools. The freshman year at college is too late. By that time bad habits have become ingrained and prejudices against writing have been established in the mind of the student who writes badly or has never written at all. But there is a more urgent reason: freshman English does not help the boys and girls who do not go on to college. Even without benefit of the college instructor, they should still somehow be taught the power of articulate speech and articulated writing.

All in all, the high school teacher of composition has his work cut out for him. He is half inventor and explorer, pushing into new territory with whatever tools he can devise. He is half repairman, doing what he can to mend the damage done both in the school itself and in the world of which it is a part. At the moment, he does not appear to be holding his own. He may even be resigned to a retreat so gradual that nobody will recognize it as ultimately a defeat, especially if he calls it "Keeping abreast of the times" or "Adjustment to the modern world."

Paul Diederich, of the Research Division of the Educational Testing Service, writes: "Since I am skeptical of the possibility of widespread improvement in writing except at a rate that is truly glacial, I find myself in sympathy with our committees of outstanding school and college teachers who devise our College Board examinations in writing. They expect very little, they get less, and our scores are based on what college-entering students do, not on what we wish they could do."

It may be that we shall have to accept with grace and a show of gratitude downward-spiraling standards dictated by high school students. It may be that we shall have to rest content with examinations that test a smaller remnant of writing with greater accuracy.

It may be getting late. But it is still far too early to give it all up with a shrug. English teachers are a resourceful, resilient, determined breed. Parents want the best for their children and are willing to find out what that best is.

More and more people are hearing the alert and beginning to realize how much is at stake. It is no less than our survival as a civilized people—perhaps even as a people at all.

For, menacing and obdurate, Caliban still crouches in his cave, the eternal archetype of the savage state of man:

"You taught me language, and my profit on't
Is, I know how to curse."

Questions

1. Can you compare what Zahner says about grammar with what Maugham implied in *Summing Up?*
2. What is immoral about "teaching the mechanics and techniques of writing to empty students"?
3. Besides mechanics and techniques, of what does writing consist? In other words, how does an empty student with a theme topic become a full student?

Assignments

1. Review the papers you have written for this course, or for some other course. Choose two different kinds and rewrite them completely, including a short note on your new approach.
2. Review the papers you have written for this course and write a critical analysis of yourself as a writer. Be specific.

CHAPTER 11

WHAT YOUR LANGUAGE

DOES TO OTHERS AND

WHAT IT CAN DO

Language, like air and rain, belongs to no one. And as we do of air and rain, we have an unconscious awareness of its value. That is why we are anxious for a baby to say its first words, and why reading and writing are the core of formal education. Recently we have discovered that children who do not receive their share of language before school can be seriously handicapped for life. Giving children the tools of language is an important part of preschool Headstart programs.

As with most things men own in common, when the property is being spoiled everybody shrugs and says, "It's not my fault. What can I do?" With water and air we can ask local, state, and national governments to make antipollution laws. But can you imagine the problems of an antipollution law for the English language?

First you would have to define pollution. Some people mean

"incorrect" or nongrammatical English; but there is no absolute grammar for English regardless of how absolute some of your teachers may have been. Some people say *usage* is the proper guide, but usage varies from group to group, region to region.

What matters most in language is its effectiveness in communication, and this will vary with what man needs to communicate. There is not now and probably never will be an idea of correctness that is comprehensive and specific enough to be used in making laws about language.

Then how do we fight language pollution? Since we have decided pollution cannot be defined in terms of correctness, we had better begin with the definition again. Let's go back to air and water. There is nothing inherently wrong with sulphur dioxide and carbon monoxide. In and of themselves, they are innocent compounds of common elements. The same is true of soap suds, bleaches, and dyes. However, when these chemicals weaken the power of air and water to support life, we call them pollutants. Language is important to our ability to survive. Regardless of its other uses, as in entertaining and idling away time, language is as basic to our social survival as water and air are to our biological survival. The basis of this importance is its power to convey many kinds of meaning, to relate ideas to things, thought to life. Therefore, anything which affects this power adversely is polluting language.

You may say we are back where we started—trying to define what weakens language. At least now we have an abstract definition. If you have now finished almost a semester or year of composition, you have already noticed many specific pollutants. Many of those errors which the class or your instructor criticized as weakening your themes were examples of pollutants. Worn-out metaphors, clichés, deceitful euphemisms, wordiness, sentimentality all pollute our language by weakening its ability to convey meaning.

Of course your particular errors are not going to shove the whole country into an error of meaninglessness any more than one car's exhaust is going to pollute all of New York City's air and infect the whole population with bronchitis. But you should be aware of your part in the big picture.

In the last chapter we tried to show how you may have been cut off from even yourself by accepting uncritically the worst elements of the language that constantly bombards you. You may have become an echo of your immediate culture.

Just as you are being bombarded, you are probably bombarding others. You may not consider yourself an influential person, but most people are so unaware of the language they use that they also are unaware when it influences themselves or others. When you first went to camp or moved to another part of the country or came to college your language probably began to change just by hearing and speaking to new people or reading new magazines and books. Your language will influence others just as others have influenced you. The way you speak limits or expands your own and others' ability to think.

If you say, "Let them fend for themselves," then think of your present or future family. However much you believe in individualism, you may be the person most responsible for denying it to your own children. The only reason we think of ourselves as individuals and see the world in our individual ways is because we can use language to extend our personalities.

If you don't consider yourself a family man, then at least think about rescuing yourself and your own language. The following selections explain how language controls thought and society. Each of the writers considers language essential to human life. For them a person without language of his own is a linguistic zombie.

SELECTIONS

The idea that our thought is limited by our language content and patterns is relatively recent, and still not widespread outside linguistic circles. But many men have used this concept in everyday life. In George Orwell's *1984* and *Animal Farm*, manipulation of language determines thought for the characters. This process of thought manipulation is common. Sometimes people argue it is necessary and beneficial. Ultimately it weakens the stabilizing effect of language and destroys people's confidence in the communicating power of language. Here, in an excerpt from Edward and

Onora Nell's *War Words*, is an explanation of language manipulation in our times.[1]

Orwell, in 1946, called attention to the impact of international politics on the language of public discussion.

> In our time, political speech and writing are largely the defense of the indefensible. [Current political events] can indeed be defended, but only by arguments which are too brutal for most people to face, and which do not square with the preferred aims of political parties. Defenseless villagers are bombarded from the air, the inhabitants driven out into the countryside, the cattle machine-gunned, the huts set on fire with incendiary bullets: this is called pacification. . . . (George Orwell, "Politics and the English Language")

Tracts for the times sometimes have relevance for all time; let us hope this one will not. But its present significance is plain, and the pressure of politics on language today all too evident. Or, worse, perhaps it is not. Perhaps we have grown so used to diplomatic evasion and politics circumlocution that we are no longer aware of the extent to which our opinions are shaped by the language in which current events are reported. Orwell's point was that the modern world calls for more than mythology and incantation. Modern technology has given us new power, new politics, and new ways to communicate their impact. To deal with this, to learn to accept it, we need an entire new political vocabulary—a Newspeak. Nor is this an unfulfilled need. It is an urgent demand of moral conscience, and in an enterprising society, given such a demand, a supply will be forthcoming.

War is seldom described literally, and the war in Vietnam is no exception. Military operations are still "missions." Captured Viet Cong are "questioned," sometimes "cooperate"; they are not interrogated, never collaborate. Captured American "fightingmen," exposed to "brain-washing," occasionally become "turn-coats." The definite description, "Allies," has been revived from World War II—with its warm associations glowing uncooled.

[1] Edward and Onora Nell, "War Words," *College English* (May 1967).

But the war in Vietnam has also produced some new turns of phrase. These often blur the line between military and non-military terminology. In this war the military depend on "hardware" to accomplish their "missions"; these include "resources control" such as "crop-spraying," "weed-killing" and "defoliation." Though regularly and successfully engaged in these ostensibly agricultural pursuits, the military have periodically to "stiffen their posture."

And, of course, the military are now largely responsible for "pacification." The art of pacification has undergone many metamorphoses since Orwell's day. In Vietnam it has included at various times the construction of "New Life Hamlets" and of "Prosperity Zones" containing "strategic hamlets." More recently a "Rural Construction Program" came on the scene, followed by a "Revolutionary Development Program" which in turn gave way to a "Rural Development Program." Another pacifically named operation, the "Open Arms Program," welcomes defectors from NLF forces. Today it is public knowledge that these programs are largely run by the military; formerly some of them were staffed only by "advisers," who were at that time responsible for the "provision of security."

By contrast some facets of "our involvement in Vietnam" which are not, or should not be, military are known under warlike names. The pacification programs sometimes reveal their other side under the title of "the other war," and to guarantee that peace is sought as energetically as the war is prosecuted we have periodic "peace offensives."

Euphemisms are not, or should not be, necessary to describe the content of peace plans and proposals, but stale metaphors seem to be essential. Peace in this war, as in others, is to be found by winning the minds and hearts of the people, bringing them (or at any rate some of them) to the conference table and proffering the olive branch. It is worth trying to visualize this composite scene. But this particular search for peace also turned up some fresh, though rapidly tiring, metaphors. Peace negotiations are offered unconditionally, subject to the necessity to keep the President's options open and the presidential posture credible.

Escalation of the war has brought an escalation of political language. A combination of carefully selected descriptions and redefinitions excludes a number of important questions from public discussion.

Sometimes this is relatively simple and obvious, as in the use of the abbreviation "Viet Cong" (Viet Nam Cong Sam) to describe all the forces that participate in the NLF, or of "enemy" to describe all the dead after a bombing raid or battle, or of "adviser" to describe U.S. military personnel in Vietnam up to 1965. Sometimes the choice of terminology is unintentionally revealing, as when the Northern generals who fought for the French, like Marshall Ky, are called "South Vietnamese," and Southerners like Ho Chi Minh are called "North Vietnamese."

But modern question-begging is often more complex. Consider the popular "we are in Vietnam to protect an independent nation against Communist aggression." This statement raises many factual questions, but it also presupposes answers to some of them. It assumes, for example, that there is a coherent *reason* for the U.S. presence in Vietnam, which therefore cannot be the result of past miscalculations or mistakes. "We are there to *protect*. . . ." Our actions are described as defensive, shielding or safeguarding, frequently with the assumption that such responsibilities have been assumed reluctantly, though manfully. "Protection," however, implies a danger; but one man's danger is another's safety. Who decides what is "danger"? "Communism" is no danger to Communists, nor to those well-disposed to its tenets, however much it may be one to us.

A claim that "we are in Vietnam to protect a military junta dependent on Western aid from a popular uprising" would carry little popular appeal, however necessary the action might be in terms of the "new political realities of the international scene." On the other hand protection of an "independent nation" (contrast "the regime in the North") helps to cast a glow of self-sufficiency and national pride on our Allies, and also implies that our actions are "assistance rendered to an ally," not, for instance, "intervention in the internal affairs of another country."

Just as U.S. actions are presented as essentially defensive, "shielding a small nation," so the other side is pictured as essentially, almost necessarily, aggressive. "Communist" and "aggression" have in some quarters become fused into one thought. Since this is so, preventive action against Communism can never itself be aggression or intervention. By definition, it is a defensive response to an aggressive threat. For example, we read that during the Tet truce:

> In Washington a State Department spokesman confirmed the U. S. was continuing resupply missions in Vietnam. Asked how this differed from North Vietnamese efforts, he said the North Vietnamese activity was "clear evidence of their intent to continue their aggressive action" while the U. S. was committed to combat aggression.
>
> *Washington Post*, February 12, 1967

At this point redescription has become stipulative redefinition.

> The Communists have developed *a new kind of aggression in which one country sponsors internal war within another.* Communist-sponsored internal war is clearly international aggression, but a form of aggression that frequently eludes the traditional definitions of international law. It means the use of native and imported guerillas to serve the interests of Communist nations. (Roger Hetsman in "Foreword," Vo Nguyen Giap, *People's War, People's Army*, New York: Praeger, 1962, p. ix).

There are many questions of fact here, but the language is more important. For once it is accepted, facts will hardly have a chance. "International aggression" as defined in treaties, the United Nations Charter, and other "traditional" documents, has, up to now, been clearly distinguishable from "civil war." Now if one country "sponsors" internal war within another and "uses" *native* guerillas to serve its interests, international aggression has been committed. What counts as "sponsoring"? "Providing men and materials" would be a clear case by the old definitions. The purpose of the new definition is evidently to cover the case of internal war fought largely by native guerillas largely with their own or captured supplies, but in the "service" of a foreign power. But what is the criterion for "being in the service of a foreign power"? In this case it appears to be adherence to Communism, which, by definition, is an "alien ideology," unlike the liberal democracy we are bringing to the villages of Vietnam.

The stipulative redefinition of such a central concept as aggression is paralleled by redefinitions of related terms—"military occupation," for example:

It [the Marine force in Danang] is not an occupation in any sense of the word because we have no selfish aims of our own in there and the people realize this . . . the longer we stay there the more the people understand this. (General Greene, Commandant, U. S. Marine Corps on ABC-TV, "Issues and Answers," April 3, 1966)

Redefinition of this sort shades into Newspeak proper, and the complete inversion of normal meaning:

Policy-makers . . . fear headlines about "highest losses of the war" will fuel the arguments of U. S. doves. . . . "It's hard to explain to people," concedes a high officer, "that the higher casualties mean we're doing a better job." (*Wall Street Journal*, "Washington Wire," March 10, 1967)

We must convince Hanoi that its cause is hopeless. Only then will Hanoi be ready to negotiate. Then, when we do negotiate, we must, Mr. President, work for an honorable peace. (Marshall Ky, at Guam, March 20, 1967)

Premier Ky's sharply pointed black shoes rested on a magnificent Chinese rug. He was drinking tea from a cup held delicately in a hand whose little finger was capped by an inch-long mandarin fingernail. "The philosophy of my government is 100 percent social revolutionary." (Interview with John B. Oakes, *New York Times*, April 3, 1967)

The Department of Defense

Another important Newspeak technique is to depersonalize the other side:

"I got me a VC, man. I got at least two of them bastards." The exultant cry followed a 10-second burst of automatic weapons fire, and the dull crump of a grenade. . . .

"A VC," the object of "search and destroy missions," the results of which are given daily in "body count" figures. The dispatch goes on:

The Marines ordered a Vietnamese corporal to go down into the grenade-blasted hole to pull out their victims . . . three children riddled with bullets. . . . (UPI dispatch, Aug. 3, 1965, from Chan Sun)

He got himself some children.

There's no better way to fight than goin' out to shoot VC's [from an airplane]. And there's nothing I love better than killin' Cong. No sir. (Brig. Gen. James F. Hollingsworth to Nicholas Tomalin, in London Sunday *Times,* June 5, 1966)

"We sterilize the area prior to the insertion of the Revolutionary Development team" . . . says the colonel. . . . (Mary McCarthy, "Report from Vietnam I," *New York Review of Books,* April 20, 1967)

One village so persistently resisted pacification that finally it was destroyed. . . . (AP Survey, in Baltimore *Sun,* Nov. 6, 1966)

The overriding question about a Vietnamese is: is he or she a Viet Cong?

Two weeks before, a Vietcong guerilla was shot and killed in this yard. . . . He was the grandson of the old man and woman. The Marines are not sure whether he was the girl's brother or her husband; it doesn't matter, for the family admits that she was serving dinner to a group of Vietcong when the shooting took place. . . . (Sherwood Dickerman, "How the Marines Fight the 'Other War'," *Reporter,* April 6, 1967)

Cheerful and familiar metaphors help to present the enemy as targets, rather than people, and to focus our sympathies on the difficult situation, for example, of a young pilot:

A pilot going into combat for the first time is a bit like a swimmer about to dive in an icy lake . . . it is fortunate that young pilots can get their first taste of combat under the direction of a forward air controller over a flat country in bright sunshine where nobody is shooting back. . . . He learns how it feels to drop bombs on human beings and watch huts go up in a boil of orange flame when his aluminum napalm tanks tumble into them. He gets hardened to pressing the firing button and cutting people down like little cloth dummies as they sprint frantically. . . . (Frank Harvey, in *Flying*, Nov., 1966)

The pilot must become hardened; he must learn to bear the suffering of others stoically. Tough-mindedness should not prevent an officer from helping in the war for the hearts of the people, but he must take the accidents of war in his stride.

. . . the largest single group of casualties . . . was five Vietnamese civilians, three old people and a baby boy and girl, who had been seriously burned by a Marine grenade. American officers were regretful, but they were not surprised by . . . these developments. "That," said a colonel, "is the Delta." (Sherwood Dickerman, "A Taste of What's to Come in the Ugly Delta War," *Reporter*, February 23, 1967)

Tough-mindedness also suggests judging things pragmatically, by quantitative measures. A correspondent has referred to "the smile quotient" (The people here don't smile at us much but they smile more than they used to") which he thinks "as good an indicator as any of the Marines' success in winning hearts and minds. . . ." (*Reporter*, April 6, 1967)

Sentimentalism is also avoided by speaking in terms of "challenge" and "response." The challenge is to root the enemy out of his own villages and win the villages over. The response is, for example, the Marines' combined-action program of military mission and civic action, providing sterilized and regrouped villages with security and barbed wire, to keep the enemy out.

Morale is important both in the field and at home, and progress is necessary to maintain morale. Progress can be provided partly by a careful choice of modifier and metaphor and partly through using certain appropriate and convenient constructions, such as the present continuous tense:

South Vietnam is increasingly coming to grips with the need to modernize its society, bolster its civil economy, develop its repre-

sentative institutions, and provide a better life for its people. . . .
(Report by R. W. Komer, White House Press Release, September 13, 1966)

Sometimes we hear that, even now, South Vietnam has still not carried through a fully adequate program of land reform, but this should not discourage us. There has not been enough effort yet in that direction, and it is a pressing concern. Things are improving, though the pace is still too slow.

Many other ways to improve the war's image have been used, and we can hardly begin to list them all. Vagueness—"the U.S. involvement"; jargon—"scenarios of escalation"; abstraction—"B 52s perform a useful and important combat function"; misleading descriptions—"anti-personnel bombs" ("personnel" suggests "military personnel," but bombs do not discriminate against civilians); attractive or homely names—"Lazy dog," "Junction City"; all perform useful and important combat functions in the battle for men's minds.

Criticism of the war, if it is to be politically effective, must be informed and responsible, couched in moderate language, avoiding emotion, while recognizing and respecting the burdens resting on the shoulders of high policy-makers. By analogy, criticism of the language of war must avoid extremist charges and must recognize and respect the responsibilities and burdens resting on the agencies and media whose duty it is to manage the news. In this spirit one might say that political language appears designed to eliminate the appearance of a credibility gap and to reduce the onus of social disapproval falling on the unavoidably severe methods required to root out enemy sympathizers, while at the same time improving the image of insufficiently verified data.

Orwell, less sensitive to the burdens of policy-making, wrote, "Political language . . . is designed to make lies sound truthful and murder respectable, and to give an appearance of solidity to pure wind."

Questions

1. Look in newspapers, magazines, or college publications for examples of Newspeak.
2. Look through your past themes for Newspeak.
3. Why will facts have little chance if the language of Newspeak is accepted?
4. What are good ways of fighting Newspeak in your writing and in others'?

You may think that if you knew all the words in English, you could express any idea in the world (given unlimited talent for articulation). Not so. Because you speak English, there are some concepts that can never enter your mind. Completely "uneducated" Australian aborigines may think about some things more accurately than you. Having names for things is only one part of language and thought. Another part is the patterns of relationships. In his book *Language, Mind and Reality,* pioneer linguist Benjamin Whorf describes how the pattern of language limits our thought almost as if pattern were a higher mind, meaning nothing itself, but ruling all our meanings.[2]

Because of the systematic, configurative nature of higher mind, the "patternment" aspect of language always overrides and controls the "lexation" (*Nāma*) or name-giving aspect. Hence the meanings of specific words are less important than we fondly fancy. Sentences, not words, are the essence of speech, just as equations and functions, and not bare numbers, are the real meat of mathematics. We are all mistaken in our common belief that any word has an "exact meaning." We have seen that the higher mind deals in symbols that have no fixed reference to anything, but are like blank checks, to be filled in

[2] Benjamin Lee Whorf, *Language, Mind and Reality* (Cambridge: The M.I.T. Press, 1956), pp. 258–267.

as required, that stand for "any value" of a given variable, like the C's and V's in the formula cited in Part I, or the x, y, z of algebra. There is a queer Western notion that the ancients who invented algebra made a great discovery, though the human unconscious has been doing the same sort of thing for eons! For the same reason the ancient Mayas or the ancient Hindus, in their staggering cycles upon cycles of astronomical numbers, were simply being human. We should not however make the mistake of thinking that words, even as used by the lower personal mind, represent the opposite pole from these variable symbols, that a word DOES have an exact meaning, stands for a given thing, is only ONE value of a variable.

Even the lower mind has caught something of the algebraic nature of language; so that words are in between the variable symbols of pure patternment (*Arūpa*) and true fixed quantities. That part of meaning which is in words, and which we may call "reference," is only relatively fixed. Reference of words is at the mercy of the sentences and grammatical patterns in which they occur. And it is surprising to what a minimal amount this element of reference may be reduced. The sentence "I went all the way down there just in order to see Jack" contains only one fixed concrete reference: namely, "Jack." The rest is pattern attached to nothing specifically; even "see" obviously does not mean what one might suppose, namely, to receive a visual image.

Or, again, in word reference we deal with size by breaking it into size classes—small, medium, large, immense, etc.—but size objectively is not divided into classes, but is a pure continuum of relativity. Yet we think of size constantly as a set of classes because language has segmented and named the experience in this way. Number words may refer not to number as counted, but to number classes with elastic boundaries. Thus English 'few' adjusts its range according to the size, importance or rarity of the reference. A 'few' kings, battleships, or diamonds might be only three or four, a 'few' peas, raindrops, or tea leaves might be thirty or forty.

You may say, "Yes, of course this is true of words like large, small, and the like; they are obviously relative terms, but words like dog, tree, house, are different—each names a specific thing." Not so; these terms are in the same boat as 'large' and 'small.' The word 'Fido' said by a certain person at a certain time may refer to a specific thing, but the word 'dog' refers to a class with elastic limits. The limits of such classes are different in different languages. You might think that 'tree' means the same thing, everywhere and to everybody. Not at all. The Polish word that means 'tree' also includes the meaning 'wood.' The context or sentence pattern determines what sort of object the Polish word (or any word, in any language) refers to. In Hopi, an American Indian language of Arizona, the word for 'dog,' *pohko*, includes pet animal or domestic animal of any kind. Thus 'pet eagle' in Hopi is literally 'eagle-dog'; and having thus fixed the context a Hopi might next refer to the same eagle as so-and-so's *pohko*.

But lest this be dismissed as the vagary of a "primitive" language (no language is "primitive"), let us take another peep at our own beloved English. Take the word "hand." In 'his hand' it refers to a location on the human body, in 'hour hand' to a strikingly dissimilar object, in 'all hands on deck' to another reference, in 'a good hand at gardening' to another, in 'he held a good hand (at cards)' to another, whereas in 'he got the upper hand' it refers to nothing but is dissolved into a pattern of orientation. Or consider the word 'bar' in the phrases: 'iron bar, bar to progress, he should be behind bars, studied for the bar, let down all the bars, bar of music, sand bar, candy bar, mosquito bar, bar sinister, bar none, ordered drinks at the bar'!

But, you may say, these are popular idioms, not scientific and logical use of language. Oh, indeed? "Electrical" is supposed to be a scientific word. Do you know what its referent is? Do you know that the "electrical" in "electrical apparatus" is not the same "electrical" as the one in "electrical expert"? In the first it refers to a current of electricity in the apparatus, but in the second it does not refer to a current of electricity in the expert. When a word like "group" can refer either to a sequence of phases in time or a pile of articles on the floor, its element of reference is minor. Referents of scientific words are often con-

veniently vague, markedly under the sway of the patterns in
which they occur. It is very suggestive that this trait, so far from
being a hallmark of Babbittry, is most marked in intellectual
talk, and—*mirabile dictu*—in the language of poetry and love!
And this needs must be so, for science, poetry, and love are
alike in being "flights" above and away from the slave-world of
literal reference and humdrum prosaic details, attempts to
widen the petty narrowness of the personal self's outlook, lift-
ings toward *Arūpa*, toward that world of infinite harmony,
sympathy and order, of unchanging truths and eternal things.
And while all words are pitiful enough in their mere "letter
that killeth," it is certain that scientific terms like 'force, average, sex, allergic, biological' are not less pitiful, and in their
own way no more certain in reference than 'sweet, gorgeous,
rapture, enchantment, heart and soul, star dust.' You have
probably heard of 'star dust'—what is it? Is it a multitude of
stars, a sparkling powder, the soil of the planet Mars, the Milky
Way, a state of daydreaming, poetic fancy, pyrophoric iron, a
spiral nebula, a suburb of Pittsburgh, or a popular song? You
don't know, and neither does anybody. The word—for it is one
LEXATION, not two—has no reference of its own. Some words
are like that.° As we have seen, reference is the lesser part of
meaning, patternment the greater. Science, the quest for truth,
is a sort of divine madness like love. And music—is it not in the
same category? Music is a quasilanguage based entirely on patternment, without having developed lexation.

Sometimes the sway of pattern over reference produces
amusing results, when a pattern engenders meanings utterly
extraneous to the original lexation reference. The lower mind is
thrown into bewilderment, cannot grasp that compelling for-
mulas are at work upon it, and resorts wildly and with glad relief to its favorite obvious type of explanation, even "seeing
things" and "hearing things" that help out such explanation.
The word 'asparagus,' under the stress of purely phonetic English patterns of the type illustrated in the formula cited in Part

° Compare 'kith' and 'throe,' which give no meaning, and a bewildering
effect, without the patterns 'kith and kin' and 'in throes of.'

I, rearranges to 'sparagras'; and then since 'sparrer' is a dialectical form of 'sparrow,' we find 'sparrow grass' and then religiously accepted accounts of the relation of sparrows to this 'grass.' 'Cole slaw' came from German *Kohlsalat,* 'cabbage salad,' but the stress of the pattern tending to revamp it into 'cold slaw' has in some regions produced a new lexation 'slaw,' and a new dish 'hot slaw'! Children of course are constantly repatterning, but the pressure of adult example eventually brings their language back to the norm; they learn that Mississippi is not Mrs. Sippy, and the equator is not a menagerie lion but an imaginary line. Sometimes the adult community does not possess the special knowledge needed for correction. In parts of New England, Persian cats of a certain type are called Coon cats, and this name has bred the notion that they are a hybrid between the cat and the 'coon' (raccoon). This is often firmly believed by persons ignorant of biology, since the stress of the linguistic pattern (animal-name 1 modifying animal-name 2) causes them to "see" (or as the psychologists say "project") objective raccoon quality as located on the body of the cat—they point to its bushy tail, long hair, and so on. I knew of an actual case, a woman who owned a fine "Coon cat," and who would protest to her friend: "Why, just LOOK at him—his tail, his funny eyes—can't you see it?" "Don't be silly!" quoth her more sophisticated friend. "Think of your natural history! Coons cannot breed with cats; they belong to a different family." But the lady was so sure that she called on an eminent zoologist to confirm her. He is said to have remarked, with unwavering diplomacy, "If you like to think so, just think so." "He was even more cruel than you!" she snapped at her friend, and remained convinced that her pet was the outcome of an encounter between a philandering raccoon and a wayward cat! In just such ways on a vaster scale is woven the web of Māyā, illusion begotten of intrenched selfhood. I am told that Coon cats received their name from one Captain Coon, who brought the first of these Persian cats to the State of Maine in his ship.

In more subtle matters we all, unknowingly, project the linguistic relationships of a particular language upon the universe, and SEE them there, as the good lady SAW a linguistic relation (Coon = raccoon) made visible in her cat. We say 'see that wave'—the same pattern as 'see that house.' But without the projection of language no one ever saw a single wave. We see a surface in everchanging undulating motions. Some languages cannot say 'a wave'; they are closer to reality in this respect. Hopi say *walalata,* 'plural waving occurs,' and can call attention to one place in the waving just as we can. But, since actually a wave cannot exist by itself, the form that corresponds to our singular, *wala,* is not the equivalent of English 'a wave,' but means 'a slosh occurs,' as when a vessel of liquid is suddenly jarred.

English pattern treats 'I hold it' exactly like 'I strike it,' 'I tear it,' and myriads of other propositions that refer to actions effecting changes in matter. Yet 'hold' in plain fact is no action, but a state of relative positions. But we think of it, even see it, as an action, because language sets up the proposition in the same way as it sets up a much more common class of propositions dealing with movements and changes. We ASCRIBE action to what we call "hold" because the formula, substantive + verb = actor + his action, is fundamental in our sentences. Thus we are compelled in many cases to read into nature fictitious acting-entities simply because our sentence patterns require our verbs, when not imperative, to have substantives before them. We are obliged to say 'it flashed' or 'a light flashed,' setting up an actor IT, or A LIGHT, to perform what we call an action, FLASH. But the flashing and the light are the same; there is no thing which does something, and no doing. Hopi says only *rehpi.* Hopi can have verbs without subjects, and this gives to that language power as a logical system for understanding certain aspects of the cosmos. Scientific language, being founded on western Indo-European and not on Hopi, does as we do, sees sometimes actions and forces where there may be only states. For do you not conceive it possible that scientists as well as ladies with cats all unknowingly project the linguistic patterns of a particular type of language upon the universe, and SEE them there, rendered visible on the very face of nature? A change in language can transform our appreciation of the Cosmos.

All this is typical of the way the lower personal mind, caught in a vaster world inscrutable to its methods, uses its strange gift of language to weave the web of Māyā or illusion, to make a provisional analysis of reality and then regard it as final. Western culture has gone farthest here, farthest in determined thoroughness of provisional analysis, and farthest in determination to regard it as final. The commitment to illusion has been sealed in western Indo-European language, and the road out of illusion for the West lies through a wider understanding of language than western Indo-European alone can give. This is the "Mantra Yoga" of the Western consciousness, the next great step, which it is now ready to take. It is probably the most suitable way for Western man to begin that "culture of consciousness" which will lead him to a great illumination.

Again, through this sort of understanding of language is achieved a great phase of human brotherhood. For the scientific understanding of very diverse languages—not necessarily to speak them, but to analyze their structure—is a lesson in brotherhood which is brotherhood in the universal human principle—the brotherhood of the "Sons of Manas." It causes us to transcend the boundaries of local cultures, nationalities, physical peculiarities dubbed "race," and to find that in their linguistic systems, though these systems differ widely, yet in the order, harmony, and beauty of the systems, and in their respective subtleties and penetrating analysis of reality, all men are equal. This fact is independent of the state of evolution as regards material culture, savagery, civilization, moral or ethical development, etc., a thing most surprising to the cultured European, a thing shocking to him, indeed a bitter pill! But it is true; the crudest savage may unconsciously manipulate with effortless ease a linguistic system so intricate, manifoldly systematized, and intellectually difficult that it requires the lifetime study of our greatest scholars to describe its workings. The manasic plane and the "higher ego" have been given to all, and the evolution of human language was complete, and spread in its proud completeness up and down the earth, in a time far anterior to the oldest ruin that molders in the soil today.

Linguistic knowledge entails understanding many different

beautiful systems of logical analysis. Through it, the world as seen from the diverse viewpoints of other social groups, that we have thought of as alien, becomes intelligible in new terms. Alienness turns into a new and often clarifying way of looking at things. Consider Japanese. The view of the Japanese that we get outwardly from their governmental policy seems anything but conducive to brotherhood. But to approach the Japanese through an aesthetic and scientific appreciation of their language transforms the picture. THAT is to realize kinship on the cosmopolitan levels of the spirit. One lovely pattern of this language is that its sentence may have two differently ranked subjects. We are familiar with the idea of two ranks of OBJECTS for our verbs, an immediate and a more remote goal, or direct and indirect object as they are commonly called. We have probably never thought of the possibilities of a similar idea applied to SUBJECTS. This idea is put to work in Japanese. The two subjects —call them subject 1 and subject 2—are marked by the particles *wa* and *ga*, and a diagram might show them with a line drawn from each subject word, the two lines converging upon the same predication, whereas our English sentence could have only one subject with one line to the predicate. An example would be the way of saying "Japan is mountainous": "Japan$_1$ mountain$_2$ (are) many"; ° or: "Japan, in regard to its mountains are many." "John is long-legged" would be "John$_1$ leg$_2$ (are) long." This pattern gives great conciseness at the same time with great precision. Instead of the vagueness of our "mountainous," the Japanese can, with equal compactness of formulation, distinguish "mountainous" meaning that mountains not always high are abundant, from "mountainous" meaning that mountains not abundant relative to the whole area are high. We see how the logical uses of this pattern would give to Japanese great power in concise scientific operations with ideas, could this power be properly developed.

The moment we begin scientific, unbiased RESEARCH into language we find, in people and cultures with the most unpre-

---

° "Are" is in parentheses because "be many" is expressed by a single verb-like word. The Japanese ordinarily does not use a plural.

possessing exteriors, beautiful, effective, and scientific devices of expression unknown to western Indo-European tongues or mentalities. The Algonkian languages are spoken by very simple people, hunting and fishing Indians, but they are marvels of analysis and synthesis. One piece of grammatical finesse peculiar to them is called the obviative. This means that their pronouns have four persons instead of three, or from our standpoint two third persons. This aids in compact description of complicated situations, for which we should have to resort to cumbersome phraseology. Let us symbolize their third and fourth persons by attaching the numerals 3 and 4 to our written words. The Algonkians might tell the story of William Tell like this: "William Tell called his$_3$ son and told him$_4$ to bring him$_3$ his$_3$ bow and arrow, which$_4$ he$_4$ then brought to him$_3$. He$_3$ had him$_4$ stand still and placed an apple on his$_4$ head, then took his$_3$ bow and arrow and told him$_4$ not to fear. Then he$_3$ shot it$_4$ off his$_4$ head without hurting him$_4$." Such a device would greatly help in specifying our complex legal situations, getting rid of "the party of the first part" and "the aforesaid John Doe shall, on his part, etc."

Chichewa, a language related to Zulu, spoken by a tribe of unlettered Negroes in East Africa, has two past tenses, one for past events with present result or influence, one for past without present influence. A past as recorded in external situations is distinguished from a past recorded only in the psyche or memory; a new view of TIME opens before us. Let 1 represent the former and 2 the latter; then ponder these Chichewa nuances: I came$_1$ here; I went$_2$ there; he was$_2$ sick; he died$_1$; Christ died$_2$ on the cross; God created$_1$ the world. "I ate$_1$" means I am not hungry; "I ate$_2$" means I am hungry. If you were offered food and said: "No, I have eaten$_1$," it would be all right, but if you used the other past tense you would be uttering an insult. A Theosophical speaker of Chichewa might use tense 1 in speaking of the past involution of Monads, which has enabled the world to be in its present state, while he might use tense 2 for, say, long-past planetary systems now disintegrated and their evolution done. If he were talking about Reincarnation, he would use 2 for events of a past incarnation simply in their own frame of reference, but he would use 1 in referring to or implying their "Karma." It may be that these primitive folk are equipped with a language which, if they were to become philosophers or mathematicians, could make them our foremost thinkers upon TIME.

Or take the Coeur d'Alene language, spoken by the small Indian tribe of that name in Idaho. Instead of our simple concept of "cause," founded on our simple "makes it (him) do so," the Coeur d'Alene grammar requires its speakers to discriminate (which of course they do automatically) among three causal processes, denoted by three causal verb-forms: (1) growth, or maturation of an inherent cause, (2) addition or accretion from without, (3) secondary addition i.e., of something affected by process 2. Thus, to say "it has been made sweet" they would use form 1 for a plum sweetened by ripening, form 2 for a cup of coffee sweetened by dissolving sugar in it, and form 3 for griddle cakes sweetened by syrup made by dissolving sugar. If, given a more sophisticated culture, their thinkers erected these now unconscious discriminations into a theory of triadic causality, fitted to scientific observations, they might thereby produce a valuable intellectual tool for science. WE could imitate artificially such a theory, perhaps, but we could NOT apply it, for WE are not habituated to making such distinctions with effortless ease in daily life. Concepts have a basis in daily talk before scientific workers will attempt to use them in the laboratory. Even relativity has such a basis in the western Indo-European languages (and others)—the fact that these languages use many space words and patterns for dealing with time.

Language has further significance in other psychological factors on a different level from modern linguistic approach but of importance in music, poetry, literary style, and Eastern mantram. What I have been speaking of thus far concerns the plane of Manas in the more philosophical sense, the "higher unconscious" or the "soul" (in the sense as used by Jung). What I am about to speak of concerns the "psyche" (in the sense as used by Freud), the "lower" unconscious, the Manas which is especially the "slayer of the real," the Plane of Kāma, of emotion or rather feeling (*Gefühl*). In a serial relation containing the levels of Nāma-Rūpa and Arūpa, this level of the unconscious psyche is on the other side of Nāma-Rūpa from Arūpa, and Nāma or lexation mediates in a sense between these extremes. Hence the psyche is the psychological correlative of the phonemic level in language, related to it not structurally as is Nāma or lexation, not by using it as building blocks, as word-making uses the phonemes (vowels, consonants, accents, etc.), but related as the feeling-content of the phonemes. There is a universal, *Gefühl*-type way of linking experiences, which shows up in laboratory experiments and appears to be independent of language—basically alike for all persons.

Without a serial or hierarchical order in the universe it would have to be said that these psychological experiments and linguistic experiments contradict each other. In the psychological experiments human subjects seem to associate the experiences of bright, cold, sharp, hard, high, light (in weight), quick, high-pitched, narrow, and so on in a long series, with each other; and conversely the experiences of dark, warm, yielding, soft, blunt, low, heavy, slow, low-pitched, wide, etc., in another long series. This occurs whether the words for such associated experiences resemble or not, but the ordinary person is likely to notice a relation to words only when it is a relation of likeness to such a series in the vowels or consonants of the words, and when it is a relation of contrast or conflict it is passed unnoticed. The noticing of the relation of likeness is an element in sensitiveness to literary style or to what is often rather inaccurately called the "music" of words. The noticing of the relation of conflict is much more difficult, much more a freeing oneself from illusion, and though quite "unpoetical" it is really a movement toward Higher Manas, toward a higher symmetry than that of physical sound.

What is significant for our thesis is that language, through lexation, has made the speaker more acutely conscious of certain dim psychic sensations; it has actually produced awareness on lower planes than its own: a power of the nature of magic. There is a yogic mastery in the power of language to remain independent of lower-psyche facts, to override them, now point them up, now toss them out of the picture, to mold the nuances of words to its own rule, whether the psychic ring of the sounds fits or not. If the sounds fit, the psychic quality of the sounds is increased, and this can be noticed by the layman. If the sounds do not fit, the psychic quality changes to accord with the linguistic meaning, no matter how incongruous with the sounds, and this is not noticed by the layman.

QUESTIONS

1. According to Whorf what would be the value of a writer having many kinds of sentence structures at his command?
2. If Whorf is right about perception of reality being limited by language, how could this affect the way a writer works?
3. In your own papers or in this book find several words whose meaning varies considerably according to context or pattern. What would happen if these words were fixed to only one meaning? Suppose all English words varied like those you are asked to find?
4. Do Whorf's ideas say anything about how writing and personality are related? Writing and culture?

It is true that all ages have writers who bore people. And all ages have readers who are intellectually limited and are "bored" by anything beyond their limits. The most commonly heard remedy for boring writing is "more action." This is a cliché of popular criticism. The people who cry action don't realize that even *they* often enjoy "non-action" writing. Here Irish short story writer Frank O'Connor tells an interviewer what he feels is the basis of interesting writing.[3]

[3] Frank O'Connor interview, *Writers at Work: The Paris Review Interviews,* ed. Malcolm Cowley (New York: The Viking Press, 1957).

INTERVIEWER: What is the greatest essential of a story?

O'CONNOR: You have to have a theme, a story to tell. Here's a man at the other side of the table and I'm talking to him; I'm going to tell him something that will interest him. As you know perfectly well, our principal difficulty at Harvard was a number of people who'd had affairs with girls or had had another interesting experience, and wanted to come in and tell about it, straight away. That is not a theme. A theme is something that is worth something to everybody. In fact, you wouldn't, if you'd ever been involved in a thing like this, grab a man in a pub and say, "Look, I had a girl out last night, under the Charles Bridge." That's the last thing you'd do. You grab somebody and say, "Look, an extraordinary thing happened to me yesterday—I met a man—he said this to me—" and that, to me, is a theme. The moment you grab somebody by the lapels and you've got something to tell, that's a real story. It means you want to tell him and think the story is interesting in itself. If you start describing your own personal experiences, something that's only of interest to yourself, then you can't express yourself, you cannot say, ultimately, what you think about human beings. The moment you say this, you're committed.

I'll tell you what I mean. We were down on the south coast of Ireland for a holiday and we got talkin' to this old farmer and he said his son, who was dead now, had gone to America. He'd married an American girl and she had come over for a visit, alone. Apparently her doctor had told her a trip to Ireland would do her good. And she stayed with the parents, had gone around to see his friends and other relations, and it wasn't till after she'd gone that they learned that the boy had died. Why didn't she tell them? There's your story. Dragging the reader in, making the reader a part of the story—the reader is a part of the story. You're saying all the time, "This story is about you— *de te fabula.*"

INTERVIEWER: Do you think the writer should be a reformer or an observer?

O'CONNOR: I think the writer's a reformer; the observer thing is very old, it goes back to Flaubert. I can't write about something I don't admire—it goes back to the old concept of the celebration: you celebrate the hero, an idea.

QUESTIONS

1. Why is the American girl's story about the reader?
2. Why is the idea of a reformer linked to the idea of admiration?
3. What *themes* have you had in your own writing?

How can science and art serve each other? Gyorgy Kepes, a scientist at Massachusetts Institute of Technology, believes that art is essentially a bridge-building between the individual and his world. What he says about art's power to create unity, in the following *Saturday Review* article, "Where Is Science Taking Us?" is also true of your writing.[4]

Science has opened up immense new vistas, but we shrink from accepting the deeper and richer sense of life uniquely inherent in the new parameters of our twentieth-century world. Where our age falls short is in the harmonizing of our outer and our inner wealth. We lack the depth of feeling and the range of sensibility needed to retain the riches that science and techniques have brought within our grasp. Consequently we lack a model that could guide us to re-form our formless world.

The formlessness of our present life has three obvious aspects:

FIRST, our environmental chaos, which accounts for inadequate living conditions, waste of human and material resources.

SECOND, our social chaos—lack of common ideas, common feelings, common purposes.

[4] Gyorgy Kepes, "Where Is Science Taking Us?," *Saturday Review Magazine* (March 12, 1966).

THIRD, our inner chaos—individual inability to live in harmony with one's self, inability to accept one's whole self and let body, feelings, and thought dwell together in friendship.

We have, then, three basic tasks before us. First of all we must build bridges between man and nature—construct a physical environment which is on a truly twentieth-century standard. Second, we must build bridges between man and man—create a new scale of social structure built from progressive common purposes. We must establish a sense of belonging, of interdependence, in order to achieve the teamwork that the first task demands. And, finally, we have to build bridges inside ourselves. Only if each individual can unify himself, so that one aspect of his life will not intercept and cancel another, can we hope to tackle the second task efficiently. Only the man who can work with himself can work with other men.

The building of these bridges—the reintegration of all aspects of our life through twentieth-century knowledge and power—is our great contemporary challenge, and in this work the imaginative power of creative vision coupled with sensibilities can have a central role. Artists are living seismographs, as it were, with a special sensitivity to the human condition. They record our conflicts and hopes, and their immediate and direct response to the qualities of the world helps us to establish an entente with the living present.

We may distinguish two fundamental values that the artist can reveal to us. First, we respond to the images of artists because of their completeness; because their harmonies, rhythms, colors, and shapes touch us, and not just on one level or another of our being. As the poet Yeats has put it, they "could not move us at all, if our thought did not rush out to the edge of our flesh, and it is so with all good art, whether the Victory of Samothrace which reminds the soles of our feet of swiftness, or the Odyssey that would send us out under the salt wind, or the young horsemen on the Parthenon that seem happier than our boyhood ever was, and in our boyhood's way. Art bids us touch and taste and hear and see the world, and shrinks from what Blake calls mathematical form, from every abstract thing, from all that is not a fountain jetting from the entire hopes, memories, and sensations of the body."

In its aspect of many-layered but unified experience, participation in a work of art often provides us with deep insight into the wholeness of the world. The physical base outside us and our sensations within us are bridged. Our sensations, feelings, and thoughts march in unison. The analogous relations, transcending both individual human beings and the work of art, become a social fact, connecting man and man through establishing a community of thought and feeling.

The other basic value that an authentic creative work of art offers to us is inherent in the proportion between its fundamental opposites: expressive vitality and formal order.

Our history suggests that human progress follows from the harmonizing of two opposite tendencies: the tendency on the one hand toward greater sociality and social discipline, and on the other toward greater individual freedom and intensity of life. There is evidence of psychological regression in the sick, whose personalities shrink as they lose the power both to integrate themselves with the world and to open themselves toward it; they retreat to a more vegetative level of existence. If not crushed, exploded, or capitated by the surges of unresolving opposites, a living system is stultified when the disproportion becomes too great.

Motor performance at the animal level, and productive work, the foundations of our social existence, are based upon the alternation of action and repose in a measure corresponding to the natural periods of breathing and neuromuscular effort. The optimum performance is defined by the worker's ability to reach a rhythmic articulation common to the body, the mind, and the task. Very early, men mastered the technique of getting work done by a unison of efforts paced by a strongly rhythmic work-song or chant. Emotional drive, muscular energy, and technical knowledge become parts of a symmetrical relation between man and man, between man and nature, when a rhythm of action and repose synchronizes ends and means, synchronizes flesh, heart, and brain so that an aggregation of men becomes a smoothly functioning labor crew, sports team, or research body. The synchronization introduces a new quality of experience; work becomes something far more than the mere fulfilment of an assigned task. The sensing of the unity is the germination of an experience basic to every art.

A work of art has both vitality and order. A shriek of agony has life, pulsating and intense, concentrated, as it were, at a single point. But Picasso's *Guernica* has organized life—absolute expression of agony and absolute discipline of form. And Grünewald's Isenheim Altar, with the most despairing of all Crucifixions, the most triumphant of all Resurrections, is grandly ordered by an orchestrated balance of color and by one of the most rigorously disciplined iconographical schemes in art. What makes a great painting far more than a well-ordered arrangement of colored surfaces, far more than an explosion of emotion, is its balanced proportioning of intense expression and disciplined structure.

Proportion, the basis of effective artistic expression, is the key to broader realms on which the conditions of our time have focused so much acute thinking.

Scientific and technical knowledge has given us an unprecedented opportunity to understand certain aspects of proportioning. Our growing knowledge of biological regulation has become a model for understanding other phenomena. There are a growing number of automatic control systems based upon symmetry and proportion which help us to understand how men stand upright without toppling, how the human heart beats, why our economic system endures slumps and booms. Automatic control devices and self-regulating mechanisms not only have become important in our economic and social life but also have philosophical and symbolic implications of the utmost significance. As we gain precision in understanding and applying automatic control, devising intricate engineering systems which maintain opposing processes in their necessary respective balance, we are the more painfully made aware of our own lack of harmony on the highest levels of our interest, personal happiness, and social equilibrium.

The poetic imagination of the ancients sought harmony in

opposites, anticipating some of the advanced scientific thought of our time. Pythagorean thinking introduced the concept of the "mean." As wine and water might be blended in a correct proportion to produce the perfect drink, a proportion completely fair to both of two opposites was thought to be possible always. To Anaximander, the mutual encroachment of opposites was unjust, and reconciliation imperative. Heraclitus not only recognized that events are generated through the struggle of opposites but also realized that change cannot be understood without a guidance of measure:

The sun will not overstep his measure; if he does, the Erinyes, handmaids of justice, will find him out.

One hundred and fifty years ago, a passionate great poet commented on the same issue, projecting it on the concrete social plane. "Our calculations have outrun conception," wrote Shelley in 1818. "We have eaten more than we can digest. The cultivation of those sciences which have enlarged the limits of the empire of man over the external world, has, for want of poetical faculty, proportionally circumscribed those of the internal world; and man, having enslaved the elements, remains himself a slave."

Nevertheless, emotional return to the archaic, ancestral cave is an obvious failure to function in contemporary terms—however necessary. This temporary standstill is not a genuine answer to our deep long-range needs. We may suffer from exposure to the new scale, but it is necessary for us to go ahead and meet its challenge.

Only complete acceptance of the world which is being born can make our lives genuinely acceptable. Such acceptance implies, above all, two concrete tasks. One, in every field of human endeavor we must advance to the furthest frontiers of knowledge possible today. Two, we must combine and intercommunicate all such knowledge so that we may gain the sense of *structure*, the power to *see*, in the deepest, richest sense, our world as an interconnected whole.

There is a reciprocal relationship between our distorted environment and our impoverished ability to see with freshness,

clarity, and joy. Fed on our deformed and dishonest environment, our undernourished artistic sensibilities can only lead us
to perpetuate the malfunctions of the inner and outer environment that we create. To counteract this spiral of self-destruc-
tion, we have to re-educate our vision and reclaim our lost
artistic and poetic sensibilities.

To meet this urgent task our universities could contribute by
creating educational conditions conducive to an effective in-
tercommunication between scientific knowledge and artistic
sensibilities.

As the twentieth century has grown older, most of our artists
have recoiled upon themselves. They lack orientation in the
total contemporary world, which, if they but knew it, holds as
much promise as it does menace. Their honest response has
been to scream their isolation. In frantic retreat, many of them
have adopted a scorched-earth policy and burned their most
valuable cultural belongings. Cornered and confused in a "horror of lost self," as the poet Robert Lowell puts it, some of them
advertise brutality as vitality and intellectual cowardice as ex-
istential self-justification.

Artists today come together in small groups in great cities.
There, in little circles that shut out the rest of the world, the
initiates share one another's images. They generate illusory
spontaneity, but miss the possible vital, deep dialogue with
contemporary intellectual and technological reality. It is un-
fashionable today, if not taboo, for artists to think and act on
the broad terms of cultural and social ideals. No doubt, moral-
izing in art can lead to creative suicide, just as market-policed
and state-policed art can lead to the murder of artistic honesty.
But the other extreme—lack of intellectual curiosity and rejection of commitment—leads to emaciation of artistic values.

QUESTIONS

1. How does the "sensing of unity" apply to the writing of your papers?
2. Why doesn't Kepes think we become modern simply by growing

up and living in a modern world? Or, if this is the Atomic Age, why isn't atomic energy a part of our art and thought?

3. Why would Kepes view the practice of art as one which protects sound personality structure?

In the presence of scientists, poets may feel somewhat apologetic, or at least very different. Here is the beginning of an essay, "The Age of Overwrite and Underthink," by English poet Stephen Spender.[5] In it, he tries to explain how all kinds of writing are part of one important task that unites scientist and poet.

In the famous controversy about the two cultures, one important point seems to have been overlooked: that if there truly is a gulf between the literary and the scientific culture, it cannot be bridged by science, but only by language. Language is the only means of communication between specialities as far apart as every individual's unique experience of his own life. Scientific specialization itself is human experience, and if it is to become part of the general culture it can only be so by communication through language. When there is a question of discussing and explaining our experiences of the other arts, music, or painting, we use words. If architecture aspires to the condition of music, all human experience aspires to words.

This very simple point, that we communicate by means of language, seems to be largely overlooked by our educators. Our own language is thought of as just one thing taught like all the others, not as an intermediary between all things taught. Before the end of the last century, English, I believe, was not a subject at English universities. There was no English school at Oxford and Cambridge. Everyone was supposed to know English literature, and apart from the grammar taught in one's childhood, how to write English was a benefit conferred by, or inferred from, a classical education. I suppose that some of

[5] Stephen Spender, "The Age of Overwrite and Underthink," *Saturday Review Magazine* (March 12, 1966).

those who hotly contested the introduction of the study of English literature must have argued, with reason, that if English becomes a subject, then reading and writing English literature becomes a specialization among other specializations. The main road of communication becomes a cellar occupied by people who make a profession of reading and writing. In our own time an attempt is being made to turn the tables on those who have made English one subject among other subjects by giving it the status of principal subject. Dr. Leavis and his followers argue that English should be the main study at the new universities. They argue that in the era of the breakdown of values, and in the absence of religion, our only connection with the past of the "organic community" is through the English books of the Great Tradition, as chosen by the Leavisite priesthood.

This seems an attempt to replace compulsory religious teaching with compulsory study of English literature. It seems an extreme position only serving to dramatize that it is a desperate one in the age of nuclear fission when the people who are studying either to reinvent us or to completely destroy us have no time for any other work than their frenetic pursuit of bigger and better means of doing one or the other.

What one may insist on, though, is that life attains significance through the consciousness of the individual who lives it, and who is able to understand that significance through comparing his own experiences with those of other people. Language is the only means of communicating experiences, realizing consciousness. One cannot, I think, reasonably argue that everyone ought to be a New Critic, or a doctrinaire of the Great Tradition, but one can point out that it is urgent for people to be able to communicate, and that they can only do this through being able to read the works that illuminate their experiences. This means developing a capacity to speak, think, and write clearly.

It seems to be universally recognized that everyone should learn to read and write. Not to be able to do so is to be illiterate. Little importance, however, is attached to *what* you read and how you write. The idea that writing is not just a physical attainment, like using a knife and fork, but is communication, and that everyone should be concerned with it to the degree that he has experiences and ideas to express, seems to be regarded as eccentric. Yet it is doubtful whether you can carry on an intelligent conversation without being able to write down the ideas conversed about. Anyone can demonstrate this to himself by simply turning on the radio or TV and listening to the dismal attempts of experts in politics and government to communicate their expertise. What one witnesses again and again is the breakdown of language.

We groan over specialization, but we accept it as inevitable, reflecting that specialists are so specialized in matters of which we are so ignorant that even if they could tell us about the things they know, we would not understand. Yet there exist, especially in France and England, a few masters of exposition who show that the most specialized subject is often far more communicable than we would anticipate its being. Moreover, it is doubtful whether what we need or want to know from the specialist is really that which is highly technical and particular to his research. What we need to know from scientists is how their scientific picture of the world should affect and qualify our life. A good deal of this can be explained. And if—as Robert Oppenheimer seems to think—there is a highly important kind of scientific experience that cannot be communicated to the nonspecialist then the significance of noncommunicability is something that also needs to be explained, because it may be a factor, or, rather a blank, in the picture of life we need to allow for. In the past it was considered important to understand that there were incommunicable mysteries. But these were communicated as *experience of the incommunicable,* in that people realized there were mysteries of knowledge and priesthood. If there is a kind of scientific experience that is central to modern life and cannot be explained, then this is something different from mere "specialization," and it can and should be understood.

Whether what scientists have to explain to us is communicable, or whether they have to explain that it is incommunicable, the fact is that the present breakdown in communication is due at least partly to the neglect of English. It is slovenly to accept without question the cliché that we cannot communicate because we live in "an age of specialization." One only has to look at the essays of most sociologists to realize that language, the medium of communication, is often the last thing that people who have very important things to tell about the state of our society have taken trouble about. We enter the era of mass communication when the study of the traditional, and the ultimate, means of communication, the English language, is looked at as a matter concerning only literary specialists.

I do not see why an attempt should not be made at school through the widened study of writing and speaking English to break down some barriers of incommunicability. The basic condition for making such an attempt possible would be that everyone, in whatever discipline, wrote an essay on some general subject once a week or fortnight. Some of these essays might take the form of communications from members of one discipline to another. For example, students on the science side of the school might be asked to write essays directed to those studying history, explaining, in words that the science student hoped the historian would understand, what some aspect of his science was about, and vice versa. The historians, or the scientists, would then read the best essays from the science students, and perhaps both classes would meet to discuss the essays.

Another exercise that I have thought about (without being able to fire anyone else with my own enthusiasm) is that a day of a term or a year should be set aside for general academic exercise in which speakers from different specialized disciplines would explain before an audience what they thought was the meaning and importance of their work. A good classroom exercise might be to make students listen to TV interviews with Senators, ex-Presidents, etc., taking with them notebooks in which they would write down sentences in the interview that strike them as particularly good, or particularly bad, considered not for their content but as language—to be followed by a general discussion of these by the class. This might prove linguistically therapeutic.

I think, then, that we should regard English literature—fiction, nonfiction, poetry, etc.—primarily as teaching people to communicate with one another and in that way helping them to live their lives. We are not, even in the university creative writing course, teaching them to be writers. We are concerned only with teaching them to read, to express themselves, to appreciate language, to discuss and talk better because they are trying to read and write. Instead of giving them a specialist view of writing, we should try to break this down, to emphasize the importance of writing everything as well as possible: a letter to a friend or to a member of the family, a private journal. We should make them think of reading and writing as two sides of the same medal. One reads better because one writes better, one writes better because one reads better.

That students often distinguish sharply between reading and writing is painfully evident. Some years ago, after reading an essay by one of my students, I suggested to her that she should read Samuel Butler's essays. "Oh, I don't read, Mr. Spender," she protested, "I write."

As I suggested above, every student at school ought to write a weekly essay. Students ought to be given a wide choice of subjects, with a view, perhaps, to their sometimes being very close to themselves and sometimes demanding that they should get away from their self-absorption, their subjectivity, into their opposite, the objective. But it is a mistake to produce the impression that this kind of belles-lettres is literature, or, at any rate, more literary, than the subject I suggested previously, of a scientist writing for a historian about his scientific studies. Everything that is well written can be literature, if literature is what we are concerned with. One of the masterpieces of English literature is a handbook on angling.

QUESTIONS

1. Look at what Spender says about scientists having to explain even what is incommunicable. Apply this to the problem of communicating emotion.

2. Listen to a public figure on television or radio and analyze the language.
3. Why isn't the creative writing course teaching students to be writers?

ASSIGNMENTS

1. Look at the papers you have written for this course and try to look at yourself, the writer, as if you were another person. Describe that writer's awareness of language. Is he too controlled by language, or is he outside the language of society completely?
2. Examine what your future will be like or could be like. Write an essay on the part language will play in that future. Use specific examples.
3. Assuming there is such a thing as "language pollution," write an essay in which you appraise the situation and present possible solutions.

Index to Authors and Titles

Adrift in New York, excerpt from, 220–21

Affluent Society, The, excerpt from, 128–30

"*Age of Overwrite and Under-think, The,*" 325–29

Agee, James, 7–8, 92

Alger, Horatio, 220–21

Anderson, Sherwood, 223–25

Anna Karenina, excerpt from, 197–204

Art and Reality, excerpt from, 256–57

Aspects of the Novel, excerpts from, 93–94, 125

"*Autopsy, The,*" 138–40

Baker, Russell, 238–41

Baudelaire, Charles, 27

Best of NBC Emphasis, The, excerpt from, 102–3

Bettelheim, Bruno, 104–15

Biography of the Unborn, excerpt from, 131–33

"*Body of an Amercian,*" 168-72

Bonanza Inn, excerpt from, 82–86

Bowen, Catherine Drinker, 123–24

Bowen, Elizabeth, 78

Cape Cod, excerpt from, 33–34

Carson, Rachel, 241–47

Cary, Joyce, 256–57

Catton, Bruce, 70–71

Chekhov, Anton, 79, 222

Colette, 152–57

Coming of Age in Samoa, excerpt from, 35–38

"*Composition at the Barricades,*" excerpt from, 286–93

"*Confession and Autobiography,*" 261–65

Confessions of an Advertising Man, excerpt from, 8–10

Crack-Up, The, excerpt from, 99–101

Darrow, Clarence, 177–82

Darrow for the Defense, excerpt from, 177–82

"*Death of the Ball Turret Gunner, The,*" 149–50

"*Disposable Man, The,*" 238–40

Dos Passos, John, 167–73

Dubos, René, 134–38

Durrell, Lawrence, 53–54, 58–59

Eastman, Max, 220

Enjoyment of Laughter, excerpt from, 220

Farb, Peter, 39–41

Farewell to Arms, A, excerpt from, 49

Fitzgerald, F. Scott, 98–102

"*Flower Dump,*" 42

Forster, E. M., 93–94, 125, 142, 234

Fredericks, Pauline, 102–4

Galbraith, John Kenneth, 127–30

Gilbert, Margaret Shea, 131–33

Green, Paul, 59–61, 63
Green Hills of Africa, excerpt from, 30–32
Guest, Edgar, 190

Hall, Caroll, 82–86
Hardy, Sir Alistair, 27–28
Harris, Mark, 253–54
Hawthorne, Nathaniel, 79–82
Hemingway, Ernest, 30–32, 48–49, 69, 191–97, 205
Heym, Georg, 138–41
"Hidden World of the Soil, The," excerpt from, 40
Housman, A.E., 180

Isherwood, Christopher, 219, 226–28
"I Want to Know Why," excerpt from, 223–25

"James Agee, by Himself," 7–8
Jarrell, Randall, 149–50
"Jealousy," 152–56
"Joey: A Mechanical Boy," 104–14

Kepes, Gyorgy, 319–25
Koestler, Arthur, 75–77

Language, Mind and Reality, excerpt from, 306–17
Lewis, Oscar, 82–86
Life on the Mississippi, excerpt from, 17–22
Lippmann, Walter, 275–86
Long and Happy Life, A, excerpt from, 70
Look Homeward, Angel, excerpt from, 51–52
Lotus and the Robot, excerpt from, 75–77

Maugham, Somerset, 48, 53–58, 260–61

Mead, Margaret, 35–39, 41
Miller, Henry, 257–58
Mills, C. Wright, 95–97, 120, 238
Mirage of Health, The, excerpt from, 134–37
"Modest Proposal, A," 158–66

Nell, Edward, 297–306
Nell, Onora, 297–306
Night Flight, excerpt from, 207–10
"Night the Bed Fell, The," 229–33
"No Telling, No Summing Up," 266–75
"Now hollow fires burn out to black," 180

O'Connor, Frank, 317–19
Ogilvy, David, 8–11, 92
Open Sea, The, excerpt from, 27–28
Orwell, George, 11–17, 297

Parkinson, C. Northcote, 234–38
Parkinson's Law, excerpt from, 234–37
Poe, Edgar Allan, 71–72
Price, Reynolds, 70, 115–18

Roethke, Theodore, 42–43

Saint-Exupéry, Antoine de, 206–11
Sansom, William, 26–27
Scarlet Letter, The, excerpt from, 80–81
Scott Fitzgerald, excerpt from, 98–99
Silent Spring, The, excerpt from, 241–46
Single Man, A, excerpt from, 226–27
Southpaw, The, excerpt from, 253–54

Spender, Stephen, 189–90, 261–66, 325–29
Steinbeck, John, 211–15
"Stereotypes," 275–86
Stewart, John, 86–89
Stories of William Sansom, excerpt from, 27
"Such, Such Were the Joys," 11–16
"Sue's Got a Baby," 190
Summing Up, The, excerpts from, 54–58, 260–61
Swift, Jonathan, 158–67

Thoreau, Henry David, 33–34
Thurber, James, 228–34
"To My Daughter," 189
Tolstoy, Leo, 197–205, 258–59
Travels with Charley, excerpt from, 211–14
Trillin, Calvin, 266–75
Turnbull, Andrew, 98–99
Twain, Mark, 17–22
Twelve Million Black Voices, excerpt from, 173–76

"Uncle Grant," 115–17
Understanding Fiction, excerpt from, 79

"University in a Nuclear Age, The," excerpt from, 59–60
"Up in Michigan," 191–95

"Vulture Country," excerpt from, 86–88

War Lords of Washington, The, excerpt from, 70–71
War Words, excerpt from, 298–305
"What Is Art," excerpt from, 258–59
"Where Is Science Taking Us?" 319–24
White Collar, excerpt from, 95–97
Whorf, Benjamin Lee, 306–17
Wolfe, Thomas, 51–53
Wright, Richard, 173–77
Writers at Work: The Paris Review Interviews, excerpt from Lawrence Durrell interview, 53–54; excerpt from Henry Miller interview, 257–58; excerpt from Frank O'Connor interview, 317–19
Writing Biography, excerpt from, 123–24

Zahner, Louis, 286–94